Jean —

Best wishes
for a future
of great theatre
and good food

Jane Langton 7/22/03

Cooking for the Health of It

A No-Nonsense Guide & Cookbook
for Optimizing Health & Wellness

by
Jane M. Livingston, RD, CDE
Registered Dietitian
Certified Diabetes Educator

First Edition
ISBN 0-9725309-0-8

Artwork by Donna Livingston-Smith, MFA, Maryland Institute College of Art. Donna teaches art at Aberdeen High Shool in Aberdeen Maryland.

Cover Design by Barry Bittman, MD.

Photography by Roxanne Photography LLC, Meadville Pennsylvania.

Forward

An apple a day keeps the doctor away. Can eating and cooking for better health really be this simple? It's not as hard as you think — just throw out the fads and focus on the facts.

Cooking for the Health of It is not just another cookbook. This unique nutrition guide and cookbook serves up a new perspective on health and wellness you may never before have considered. **Cooking for the Health of It** will help you maximize your health and feel the best you've felt in your entire life. It's also an exceptional guide for individuals who want to manage or prevent diabetes, heart disease, high blood pressure, high cholesterol, cancer, osteoporosis or excess weight.

And best of all you don't have to give up the foods you love or abandon your favorite recipes. My top 10 tips for **Eating for the Health of It** combined with my **Cooking for the Health of It 10 No-Nonsense Steps** will enable you to prepare and savor over **180 delicious and healthy** recipes.

Experience the power of great nutrition today and enjoy mouth-watering "good-for-you" food beginning with your next bite. When healthy food tastes this good, you won't know how you lived without it!

It's time to cook for the health of it. *Nothing ventured, nothing gained.*

To Great Food and Better Health,
Jane M. Livingston, RD, CDE

He that takes medicine and neglects diet
wastes the skills of the physician.
Chinese Proverb

A healthy man is a successful man.
French Proverb

A man too busy to take care of his health
is like a mechanic too busy to take care of his tools.
Spanish Proverb

It is useless for the sheep to
pass resolutions in favor of vegetarianism
while the wolf remains of a different opinion.
W.R. Inge

Cooking for the Health of It

A No-Nonsense Guide & Cookbook for Optimizing Health & Wellness

Table of Contents

Fear less, hope more.
Eat less, chew more.
Sigh less, breathe more.
Hate less, love more.
And all good things are yours.
Swedish Proverb

Our bodies are our gardens
to which our wills are gardeners.
Shakespeare

A healthy future begins with your next bite.
Jane Livingston, RD, CDE

Don't dig your grave with your own knife and fork.

English Proverb

I like to eat. Who doesn't? I like to eat healthy food. Who wouldn't? And I like to eat good tasting, healthy food. Who doesn't and who wouldn't?

Good tasting, healthy food is not an oxymoron. Good tasting, healthy food is a goal that we all should embrace to achieve optimal health. Unfortunately, the prevailing attitude seems to be: "If it's good for you, it tastes bad. If it's bad for you, it tastes good."

We use food for many reasons. Food is nourishment. Food is fuel for energy. Food is health. Food is vitality. Food is wellness. Food is therapeutic. But food has also turned into a national past time — a hobby. We use food in times of stress. We turn to food in times of emotional need . . . from happiness to sadness . . . from celebration to mourning.

We are what we eat. *Garbage in, garbage out.* Our bodies build the foundation of our health from what we eat. Are we satisfied with our health? Do we feel as good as we possibly could feel? Do we optimally manage our existing health conditions? Are we practicing health care or disease care? Are we waiting until we develop a health problem to make changes in our diets and lifestyles? As the Scottish Proverb goes — *we'll never know the worth of water till the well goes dry.*

We are a nation obsessed with beauty and thinness, yet we are a nation obsessed with food, fat and big portions — the bigger the better! We are in the era of the "supersize" portions, the "value meal" deal, the "biggie" drinks and the "all-you-can-eat" buffets. Years ago restaurants and fast food chains began competing for our consumer dollars by offering larger portions. Normal, modest portion sizes began to disappear. Huge muffins, four times the size of normal, were introduced to our bakery shelves. Microwave popcorn, which once served eight people, was suddenly a single-portion bag. Even *Seinfeld* had a show on "big salads."

According to statistics from the U.S. Department of Agriculture (USDA), the average daily calorie consumption of Americans has increased from 1,854 calories to 2,002 calories over the past 20 years— almost a 10 percent increase or 148 extra daily calories, which equates to a 15 pound weight gain per year.

In the 21st century we are a nation whose health is in crisis. Our American health has begun to pay for our poor nutrition habits and sedentary lifestyles. All major chronic diseases, cardiovascular disease, diabetes mellitus, obesity, osteoporosis and cancer, are nutrition and lifestyle related.

In his *1986 Report on Nutrition and Health*, C. Everett Koop, M.D., the former U.S. Surgeon General, stated, "If you are among the 4 out of 5 Americans who do not smoke or drink excessively, your choice of diet can influence your long-term health prospects more than any other action you might take."

More recently, in *The Surgeon General's Call To Action To Prevent and Decrease Overweight and Obesity*, Health and Human Services Secretary Tommy G. Thompson stated, "Our modern environment has allowed [overweight and obesity] to increase at alarming rates and become a growing health problem for our nation. By confronting these conditions, we have tremendous opportunities to prevent the unnecessary disease and disability they portend for our future."

Healthy eating is quite simple. As the proverb goes— *one pound of learning requires ten pounds of common sense to apply it.* You've heard it before— balance, variety and moderation. Credible nutrition and health authorities promote diets of selectiveness and moderation— choosing more of certain foods while limiting our selections of other foods associated with increased risk of chronic health conditions. They do not recommend diets of deprivation or total abstinence of foods and nutrients. Why does the concept of healthy eating conger up thoughts of bland, boring and tasteless food and diets of deprivation?

What does good tasting, healthy food mean? It doesn't mean you have to cut out all the sugar . . . all the fat . . . all the cholesterol . . . all the sodium . . . and all the calories. If we eliminated these ingredients from our foods, we would cut out much of the taste and pleasure of the eating experience. The food might be healthy but it wouldn't be enjoyable.

The misconceptions associated with healthy eating may be attributed to the confusion created and sustained by the $33 billion diet and $700 million nutrition supplement industries. Fad diets, diet books, infomercials, diet programs, diet pills, nutrition supplements and herbal supplements cloud the facts about what we know to be credible nutrition information. They continue to generate controversy regarding healthy eating and dieting in order to support their industries. We are quick to spend money on fad diets from less than credible sources — diets that promote deprivation, exclusion, excessiveness and unreasonableness.

When we scrutinize the diet industry, there is no consensus regarding what to eat to achieve a optimal weight or health. Fad diets include high protein/low carb diets, grapefruit diets, cabbage soup diets, 7-day diets, meal replacement drinks, macrobiotic diets, "live-food" diets, blood-type diets, caveman diets, food combination diets, Hollywood star diets and so on. These diets are not founded on evidence-based research. They are based on anecdote, opinion and conjecture — not science, research and fact.

Fad diets promote the idea that certain foods or nutrients are "bad" and should be avoided. Many plans urge you to indulge in large or unlimited quantities of high saturated fat foods (foods associated with many chronic health conditions) and abandon fruits, whole grains and vegetables (foods associated with the prevention of many chronic health conditions.) Shouldn't we question diet plans that promote bacon and pork rinds and shun carrots?

Rather than focus on a diet of deprivation or exclusion, let's focus on a diet of selectiveness and inclusion— a focus on what TO eat, rather than what NOT to eat. Credible nutrition and health authorities are in consensus regarding what to eat to achieve and maintain good health. Here are six examples of concensus regarding fruit and vegetable consumption:

"Diets containing substantial and varied amounts of vegetables and fruits will prevent 20 percent or more of all cases of cancer"
American Institute for Cancer Research

"A diet high in fruits and vegetables usually leads to a reduction in total calories and fat which enhances weight management."
American Obesity Association

"Higher intake of fruits, vegetables and other foods rich in vitamin C and potassium have been associated with lower stroke rates."
American Stroke Association

"Eating high amounts of vegetables, vitamin E and vitamin C is associated with lower risks of dementia and Alzheimer's disease."
Alzheimer's Association

"Consumption of fruits and vegetables containing two carotenoid pigments may be linked to a reduced risk for age-related macular degeneration."
American Macular Degeneration Foundation

"Dietary patterns characterized by high intake of fruits and vegetables are associated with a lower risk of developing heart disease, stroke and hypertension."
American Heart Association

The road to health is paved with good information.

Taking It to Heart

According to the 2002 American Heart Association (AHA) *Heart and Stroke Statistical Update*, 81,200,000 Americans have one or more forms of **heart disease** — high blood pressure, coronary heart disease, heart attack, angina and stroke. The cost of cardiovascular diseases and stroke in the U.S. in 2002 is estimated at $329.2 billion. Since 1999 estimates, the number of people with heart disease has grown by almost 20,000,000.

Coronary heart disease is the single leading cause of death in the U.S. — one in every 2.5 deaths. Stroke is the leading cause of serious, long-term disability in the U.S. According to the most recent Center for Disease Control computations, if all forms of heart disease were eliminated, life expectancy would increase by about 7 years.

An elevated blood cholesterol level is a major modifiable risk factor for heart disease. Diet, exercise and weight status influence blood cholesterol levels. According to the National Health and Nutrition Examination Survey (NHANES) III, an estimated 102,340,000 American adults have total blood cholesterol levels of 200 mg/dL and higher.

Good nutrition and a healthy lifestyle are important for the prevention and management of heart disease. Healthy eating habits help maintain normal blood pressure, optimal blood cholesterol levels and a healthy body weight. They also may aid blood clotting, oxidation, maintaining a normal heart rhythm and other effects. The *2001 National Cholesterol Education Program Expert Panel on Detection, Evaluation and Treatment of High Blood Cholesterol in Adults* [Adult Treatment Panel III (ATP III)] provides recommendations for cholesterol testing and management for the prevention of heart

11

disease. ATP III recommends lowering low density lipoproteins (LDL) levels and keeping them low by adopting a low saturated fat and low cholesterol diet, maintaining a healthy body weight and participating in regular physical activity. Elevated triglyceride levels and low high density lipoprotein (HDL) levels are also strongly associated with increased risk for heart disease. See Table 1.

Table 1. ATP III Lipid Goals

Category	ATP III Levels	Classification
Total Cholesterol	Less than 200 mg/dL	Desirable
LDL Cholesterol	Less than 100 mg/dL	Optimal
HDL Cholesterol	Less than 40 mg/dL	Low
HDL Cholesterol	60 mg/dL or greater	High
Triglycerides	Less than 150 mg/dL	Normal

High blood pressure, cigarette smoking, obesity, physical inactivity and a high saturated fat, high cholesterol diet are other major modifiable risk factors for heart disease. People who consume diets high in fruits, vegetables, whole grains and unsaturated fats have an apparent lower risk for heart disease. According to the *AHA Dietary Guidelines: Revision 2000*, antioxidant nutrients, folic acid, other B vitamins, omega 3 fatty acids and other micronutrients may explain this lower risk. ATP III asserts that certain dietary habits reduce the risk for heart disease, independent of LDL cholesterol levels.

If you have elevated cholesterol levels or a strong family history, ATP III recommends a multifactorial lifestyle approach for reducing risk for heart disease. This approach has been designated as *Therapeutic Lifestyle Changes* (TLC). TLC guidelines address: (1) reduced intakes of saturated fats and cholesterol, (2) therapeutic dietary options for enhancing LDL lowering [use of plant stanols/sterols (components of soy and flax) and increased soluble fiber], (3) weight reduction and (4) increased regular physical activity. See Tables 2 and 3.

Table 2. Components for the TLC Diet

Component	Recommendation
LDL-Raising Nutrients	
Saturated Fats	Less than 7% of total calories
Dietary Cholesterol	Less than 200 milligrams per day
Therapeutic Options to Lower LDL	
Plant Stanols/Sterols	2 grams per day
Increased Soluble Fiber	10 to 25 grams per day
Total Calories	Adjust calorie intake to maintain or achieve healthy body weight
Physical Activity	Exercise moderately to expend at least 200 calories per day

Table 3. Nutrition Recommendations for the TLC Diet

Component	Recommendation
Total Fat	25 to 35% of total calories
Monounsaturated Fat	Up to 20% of total calories
Polyunsaturated Fat	Up to 10% of total calories
Carbohydrate	50 to 60% of total calories
Dietary Fiber	20 to 30 grams per day
Protein	Approximately 15% of total calories

Nutrition recommendations for the prevention and management of heart disease are summarized as follows:

1. Choose a diet low in saturated fat, trans fats, cholesterol and other LDL-raising foods.
2. Substitute moderate amounts of monounsaturated fats in place of saturated and other LDL-raising fats.
3. Eat plenty of vegetables, fresh fruits, whole grains, legumes and other foods low in fat and high in fiber. Increase soluble fiber intake to 10 to 25 grams daily.
4. Include 2 grams of plant stanols/sterols daily — soy products, ground flax seed and special cholesterol-lowering margarines.
5. Adjust calorie intake to maintain or achieve a healthy weight.

The Diabetes Epidemic

According to NHANES, over 17 million people have been diagnosed with **diabetes mellitus**. An additional 16 million individuals have "**pre-diabetes**" or "metabolic syndrome," a condition that sharply raises the risk for developing type 2 diabetes and increases the risk of heart disease by 50 percent.

A recent diabetes expert panel, which included the American Diabetes Association and representatives from the National Institute of Diabetes and Digestive and Kidney Diseases and Centers for Disease Control and Prevention, issued a strong warning regarding pre-diabetes. The expert panel sited research that shows the development of type 2 diabetes can be delayed or prevented through modest lifestyle improvements. For many people, modest lifestyle changes can "turn back the clock" and normalize blood glucose levels. Diabesity™ is an initiative from Shape Up America!, which focuses on the causal connection between obesity and type 2 diabetes.

If you have diabetes or pre-diabetes, the American Diabetes Association recommends a healthy diet similar to guidelines for all Americans. A healthy eating plan for diabetes management depends on diabetes goals, calorie and nutritional needs, lifestyle, physical activity and food preferences.

Nutrition recommendations for the prevention and management of diabetes and pre-diabetes are summarized as follows:

1. Balance and moderate total carbohydrate intake to achieve and maintain blood glucose control near normal levels. Reduce consumption of refined, processed carbohydrates.
2. Reduce overall calorie intake and portion sizes to maintain or achieve a healthy body weight. Choose a diet high in dietary fiber and vegetables.
3. Select a diet low in fat, saturated fat and cholesterol to achieve normal lipid levels to prevent or manage heart disease.
4. Choose a diet moderate in salt and sodium to maintain blood pressure control.

Those Extra Pounds

The number of U.S. adults who are **overweight** or **obese** has reached 64.5 percent according to the latest figures from NHANES. Weight status is determined by Body Mass Index (BMI). A healthy body mass index is 20 to 25. To calculate your BMI:

$$\frac{\text{Weight (in pounds)}}{\text{Height (in inches)}^2} \times 703 = \text{BMI}$$

The prevalence of obesity (BMI 30) has risen to 30.5 percent, while extreme obesity (BMI 40) has risen to 4.7 percent. In adolescents, the prevalence of obesity has nearly tripled in the past 20 years. The number of overweight individuals in the U.S. is on the rise for all age groups and all racial/ethnic groups.

Overweight and obesity are known risk factors for diabetes, heart disease, stroke, high blood pressure, gallbladder disease, osteoarthritis, sleep apnea and other breathing problems and some forms of cancer (uterine, breast, colorectal kidney and gallbladder). Obesity is associated with high blood cholesterol, complications of pregnancy, menstrual irregularities, hirsutism (presence of excess body and facial hair), stress incontinence, psychological disorders (depression) and increased surgical risk.

Epidemiological studies show an increase in death associated with overweight and obesity. Individuals who are obese have a 50 to 100 percent greater risk of premature death from all causes compared to individuals with healthy BMI's. An estimated 300,000 deaths may be attributable to obesity annually.

If you are overweight, a loss of just 5 to 15 percent of your body weight will improve your overall health, reduce risk for chronic health conditions and improve your quality of life. Even modest weight reduction improves the management of chronic health conditions and allows us to participate in and enjoy the activities of life.

Body weight and the prevalence of obesity are rising so rapidly worldwide that the World Health Organization (WHO) has acknowledged a "global epidemic of obesity." The *WHO Expert Panel on Obesity, Exercise and Cancer* has issued these nutrition and lifestyle recommendations for the prevention and management of overweight and obesity:

1. Focus on proper weight early in life.
2. Maintain weight as a lifelong strategy.
3. Ensure adequate physical activity to promote energy balance and weight control.
4. Limit the purchase and availability of high calorie foods and beverages with low nutritional value and provide an abundant supply of fruits, vegetables and whole grains.

Boning Up

The National Osteoporosis Foundation estimates that **low bone mass** and **osteoporosis** are major public health threats for almost 44 million or 55 percent of U.S. women and men age 50 and older. Eighty percent of these people are women.

Osteoporosis is not part of normal aging. It is mostly preventable with nutrition and lifestyle modifications. Building strong bones before age 30 is the best defense against developing osteoporosis. National nutrition surveys have shown that many women and young girls consume less than half the recommended amount of calcium to grow and maintain healthy bones. A healthy lifestyle also keeps bones strong. Recommendations for preventing osteoporosis include:

1. Eat a balanced diet rich in calcium. Choose lowfat and fat-free milk and milk products to consume between 1,000 and 1,300 milligrams of calcium daily. Other calcium sources include tofu, calcium-fortified orange juice, calcium-fortified soy milk, soybeans, canned fish with bones and dark-green leafy vegetables.

2. Take a calcium supplement if necessary. For optimal absorption of calcium supplements:
    *   Take with food and space the dose throughout the day.
    *   Drink plenty of fluids to avoid constipation.
    *   Do not take with soft drinks, coffee or iron supplements.
3. Consume a balanced diet rich in vitamin D to ensure absorption of calcium. Choose fortified dairy products, eggs and fish and get plenty of exposure to sunlight. Experts recommend an intake between 400 and 800 IU daily.
4. Participate in lifelong regular weight-bearing exercise such as walking, jogging, dancing, stair-climbing and racquet sports.
5. Do not smoke or use tobacco in any form.
6. Do not consume excess alcohol, coffee, caffeine or soft drinks.
7. Discuss bone mineral density testing and osteoporosis medications with your health care provider.

The Silent Killer

High blood pressure often has no warning signs or symptoms. If uncontrolled it can lead to stroke, heart and kidney disease. High blood pressure affects about 1 in 4 or 50 million adult Americans.

Research has found that diet affects the development of high blood pressure. Following the *DASH Diet* (Dietary Approaches to Stop Hypertension) and reducing the consumption of sodium has been shown to lower blood pressure and may help prevent the development of high blood pressure. The DASH Diet is low in saturated fat, cholesterol and total fat and emphasizes fruits, vegetables and lowfat dairy foods.

Lifestyle and nutrition guidelines for controlling high blood pressure include:
1. Maintain a healthy weight.
2. Be physically active.
3. Follow a healthy eating plan, lower in salt and sodium.
4. Drink alcoholic beverages only in moderation if at all.
5. Take high blood pressure medication as prescribed.

The DASH diet includes specific nutrition recommendations:
1. Select more whole grain products, fish, poultry and nuts.
2. Choose foods low in saturated fat, cholesterol and total fat; reduce consumption of red meat.
3. Choose fewer sweets and sugar-containing beverages.
4. Emphasize fruits, vegetables and lowfat dairy foods to ensure a diet rich in magnesium, potassium and calcium.
5. Consume adequate protein and fiber.
6. Limit daily sodium intake to 2,400 milligrams (the upper limit of current recommendations by the National High Blood Pressure Education Program).

Preventing Cancer

Experts agree that **cancer** is mostly a preventable disease. According to the American Institute for Cancer Research, a healthy lifestyle, which includes diet, exercise, healthy body weight and not smoking, could reduce global cancer incidence by 60 to 70 percent. Diets high in amount and variety of vegetables and fruits may prevent 20 percent or more of all cases of cancer. In 1997, the American Institute for Cancer Research, in collaboration with the World Cancer Research Fund, published *Food, Nutrition and the Prevention of Cancer: a global perspective*. Based on 4,500 research studies with 120 contributors and peer-reviewers, this report is the most comprehensive review of studies related to diet, nutrition and cancer.

The American Institute for Cancer Research offers 15 dietary and health recommendations, which encompass foods and drinks, eating patterns, dietary supplementation, physical activity, obesity and tobacco. They are summarized as follows:
1. Choose a diet rich in a variety of plant-based foods.
2. Eat plenty of vegetables and fruits.
3. Maintain a healthy weight and be physically active.
4. Drink alcohol only in moderation if at all.
5. Select foods low in fat and salt.
6. Prepare and store food safely.
7. *And always remember* — do not use tobacco in any form.

18

American Institute for Cancer Research

Nutrition & Health Recommendations

1. **Food Supply and Eating:** Choose a nutritionally adequate, varied and predominantly plant-based diet rich in a variety of vegetables and fruits, legumes and minimally-processed starchy foods.

2. **Healthy Body Weight:** Achieve and maintain a healthy body mass index between 18.5 and 25. Avoid being underweight or overweight and limit adult weight gain to less than 11 pounds.

3. **Regular Physical Activity:** Maintain an active lifestyle equivalent to at least one hour of brisk walking or moderate exercise daily. In addition, plan at least one hour of vigorous exercise per week.

4. **Fruits and Vegetables:** Consume a variety of fruits and vegetables year round striving for five or more servings daily.

5. **Other Plant Foods:** Eat seven or more servings daily of a variety of cereals (whole grains), legumes, roots, tubers and other minimally-processed foods. Limit consumption of refined sugars.

6. **Alcoholic Drinks:** Alcohol consumption is not recommended. If consumed at all, limit alcoholic drinks to less than two drinks daily for men and one for women.

7. **Meat:** If eaten at all, limit red meat intake to less than three ounces daily. Fish, poultry and meat from non-domesticated animals are preferable to red meat.

8. **Total Fats and Oils:** Limit consumption of fatty foods particularly those of animal origin. Choose modest amounts of appropriate vegetable oils.

9. **Salt and Salting:** Limit consumption of salted foods and use of cooking and table salt. Use herbs and spices to season foods.

10. **Storage:** Store perishable food in ways that minimize fungal contamination.

11. **Preservation:** Practice safe food handling techniques. Use refrigeration and other appropriate methods to preserve perishable food.

12. **Additives and Residues:** When levels of additives, contaminants and other residues are properly regulated, their presence in food and drink is not known to be harmful. Unregulated or improper use can be a health hazard, and this applies particularly to foods from economically developing countries.

13. **Preparation:** Do not eat charred or burned foods. For meat and fish eaters, avoid the burning of meat juices. Limit consumption of meat and fish grilled in direct flame and cured and smoked meats.

14. **Dietary Supplements:** Focus on eating a healthful diet rather than relying on dietary supplements. For those who follow these recommendations, dietary supplements are probably unnecessary and possibly unhelpful for reducing cancer risk.

15. **Tobacco Use:** Do not smoke or chew tobacco in any form.

The American Institute for Cancer Research recently unveiled their "New American Plate." The New American Plate emphasizes the kinds of foods that can significantly reduce risk for disease and promotes the 2/3 to 1/3 portions— two-thirds of our plate from plant-based foods and one-third from protein and animal-based foods.

USDA Dietary Guidelines

The fifth edition of **Nutrition and Your Health: Dietary Guidelines for Americans** was released by the U.S. Departments of Health and Human Services and Agriculture in May 2000. The new 10 dietary guidelines promote three basic messages designed to promote overall good health and reduce risk for chronic diseases. The *Dietary Guidelines* are:

AIM FOR FITNESS–
1. Aim for a healthy weight.
2. Be physically active each day.

BUILD A HEALTHY BASE–
3. Let the Pyramid guide your food choices.
4. Choose a variety of grains daily especially whole grains.
5. Choose a variety of fruits and vegetables daily.
6. Keep food safe to eat.

CHOOSE SENSIBLY–
7. Choose a diet low in saturated fat and cholesterol and moderate in total fat.
8. Choose beverages and foods to moderate your intake of sugars.
9. Choose and prepare foods with less salt.
10. If you drink alcoholic beverages, do so in moderation.

Food Guide Pyramid

The **Food Guide Pyramid** is a general guide for choosing a healthful diet based on the Dietary Guidelines. The Food Guide Pyramid emphasizes eating a variety of foods from each food group to get adequate nutrients without excessive calories, fat, saturated fat, cholesterol, sugar, sodium or alcohol. The Pyramid focuses on a foundation of plenty of breads, cereals, rice, pasta, vegetables and fruits, with less emphasis on meat, poultry, fish, milk and milk products. The Pyramid does not promote excess. It promotes that no one food group is more important than another. The Food Pyramid guidelines are based on the fourth edition of the Dietary Guidelines for Americans:

1. Eat a variety of foods to get the energy, protein, vitamins, minerals and fiber you need for good health.
2. Balance your food consumption with physical activity to maintain or improve weight to reduce risk of high blood pressure, heart disease, stroke, certain cancers and type 2 diabetes.
3. Choose a diet with plenty of grain products, vegetables and fruits, which provide vitamins, minerals, fiber and complex carbohydrates and little fat.
4. Choose a diet low in fat, saturated fat and cholesterol to reduce your risk of heart attack, certain cancers and obesity.
5. Choose a diet moderate in sugars. A diet high in sugars has too many calories and too few nutrients for most people and can contribute to tooth decay.
6. Choose a diet moderate in salt and sodium, using less salt in cooking and at the table to reduce risk of high blood pressure.
7. If you drink alcoholic beverages, do so in moderation. Alcoholic beverages supply calories but little or no nutrients.

Healthy People 2010

Health People 2010 is the prevention agenda for the U.S. It is a comprehensive set of national health objectives designed to identify the most significant, preventable threats to health and to establish national goals to reduce these threats. Leading health indicators include cancer, chronic kidney disease, diabetes, heart disease and stroke, nutrition and overweight, physical activity and fitness and tobacco use. Specific nutrition and lifestyle guidelines include:

1. Maintain or achieve a healthy body weight (BMI <25).
2. Reduce saturated fat intake to less than 10% of total calories.
3. Increase vegetable intake to at least three servings daily with at least one serving of dark green or orange vegetables.
4. Increase fruit intake to at least two servings daily.
5. Consume at least six servings of grains daily with at least two servings from whole grains.
6. Do not smoke.
7. Participate in regular physical activity of moderate intensity.

The proof of the pudding is in the eating.

American Proverb

Would I like to see everyone cooking from scratch much like my mother did while growing up in rural northwestern Pennsylvania? The unequivocal ideal answer would have to be "yes." But the realistic answer would be "not in today's society." This was illustrated to me recently when my nephew's second grade class wrote cookbooks of their favorite recipes made by their mothers. Here are two examples:

"Chalupas" by Malik's Mom — "First we go to Taco Bell. Then we go through the drive away. Then I give them the coupons. Then they give me the chalupa. Then we go back home. And I eat it!"

"Cheese Pizza" by Natalie's Mom — "First she goes to the [grocery store] to get pizza. Then she goes home and then she puts it in the oven without the box. Then she puts the pizza in there for about a half an hour. And then when she takes it out, you put cheese on it. Then we get to eat the yummy pizza!"

I cannot help but wonder if houses will someday be built without kitchens. How will our concept of meals change in the next 20 years?

Based on what I've learned — it's doubtful we can live in the fast food lane and still maintain a healthy weight or optimal cholesterol levels. And a diet absent of fruits and vegetables is unlikely to help us achieve optimal health and wellness.

Fortunately, we do not have to spend hours in the kitchen, slaving over a hot stove, to prepare or plan a balanced meal. We don't have to gather the family around the traditional kitchen table to eat a balanced meal. Meals of the 21st century are vastly different than meals of the 20th century. Schedules, priorities and goals of the 21st century are vastly different than the schedules, priorities and goals of the 20th century. For these reasons, it is appropriate that nutrition, cooking and lifestyle recommendations reflect our 21st century schedules, priorities and goals.

Better eating habits begin with better shopping habits. We can't prepare healthy meals without shopping for and selecting healthy foods and ingredients. I am frequently asked the question, "Why aren't there more healthy foods to buy [at the grocery store or restaurant]?" There are endless good, healthy choices— we just need to look and think beyond our usual grocery list or menu selections. At first, it may take a little more time to do your food shopping, but new shopping habits become easy with practice and repetition. *Practice makes perfect.*

On the other hand, we can't eat healthy meals if we don't prepare foods using healthy cooking methods. But we can learn better cooking habits— we just need to think beyond our usual repertoire of preparation methods and cooking techniques. With practice, it becomes easy to modify recipes to be healthy, taste delicious and provide pleasurable eating experiences.

It's time we focus on the facts and stop being lured by the fads. We've identified ten common themes in the national nutrition recommendations. Let's use the best information medical science has to offer to build better eating and cooking habits. You don't have to give up the foods you love or abandon your favorite recipes. Just follow my guidelines for the **Eating for the Health of It** and **Cooking for the Health of It** "10 No-Nonsense Steps."

You'll soon be preparing and enjoying great tasting, healthy meals and feeling the power of better nutrition for a lifetime.

You can have your cake and eat it too!

Eating for the Health of It

One pound of learning requires
ten pounds of common sense to apply it.
Persian Proverb

1. Healthy people consume a diet rich in a variety of fruits and vegetables.

2. Healthy people select high fiber foods and prepare recipes using more whole grains and other minimally-processed foods.

3. Healthy people select more plant-based meals including more soy products, legumes and other vegetarian alternatives.

4. Healthy people choose foods and recipes low in saturated fats and other processed fats such as hydrogenated and trans fats.

5. Healthy people consume more fish and other foods rich in omega 3 fatty acids.

6. Healthy people choose and cook with fewer processed sugars and limit ingredients high in refined sugars.

7. Healthy people use moderate amounts of monounsaturated, nut and plant oils in place of saturated and other fats.

8. Healthy people balance their calorie intake to achieve or maintain a healthy body weight throughout their lifetime.

9. Healthy people ensure an adequate daily calcium intake to build adequate bone mass and prevent osteoporosis.

10. Healthy people enjoy the natural flavor of foods without excessively using salt and sodium.

Cooking for the Health of It
10 No-Nonsense Steps

Step 1

A preparation method or cooking technique can be changed. The sauté cooking method using nonstick cooking spray is an excellent alternative to frying. Use olive or canola oil nonstick cooking sprays on pans and directly on foods.

Step 2

An ingredient may be reduced or eliminated. In most recipes, fat may be cut by 1/4 without changing the final product. Sugar, in its various forms, may be cut by 1/3 without sacrificing flavor or function. Consider eliminating certain ingredients that provide empty calories.

Step 3

One ingredient may be substituted for another. A lowfat ingredient or product may be substituted for its high fat counterpart. A lowfat food contains 0 to 3 grams of fat per serving. A sugarfree product made without sugar or with a sugar substitute may be substituted for sugar in its various forms.

Step 4

Cook with only small amounts of salt and flavor with more herbs and spices. Salt may be eliminated from most recipes except those with yeast. Rinse canned vegetables and beans to reduce the sodium content by 40 percent. Check with your physician or registered dietitian before using a salt substitute due to potential nutrient-drug interactions.

Step 5

Add more vegetables to recipes to extend portions and reduce calories. Double vegetables in recipes. Take advantage of fresh and frozen pre-prepped vegetables that are shredded, chopped and diced. Thaw frozen vegetables before using in recipes.

Step 6

Look for ways to increase fiber in recipes. Choose whole grains and add legumes, nuts, ground flax seed, wheat germ and bran to favorite recipes. Good fiber sources provide at least 3 grams of dietary fiber per serving.

Step 7

Apply sound cooking principles when *Cooking for the Health of It.* Heat pans and skillets before coating with nonstick cooking spray or adding oil. Heat oils before adding food or seasonings. Do not cover foods before the searing or carmelization process occurs. Adjust seasonings at the end of the cooking process.

Step 8

Consider the function of ingredients when modifying recipes. Fat is a cooking medium, plus it provides taste, structure, moisture, volume, tenderness, plasticity (the ability to mold and hold shape), crispness, spread-ability and whip-ability. Sugar provides sweetness, moisture, volume, tenderness, browning and preservation.

Step 9

Blend textures, tastes, shapes and colors to add dimension, diversity and interest to healthy cooking. The "bland and boring" perception of healthy eating is often a result of poor planning, lack of creativity, misconceptions and stereotypes. Healthy eating is only limited by the cook's imagination. The concept of "less" does not mean "eliminate."

Step 10

Make recipe modifications that result in significant improvements in the overall health contribution of the recipe. Do not sacrifice flavor, appeal and quality for minimal health benefits. Consider portions before reducing or eliminating ingredients.

A Brief History of Medicine

'Doctor, I have an earache' . . .
2000 BC — Here, eat this root.
1000 AD — That root is heathen.
Here, say this prayer.
1850 AD — That prayer is superstition.
Here, drink this potion.
1940 AD — That potion is snake oil.
Here, swallow this pill.
1985 AD — That pill is ineffective.
Here, take this antibiotic.
2000 AD — That antibiotic is artificial.
Here, eat this root.

Anonymous

Cooking for the Health of It

Good-for-You Recipes

*Good, better, best—
never rest till good be better
and better, best.*
Anonymous

29

*Better a meal of vegetables where there is love
than a fattened calf with hatred.*
Proverbs 15:17

*Having a good wife and rich cabbage soup,
seek not other things.*
Russian Proverb

Some prefer carrot while others like cabbage.
Chinese Proverb

*Eat vegetables and fear no creditor
rather than eat duck and hide.*
Hebrew

If there is no apple one eats a little carrot.

Russian Proverb

*Healthy people consume a diet rich
in a variety of fruits and vegetables.*

- Eat a serving fruit and/or vegetable at every meal.
- Choose a variety of fruits and vegetables— all shapes, tastes, colors and textures.
- Prepare both cooked and uncooked fruits and vegetables.
- Plan balanced meals and half-fill plates with vegetables.
- Consume a minimum of 5 servings and an optimal 10 servings of fruits and vegetables daily. One serving equals 1/2 cup cooked/canned, 1 cup raw, 1/4 cup dried or 1 medium piece.
- Snack on fresh fruits and vegetables for health and convenience.
- Select fresh fruits for dessert.
- Double the amount of fruit required in fruit recipes.
- Select canned fruit packed in fruit juice without added sugars.
- Double the amount of vegetables required in casserole, side dish or entree recipes.
- Keep pre-packaged, shredded and cut vegetables handy for quick snacks or fast food preparation.
- Save preparation time by using frozen chopped vegetables such as diced onions, peppers and carrots.
- Prepare vegetables using a variety cooking methods— stir-fry, steam, sauté or grill.
- Sauté vegetables in nonstick cooking spray to carmelize natural sugars.
- Use a variety of cutting techniques to add interest to vegetables — chop, dice, diagonal cut, julienne (matchstick), coin, shred, half-moon, cube, mince or sliver.
- Select local produce when available and take advantage of seasonal produce.
- Thoroughly wash all produce with water, a vinegar/water wash or a bleach/water wash before consuming.

Chunky Tomato Rice Soup

An updated vegetable-enhanced version of an old favorite.

1 tablespoon extra virgin olive oil
1 medium onion, chopped
2 cloves crushed garlic
1 can (28-ounce) crushed tomatoes, undrained
2 tablespoons tomato paste
1 tablespoon fresh chopped basil [or 1 teaspoon dried]
2½ cups water
1 teaspoon granulated sugar
1/3 cup long-grain white rice
1 cup chopped broccoli (fresh or frozen)
3 tablespoons dry sherry, optional
1/2 teaspoon salt
1/4 teaspoon fresh ground black pepper
1/4 teaspoon ground white pepper

In a large saucepot, combine oil, onion and garlic. Sauté over medium heat until onions are opaque. Add undrained tomatoes, tomato paste, basil, water and sugar. Bring to a boil. Cover and simmer for 30 minutes.

Bring tomato mixture back to a boil. Add rice and broccoli. Reduce heat and simmer for 15 minutes or until rice is tender. Stir in sherry and season with salt and peppers. Adjust seasonings. Makes 4 servings (approximately 1½ cups per serving).

Nutrition Facts: Calories 148, Protein 3.1 gm, Carbohydrate 24.2 gm, Dietary Fiber 3.4 gm, Fat 4.1 gm, Saturated Fat 0.6 gm, Sodium 604 mg
Meal Planning: 1 Carbohydrate, 1 Vegetable, 1 Fat

Country Mushroom Soup

A delicious soup loaded with mushrooms– great on a cold day.

1 large vidalia onion, thinly sliced
1/3 cup brown rice
1/4 cup wild rice
6 cups low sodium vegetable or chicken broth
1 pound fresh mushrooms
1 pound fresh baby portobello mushrooms
2 tablespoons extra virgin olive oil
1 cup matchstick carrots
1/4 cup dry sherry, optional
1 tablespoon fresh chopped parsley [or 1 teaspoon dried]
1/2 teaspoon salt
1/4 teaspoon fresh ground black pepper
1/4 teaspoon ground white pepper

In a large saucepot, combine onion, brown rice, wild rice and broth. Bring to a boil. Cover, reduce heat and simmer for 25 minutes.

Meanwhile, wash and scrub mushrooms. Chop half the mushrooms and slice the other half.

Coat a large deep skillet with nonstick cooking spray. Place over medium heat. Add oil and heat. Add chopped and sliced mushrooms. Gently cook mushrooms for about 10 to 15 minutes or until golden brown and most of the moisture has evaporated.

Add mushrooms and carrots to simmering broth. Stir in sherry and parsley; season with salt and peppers. Simmer for 10 minutes. Adjust seasonings. Makes 6 servings (approximately 1½ to 2 cups per serving).

Nutrition Facts: Calories 158, Protein 6.8 gm, Carbohydrate 25.2 gm, Dietary Fiber 3 gm, Fat 3.2 gm, Saturated Fat 0.5 gm, Sodium 355 mg
Meal Planning: 1 Carbohydrate, 2 Vegetable, 1/2 Fat

Vermicelli Minestrone

A chunky soup loaded with vegetables and fiber.

1 medium onion, chopped
1 large fresh tomato, diced
2 cups cut green beans (fresh or frozen)
2 small zucchini squash, unpeeled, diced
4 ounces snow pea pods (fresh or frozen)
1 bag (10-ounce) fresh baby spinach
4 ounces whole wheat vermicelli or thin spaghetti
2 teaspoons extra virgin olive oil
4 cups low sodium vegetable or chicken broth
1 cup water
1 can (15-ounce) dark red kidney beans, drained and rinsed
1 can (15-ounce) cannellini (white kidney) beans, drained and rinsed
1/2 cup freshly grated Parmesan cheese
1/2 teaspoon salt
1/4 teaspoon fresh ground black pepper
1/4 teaspoon ground white pepper

Wash and prepare vegetables. Remove stems and strings along both edges of pea pods.

Break vermicelli into thirds. In a large stockpot, cook vermicelli in a large amount of boiling water until al dente, about 5 minutes; drain. Set aside.

Coat same stockpot with nonstick cooking spray. Add oil and heat over medium heat. Add onion and tomato. Cook until tender, about 4 to 5 minutes. Stir in broth, green beans, zucchini and 1 cup water. Bring to a boil over high heat. Reduce heat to low. Cover and simmer for 10 minutes or until beans and zucchini are tender. Stir in pea pods, spinach and kidney beans. Cook just until spinach wilts. Stir in cooked vermicelli and heat through. Season with salt and peppers. Sprinkle with Parmesan cheese. Adjust seasonings. Makes 8 servings (approximately 1 cup per serving).

Nutrition Facts: Calories 207, Protein 13.4 gm, Carbohydrate 32.2 gm, Dietary Fiber 6.5 gm, Fat 3.4 gm, Saturated Fat 1.5 gm, Sodium 592 mg
Meal Planning: 2 Lean Meat/Protein, 1 Carbohydrate, 2 Vegetable

Fresh Vegetable Stew

The roasting process makes this stew sweet and tasty.

1/2 head cauliflower, cut into florets
2 medium red skin potatoes, unpeeled, diced
2 medium carrots, peeled and thinly sliced [or 2 cups frozen cut carrots]
1/2 medium eggplant, unpeeled, diced
1 can (16-ounce) Italian plum tomatoes, drained
2 medium onions, thinly sliced
2 medium zucchini squash, thinly sliced
2 medium yellow squash, thinly sliced
1/2 cup frozen green peas
1/2 cup cut green beans
2 celery ribs, finely chopped
1/2 teaspoon salt
1/4 teaspoon fresh ground black pepper
1/2 cup fresh chopped dill [or 1/4 cup dried]
1/2 cup fresh chopped parsley [or 1/4 cup dried]
3 bay leaves
1½ cups low sodium vegetable broth
2 tablespoons extra virgin olive oil

Coat a large roaster with nonstick cooking spray. Arrange 1/3 vegetables in a single layer. Sprinkle with salt, pepper, dill and parsley. Top with a bay leaf. Make 2 more layers with remaining vegetables and seasonings.

Combine broth and oil and pour over vegetables. Cover and bake at 350 degrees F for 3 hours or until the vegetables are tender. May also be prepared in a large crockpot. Makes 8 servings (approximately 1½ cups per serving).

Nutrition Facts: Calories 106, Protein 3.9 gm, Carbohydrate 16.4 gm, Dietary Fiber 4.7gm, Fat 3.9 gm, Saturated Fat 0.5 gm, Sodium 211 mg
Meal Planning: 1 Carbohydrate, 1 Fat

Steamed Won-Tons

A little fussy but worth the fuss.

1 cup shredded carrots
1 head bok choy, finely chopped
1 large onion, chopped
2 cups fresh bean sprouts
1/4 cup chopped green onions
1/8 teaspoon fresh ground black pepper
1 package (10-ounce) won-ton wrappers
3 tablespoons cornstarch
1 tablespoon rice wine
2 tablespoons cold water
1/2 cup low sodium soy sauce
2 tablespoons honey [or 1 tablespoon brown sugar]

Coat a wok or large skillet with nonstick cooking spray. Place over high heat. Add carrots, bok choy, onion and bean sprouts to hot wok. Cook over medium heat until vegetables are tender and liquid has mostly evaporated. Stir in green onions and black pepper.

In a small bowl, combine cornstarch, rice wine and water. Stir into vegetables and cook for 1 to 2 minutes until thickened.

Place 1 teaspoon filling into center of a won-ton wrapper. Moisten edges with water, fold four corners into center and seal. Place won-ton in a lettuce-lined bamboo steamer. Continue filling until all wrappers are used.

Cover prepared won-tons in bamboo steamer and place over simmering water in a wok or steamer for 10 minutes.

Combine soy sauce and honey and serve as a dipping sauce, if desired. Makes 8 servings (approximately 4 to 5 won-tons per serving).

Nutrition Facts: Calories 131, Protein 5.7 gm, Carbohydrate 26 gm, Dietary Fiber 1.5 gm, Fat 0.7 gm, Saturated Fat 0.1 gm, Sodium 293 mg
Meal Planning: 1 Carbohydrate, 2 Vegetable

Savory Vegetable Pancakes

A unique departure from a favorite comfort food.

1 package (10-ounce) frozen mixed vegetables, thawed
2 tablespoons fresh minced cilantro [or 1 tablespoon dried]
Dash salt
1/2 cup whole wheat pastry flour
1 teaspoon curry powder
1/2 teaspoon baking soda
1/2 teaspoon baking powder
2 teaspoons honey
1 egg plus 1 egg white
1/2 cup plain nonfat yogurt
2 tablespoons water
Nonfat sour cream
Chives, optional

Stir cilantro and salt into thawed mixed vegetables. Set aside.

In a large bowl, combine flour, curry, baking soda and baking powder. Set aside.

In a medium bowl, beat together honey, egg and egg white with a wire whisk; add yogurt and water. Stir this mixture into reserved dry ingredients. Fold in prepared mixed vegetables.

Coat a large griddle with nonstick cooking spray. Heat over medium-low heat for a several minutes to evenly heat. Pour 1/3 cup batter per pancake onto hot griddle. Cook until lightly browned on bottom. Turn to cook the other side. Recoat griddle with nonstick cooking spray before each new batch. Serve hot with nonfat sour cream mixed with dried chives. Makes 12 medium pancakes (3 pancakes per serving).

Nutrition Facts: Calories 143, Protein 8.3 gm, Carbohydrate 25.9 gm, Dietary Fiber 5.7 gm, Fat 1.8 gm, Saturated Fat 0.9 gm, Sodium 352 mg
Meal Planning: 1 Lean Meat/Protein, 1 Carbohydrate, 1 Vegetable

Marinated Vegetable Salad

Quick and easy— great for a pot-luck dinner or picnic.

1 medium head broccoli, cut into florets
1 small head cauliflower, cut into florets
1 large red bell pepper, seeded and cut into 1-inch strips
1 large green bell pepper, seeded and cut into 1-inch strips
12 fresh mushrooms, sliced
2 large carrots, peeled and sliced on the diagonal
10 cherry or grape tomatoes
1 can (8-ounce) marinated artichoke hearts, drained
1 to 2 cloves crushed garlic
1 cup fat-free Italian dressing

Wash all vegetables thoroughly. Combine vegetables in a large bowl.

Add dressing and garlic. Toss to coat.

Cover and refrigerate overnight or for several hours to blend flavors.
Makes 12 servings (approximately 1 cup per serving).

Nutrition Facts: Calories 38, Protein 1.9 gm, Carbohydrate 11.5 gm,
Dietary Fiber 2.5 gm, Fat 0.2 gm, Saturated Fat 0 gm, Sodium 311 mg
Meal Planning: 2 Vegetable

Relish Salad

A delicious salad that keeps for days in the refrigerator.

1 package (10-ounce) frozen English (petite) peas, thawed
1 package (10-ounce) frozen white shoepeg corn, thawed
1 package (10-ounce) frozen French cut green beans, thawed
2 cups fresh bean sprouts [or 2 cups canned, drained and rinsed]
1/2 cup finely chopped red bell pepper
1/2 cup finely chopped green bell pepper
1 cup finely chopped vidalia onion
1 cup finely chopped celery
1/4 cup canola oil
1/4 cup water
3/4 cup white balsamic or apple cider vinegar
1/2 teaspoon salt
1/4 teaspoon fresh ground black pepper
1/4 teaspoon ground white pepper
1/4 cup granulated sugar
3/4 cup Splenda® sugar substitute

In a large bowl, combine all vegetables.

In a medium saucepan, combine canola oil, water, vinegar, salt, peppers, sugar and Splenda®. Bring to a boil then cool slightly.

Pour warm dressing over vegetables, tossing to combine. Cover and refrigerate for 24 hours before serving. Makes 24 servings (approximately 1/2 cup per serving).

Nutrition Facts: Calories 60, Protein 1.7 gm, Carbohydrate 8.6 gm, Dietary Fiber 1.7 gm, Fat 2.5 gm, Saturated Fat 0.2 gm, Sodium 52 mg
Meal Planning: 1 Vegetable, 1/2 Fat

Original Relish Salad recipe from my sister-in-law Sandra Livingston from Jamestown, Pennsylvania

Broccoli Cauliflower Slaw

A lighter version of a salad bar favorite.

1 large head broccoli, cut into florets
1 medium head cauliflower, cut into florets
3/4 cup shredded lowfat extra sharp Cheddar cheese
1 medium onion, finely chopped
2 cups fat-free mayonnaise
6 tablespoons apple cider vinegar
1/4 teaspoon fresh ground black pepper
1/3 to 1/2 cup Splenda® sugar substitute – to taste

Combine broccoli, cauliflower, cheese and onion in a large bowl. Set aside.

In a small bowl, combine mayonnaise, vinegar, black pepper and Splenda. Whisk with a wire whisk to thoroughly combine.

Pour sauce over broccoli-cauliflower mixture immediately before serving. Toss to combine. This slaw may be made the night before if kept in separate bowls. Makes 10 servings (approximately 1 cup per serving).

Nutrition Facts: Calories 84, Protein 4.2 gm, Carbohydrate 14.1 gm, Dietary Fiber 2 gm, Fat 1.7 gm, Saturated Fat 0.9 gm, Sodium 521 mg
Meal Planning: 1 Carbohydrate

Cauliflower Apple Salad

A wonderful blend of strong flavors and textures.

2 red delicious apples, unpeeled, cored and cut into cubes
2 tablespoons lemon juice
3 cups cauliflower, cut into florets
1 cup shredded lowfat extra sharp Cheddar cheese
1/4 cup chopped pecans
1/4 cup nonfat plain yogurt
1/4 cup lite mayonnaise
1 tablespoon prepared yellow mustard
1 tablespoon honey
1/4 teaspoon paprika

Place apple cubes in a large bowl. Drizzle with lemon juice. Toss to combine.

Add the cauliflower, cheese and pecans to the apples. Toss to combine.

In a small bowl, combine yogurt, mayonnaise, mustard, honey and paprika. Pour over the cauliflower-apple mixture and gently toss. Serve immediately. Makes 8 servings (approximately 3/4 cup per serving).

Nutrition Facts: Calories 95, Protein 5.2 gm, Carbohydrate 9.6 gm, Dietary Fiber 1.4 gm, Fat 4.3 gm, Saturated Fat 1.8 gm, Sodium 151 mg
Meal Planning: 1 Lean Meat/Protein, 2 Vegetable

Grape Apple Waldorf Salad

You'll never make traditional Waldorf salad again.

2 large red delicious apples, unpeeled, cored and cut into cubes
1/2 cup green grapes, cut in half
1/4 cup diced celery
1/4 cup chopped pecans, toasted
2 tablespoons 100% apple juice
2 tablespoons plain nonfat yogurt
2 tablespoons lite mayonnaise

Combine cubed apple, grapes, celery and pecans in a medium bowl. Set aside.

In a small bowl, combine juice, yogurt and mayonnaise. Stir with a wire whisk until smooth. Pour over prepared apple mixture. Toss well. Makes 4 servings (approximately 1/2 cup per serving).

Nutrition Facts: Calories 90, Protein 1.2 gm, Carbohydrate 16.3 gm, Dietary Fiber 2.4 gm, Fat 3.1 gm, Saturated Fat 0.5 gm, Sodium 50 mg
Meal Planning: 1 Carbohydrate, 1/2 Fat

Time Saver Tip: To quickly toast pecans and other nuts, place pecans in a single layer in a glass pie or cake pan. Lightly spray top of nuts with nonstick cooking spray and toss to coat. Microwave on high for 2 minutes. Stir and repeat for an additional 1 to 2 minutes or until pecans are toasted. Stir after each 1 minute of cooking time.

Spinach Korean Salad

A long-time favorite at family picnics.

1 bag (16-ounce) fresh baby spinach, washed
2 cups fresh bean sprouts, washed
1 can (6-ounce) water chestnuts, drained and rinsed
2 cups sliced fresh mushrooms, washed
1 cup coarsely shredded carrots
2 tablespoons extra virgin olive oil
1/3 cup ketchup
1/3 cup apple cider vinegar
2/3 cup water
1/4 to 1/3 cup Splenda® sugar substitute – to taste
1 small red onion, chopped
1/2 teaspoon salt
1/4 teaspoon fresh ground black pepper

Combine all vegetables in a large salad bowl.

In a small bowl or jar, combine remaining ingredients. Pour over vegetable mixture and toss to combine.

Refrigerate for 1 to 2 hours before serving. Makes 10 servings (1 to 1½ cups per serving).

Nutrition Facts: Calories 67, Protein 2.4 gm, Carbohydrate 9.5 gm, Dietary Fiber 2.5 gm, Fat 3 gm, Saturated Fat 0.4 gm, Sodium 234 mg
Meal Planning: 2 Vegetable, 1/2 Fat

Strawberry-Spinach Salad

Combining fruits and vegetables into one salad saves time.

1 pint fresh strawberries
1 bag (16-ounce) baby spinach, washed
1 small bunch broccoli rabe, trimmed and coarsely chopped
1 small red onion, thickly sliced
1/4 cup lite mayonnaise
1/4 cup Miracle Whip® Free® Nonfat Dressing
2 tablespoons white balsamic vinegar
3 tablespoons honey [or 1/4 cup Splenda® Sugar Substitute]
1/4 cup fat-free or 1% milk
2 tablespoons poppy seeds

Wash strawberries. Remove tops and slice thickly. Set aside.

Toss spinach, broccoli rabe and red onion in a large bowl. Set aside.

In a small bowl, blend together mayonnaise, Miracle Whip®, vinegar, honey, milk and poppy seeds with a wire whisk until well combined.

Add sauce to spinach mixture and fold gently. Gently fold in prepared strawberries. Serve immediately. Makes 6 servings (approximately 1 to 1½ cups per serving).

Nutrition Facts: Calories 110, Protein 4 gm, Carbohydrate 20.9 gm,
Dietary Fiber 3.6 gm, Fat 2.3 gm, Saturated Fat 0.5 gm, Sodium 192 mg
Meal Planning: 1 Carbohydrate, 1/2 Fat

Lemon Broccoli Salad

A refreshing taste with the crunchy surprise of sunflower seeds.

4 cups fresh broccoli florets
2 cups fresh cauliflower florets
1/2 cup water
1 cup matchstick carrots
1 small red onion, chopped
2 tablespoons dark raisins
1/4 cup toasted sunflower seeds
1/2 cup plain nonfat yogurt
2 tablespoons honey mustard
1 tablespoon lite mayonnaise
3 tablespoons honey
1/2 teaspoon grated lemon peel

In a medium casserole, combine broccoli, cauliflower and water. Cover. Microwave on HIGH for 3 to 4 minutes or until vegetables are very hot and color brightens. Rinse briefly with cold water to stop cooking. Drain well.

In a large bowl, combine broccoli, cauliflower, carrot, onion, raisins and sunflower seeds. Set aside.

In a small bowl, combine yogurt, mustard, mayonnaise, honey and lemon peel. Mix well. Stir yogurt mixture into vegetable mixture. Toss to coat. Cover salad tightly. Chill at least 4 hours or overnight to blend flavors. Makes 6 servings (approximately 1 cup per serving).

Nutrition Facts: Calories 117, Protein 4.8 gm, Carbohydrate 19.2 gm, Dietary Fiber 2.6 gm, Fat 3.9 gm, Saturated Fat 0.4 gm, Sodium 155 mg
Meal Planning: 2 Carbohydrate, 1 Fat

Tomato Cucumber Bean Salad

A delightful combination of vegetables and herbs.

1 pound grape or cherry tomatoes, cut in half
1 large vidalia onion, julienned
2 cups sliced fresh mushrooms
1/2 large English cucumber, unpeeled and sliced
1 can (15-ounce) cannellini (white kidney) beans, drained and rinsed
1/2 cup balsamic vinegar
2 tablespoons extra virgin olive oil
1 to 2 tablespoons honey – to taste
3 cloves crushed garlic
2 tablespoons fresh chopped oregano [or 1 tablespoon dried]
1 tablespoon fresh chopped cilantro [or 1½ teaspoons dried]
1/4 teaspoon fresh ground black pepper
1/4 teaspoon salt

In a large bowl, combine tomatoes, onion, mushrooms, cucumbers and cannellini beans.

In a small bowl, combine balsamic vinegar, olive oil, honey, garlic, oregano, cilantro, black pepper and salt. Whisk together.

Pour dressing over prepared vegetables. Cover and refrigerate for 30 minutes before serving. Serves 6 (approximately 1 to 1½ cups per serving).

Nutrition Facts: Calories 133, Protein 5.1 gm, Carbohydrate 19.4 gm, Dietary Fiber 3.7 gm, Fat 4.9 gm, Saturated Fat 0.7 gm, Sodium 298 mg
Meal Planning: 1/2 Lean Meat/Protein, 1 Carbohydrate, 1/2 Fat

Tomato Potato Salad

It's not just your mother's potato salad.

6 large red potatoes
6 large fresh tomatoes, very firm
1 small red onion, chopped
1/4 cup fresh chopped cilantro [or 2 tablespoons dried]
1½ teaspoons ground cumin
1 clove crushed garlic
1/2 teaspoon salt
1/4 teaspoon fresh ground black pepper
1/4 teaspoon ground white pepper
1/2 cup nonfat sour cream
1/4 cup lite mayonnaise

Wash and scrub potatoes. Remove any blemishes. Place potatoes in a large saucepot with about 3 inches of water. Cover and bring to a boil over high heat. Reduce heat to medium-low and continue cooking for 20 to 40 minutes or until potatoes are tender. Drain and let cool.

Cut potatoes into cubes when cool. Do not peel. Set aside.

Wash tomatoes and cut into cubes.

In a large bowl, combine chopped tomatoes, onion, cilantro, cumin, garlic, salt and peppers. Add potatoes. Combine sour cream and mayonnaise and add to mixture, tossing gently to coat. Makes 8 servings (approximately 3/4 cup per serving).

Nutrition Information: Calories 116, Protein 3 gm, Carbohydrate 20 gm, Dietary Fiber 2.3 gm, Fat 3 gm, Saturated Fat 0.6 gm, Sodium 229 mg
Meal Planning: 1 Carbohydrate, 1 Vegetable, 1/2 Fat

Lite Macaroni Salad

A lightened up version of an American past-time.

8 ounces elbow macaroni
8 ounces whole wheat elbow macaroni
1/2 cup chopped vidalia onion
1 cup diced celery
1½ cups coarsely shredded carrot
1½ cups shredded cabbage
10 green olives, chopped
4 hard-cooked eggs (*reserve 4 egg whites and 1 yolk*), chopped
3/4 cup lite mayonnaise
3/4 cup Miracle Whip® Free® Nonfat Dressing
1 teaspoon prepared yellow mustard
1 teaspoon granulated sugar
1/2 teaspoon salt
1/4 teaspoon fresh ground black pepper
1/4 teaspoon ground white pepper
Paprika

In a large stockpot, cook pasta in a large amount of boiling water for 8 minutes or until al dente. *Do not add salt or oil.* Stir occasionally while boiling. Drain and rinse briefly with cold water. Let cool.

Transfer cooled pasta to a large bowl. Add onion, celery, carrots, cabbage, olives and egg. Toss gently to combine.

In a small bowl, combine mayonnaise, Miracle Whip, mustard, sugar, salt and peppers. Stir with a wire whisk to combine. Fold into macaroni mixture, mixing well. Adjust seasonings. Sprinkle paprika on top. Makes 16 servings (approximately 3/4 cup per serving).

Nutrition Facts: Calories 170, Protein 5.5 gm, Carbohydrate 24.6 gm, Dietary Fiber 2.5 gm, Fat 4.9 gm, Saturated Fat 1.2 gm, Sodium 307 mg
Meal Planning: 1 Carbohydrate, 2 Vegetable, 1 Fat

Recipe Tip: Using half regular macaroni and half whole wheat macaroni increases the fiber content while maintaining a mild flavor.

Glazed Carrots with Apples

Who said vegetables can't taste like dessert?

3 cups baby carrots (fresh or frozen)
1 medium yellow bell pepper, seeded and cut into chunks
1 medium red bell pepper, seeded and cut into chunks
1 medium green bell pepper, seeded and cut into chunks
3 tablespoons water
2 large Gala or Jonagold apples, unpeeled, cored and thinly sliced
3 tablespoons brown sugar
1 teaspoon cornstarch
1/2 teaspoon cinnamon
1 tablespoon lite whipped butter

Combine carrots, peppers and water in a microwave-safe casserole. Cover and microwave on HIGH for 3 minutes. Drain, add apples and toss gently.

In a small bowl, combine brown sugar, cornstarch and cinnamon. Cut in margarine using a pastry blender until mixture resembles a coarse meal. Sprinkle over carrot-apple mixture.

Cover and microwave on HIGH for 3 minutes. Stir and cook uncovered on HIGH for 2 to 3 minutes until glaze thickens. Makes 6 servings (approximately 1 cup per serving).

Nutrition Facts: Calories 84, Protein 2.1 gm, Carbohydrate 17.5 gm, Dietary Fiber 2.0 gm, Fat 1.4 gm, Saturated Fat 0.6 gm, Sodium 55 mg
Meal Planning: 1 Carbohydrate

Hash Brown Turnips

The sweet taste of curry adds new life to turnips.

3 cups peeled, grated turnips [or 3 cups peeled, grated parsnips]
2 tablespoons lite tub margarine
6 green onions, chopped
1/2 teaspoon salt
1/8 teaspoon fresh ground black pepper
1/8 teaspoon curry powder, optional
Olive oil nonstick cooking spray

Cook turnips, covered, in a small amount of boiling water for 10 minutes or until tender; drain.

Coat a medium skillet with nonstick cooking spray. Place over medium-high heat until hot. Add margarine and melt.

Add cooked turnips and onions. Season with salt, pepper and curry.

Cook, stirring occasionally, until turnips are lightly browned. Recoat with nonstick cooking spray, as needed. Makes 4 servings approximately 1/2 to 3/4 cup per serving). Shredded jicama, Dikon radish, rutabaga and carrot may also be used in place of turnips.

Nutrition Facts: Calories 50.4, Protein 1 gm, Carbohydrate 5.9 gm,
Dietary Fiber 1.8 gm, Fat 2.9 gm, Saturated Fat 0.5 gm, Sodium 258 mg
Meal Planning: 1 Vegetable, 1/2 Fat

Pristine Pears Christine

An unusual combination that melts in your mouth.

4 large ripe Barlett pears
1/4 cup crumbled gorgonzola cheese
16 pecan halves

Wash pears and cut in half lengthwise. Cut out core. Peel if desired. Place pears cut side up in a broiler-safe pan or skillet.

Divide gorgonzola cheese evenly between the 8 pear halves. Place 2 pecan halves on each pear half.

Broil prepared pears, close to heat source, until cheese begins to melt. Serve warm. Pears will soften and cook slightly. Makes 4 servings (2 halves per serving).

Nutrition Facts: Calories 152, Protein 2.8 gm, Carbohydrate 24.1 gm, Dietary Fiber 4.0 gm, Fat 6.3 gm, Saturated Fat 1.9 gm, Monounsaturated Fat 2.8 gm, Sodium 118 mg
Meal Planning: 1 Carbohydrate, 1 Fat

Original Pristine Pears Christine recipe from my friend Christine Carpenter from Townville, Pennsylvania

3 Green Bean Casserole

Inspired by a 70's favorite.

1 tablespoon extra virgin olive oil
1 clove crushed garlic
2 large vidalia onions, cut into very thin slices
1/2 cup dry whole wheat bread crumbs
1/4 teaspoon salt
1 package (10-ounce) frozen french-style green beans, thawed
1 package (16-ounce) frozen cut green beans, thawed
1 package (10-ounce) frozen whole green beans, thawed
1 can Campbell's® Healthy Request® Cream of Mushroom Soup
1 cup fat-free or 1% milk
1/4 teaspoon fresh ground black pepper
1/4 teaspoon ground white pepper
2 cans (6-ounce each) mushroom pieces, drained and rinsed
Paprika
Nonstick cooking spray

Coat a large skillet with nonstick cooking spray. Add oil and heat. Add garlic and sliced onions and sauté until translucent. Reduce heat to medium-low and continue sautéing for about 15 minutes or until onions begin to carmelize and liquid evaporates. Remove from heat and stir in dry bread crumbs and salt to evenly coat onion slices.

Drain beans. Place beans in a deep 9 x 13-inch baking pan coated with nonstick cooking spray.

In a medium bowl, combine soup, milk and peppers; whisk to combine. Stir in mushrooms. Pour mixture over beans and carefully stir to combine. Spread onion-bread crumb mixture evenly over top; sprinkle with paprika. Coat top with nonstick cooking spray. Bake at 375 degrees F for 45 minutes or until bubbly. After 15 minutes and 30 minutes of baking, remove casserole from oven and coat top of onion-bread crumb mixture with nonstick cooking spray. Serves 12 (approximately 1 cup per serving).

Nutrition Facts: Calories 88, Protein 3.4 gm, Carbohydrate 13.7 gm,
Dietary Fiber 3.7 gm, Fat 2.2 gm, Saturated Fat 0.6 gm, Sodium 337 mg
Meal Planning: 1 Carbohydrate, 1/2 Fat

Spicy Squash Bake

Take advantage of this wonderful fall vegetable.

1 pound butternut squash
2 tablespoons water
1 tablespoon olive oil tub margarine
1/4 cup finely chopped onion
1 clove crushed garlic
1/2 cup chunky salsa
1/2 cup shredded lowfat extra sharp Cheddar cheese, divided
1/8 teaspoon salt
1/8 teaspoon fresh ground black pepper

Peel squash and cut into 3/4-inch cubes. Combine squash and water in a glass casserole. Microwave, covered, on HIGH for 6 to 8 minutes or until tender, stirring once. Drain well.

In same glass casserole, combine margarine, onion and garlic. Microwave, uncovered, on HIGH for 1 to 2 minutes or until tender.

Stir salsa, 1/4 cup cheese, salt and pepper into onion mixture. Gently fold in cooked squash.

Microwave, uncovered, on HIGH for 2 to 3 minutes or until heated through. Top with remaining cheese. Let stand, covered, for 1 to 2 minutes or until cheese melts. Makes 4 servings.

Nutrition Facts: Calories 126, Protein 5.2 gm, Carbohydrate 12.7 gm, Dietary Fiber 1.8 gm, Fat 6.7 gm, Saturated Fat 2.2 gm, Sodium 213 mg
Meal Planning: 1 Carbohydrate, 1 Fat

Cranberry Buttercup Squash

A quick idea for a colorful, delicious lunch.

1 medium buttercup or acorn squash
1 tablespoon lite whipped butter
1/8 teaspoon salt
1/8 teaspoon fresh ground black pepper
2 teaspoons dark brown sugar [or brown sugar substitute]
2 tablespoons dried cranberries
2 tablespoons sliced toasted almonds

Pierce squash in several places. Place on a microwave-safe plate and microwave on HIGH for 6 minutes. Turn squash over and microwave for 5 to 8 minutes more or until squash is soft to touch. Let stand for a few minutes to finish cooking.

Cut squash in half and scoop out seeds. Place on serving a dish.

Divide margarine, salt, pepper, brown sugar, cranberries and almonds between squash halves. Serve immediately. Makes 2 servings.

Nutrition Facts: Calories 172, Protein 3.2 gm, Carbohydrate 27.9 gm, Dietary Fiber 1.6 gm, Fat 6.7 gm, Saturated Fat 1.7 gm, Sodium 168 mg
Meal Planning: 1 Carbohydrate, 2 Vegetable, 1 Fat

Upside-Down Squash Pie

A unique way to use a plentiful zucchini squash crop.

1 medium zucchini squash, unpeeled, finely chopped
1 medium yellow summer squash, unpeeled, finely chopped
1 tablespoon all-purpose flour
2 cups chopped tomatoes in juice (fresh or canned)
1 cup shoepeg (white) corn, thawed
1 clove crushed garlic
1 large vidalia onion, chopped
1 teaspoon dried basil
1/4 teaspoon salt
1/4 teaspoon fresh ground black pepper
1 package corn muffin mix (*less than 3 grams total fat per serving*)

In a large saucepan, cook squash in a small amount of water until tender, about 4 minutes. Drain well and transfer to a large bowl.

Sprinkle flour over squash and stir to combine. Combine squash, tomatoes, corn, garlic, onion, basil, salt and pepper. Transfer to a deep 9-inch baking dish coated with nonstick cooking spray.

In a medium bowl, prepare corn muffin mix according to lowfat package directions. (*Use fat-free milk, canola oil and egg whites.*) Spoon over top of prepared vegetables. Bake at 375 degrees F for 20 minutes or until corn bread is golden. Makes 8 servings.

Nutrition Facts: Calories 176, Protein 4.5 gm, Carbohydrate 27.7 gm, Dietary Fiber 2.7 gm, Fat 6.3 gm, Saturated Fat 0.6 gm, Sodium 313 mg
Meal Planning: 1 Carbohydrate, 2 Vegetable, 1 Fat

Herb Brussels Sprouts & Carrots

Try it– you might like it.

3/4 pound fresh Brussels sprouts [or 1 package (10-ounce) frozen]
2 cups low sodium vegetable broth
1/2 pound baby carrots [or 1 package (8-ounce) frozen]
1 tablespoon lemon juice
2 teaspoons lite tub margarine
1/2 teaspoon dried whole tarragon, crushed
Dash of ground nutmeg

Wash Brussels sprouts thoroughly; remove any wilted outer leaves. Cut an X in the root end of each Brussels sprout.

Bring broth to a boil in a medium saucepan. Add Brussels sprouts and carrots. Return to a boil. Cover, reduce heat and simmer for 6 to 8 minutes or until vegetables are tender.

Drain and transfer vegetables to a serving bowl. Toss with lemon juice, margarine, tarragon and nutmeg. Makes 6 servings (approximately 3/4 to 1 cup per serving).

Nutrition Facts: Calories 44, Protein 2.2 gm, Carbohydrate 8.1 gm, Dietary Fiber 2.2 gm, Fat 1 gm, Saturated Fat 0.2 gm, Sodium 55 mg
Meal Planning: 2 Vegetable

Chunky Marinara Sauce

Delicious pasta sauce doesn't have to simmer all day.

1 tablespoon extra virgin olive oil
1 medium onion, chopped
2 cloves crushed garlic
8 ounces sliced fresh mushrooms
1 cup matchstick carrots
2 celery ribs, finely chopped
1 large green bell pepper, seeded and diced
1 teaspoon dried oregano
1/2 teaspoon dried thyme
1/2 teaspoon dried basil
1/4 teaspoon salt
1/4 teaspoon fresh ground black pepper
1 teaspoon granulated sugar
1 can (28-ounce) chopped tomatoes
1 can (6-ounce) tomato paste

Coat a large saucepot with nonstick cooking spray. Add oil and heat. Add onion, garlic and mushrooms. Sauté for 2 minutes. Add carrots, celery and green pepper. Cover and continue cooking until vegetables are tender.

Add herbs, seasonings, sugar, tomatoes and tomato paste. Stir to combine. Cover, reduce heat and simmer for 10 to 15 minutes. Adjust seasonings. Serve over whole wheat pasta. Sauce becomes tastier with time. Makes 4 cups or 8 servings (1/2 cup per serving).

Nutrition Facts: Calories 70, Protein 2.6 gm, Carbohydrate 11.9 gm, Dietary Fiber 2.9 gm, Fat 2.3 gm, Saturated Fat 0.3 gm, Sodium 327 mg
Meal Planning: 2 Vegetable, 1/2 Fat

Vegetable Ragout Sauce

A sweet and sour combination of vegetable favorites.

2 tablespoons extra virgin olive oil
1 celery rib, chopped
2 large onions, coarsely chopped
1 medium young eggplant, unpeeled and diced
1 pound fresh plum tomatoes, unpeeled and diced
1/4 cup dark raisins
1/4 cup slivered almonds, toasted
2 tablespoons capers, well drained
1/4 cup coarsely chopped black olives
1/2 teaspoon salt
1/4 teaspoon fresh ground black pepper
2 tablespoons granulated sugar
2 tablespoons white wine vinegar

Coat a large skillet with nonstick cooking spray. Add oil, celery and onions and sauté over medium heat until lightly golden, about 3 minutes.

Add eggplant and cook, stirring, for 5 minutes. Add tomatoes, raisins, almonds, capers, olives, salt and pepper. Cook for 5 minutes. Remove from heat and set aside.

In a small saucepan, melt the sugar over medium heat, stirring only when the sugar starts melting at the edge of the pan. Continue heating until the sugar is a deep golden color and foams on top, about 3 minutes. Add the vinegar and mix well. Pour over vegetables. Serve over whole wheat pasta or spaghetti squash. Makes 6 servings (approximately 1 cup per serving).

Nutrition Facts: Calories 119, Protein 3.2 gm, Carbohydrate 20 gm, Dietary Fiber 3.8 gm, Fat 4.2 gm, Saturated Fat 0.5 gm, Sodium 365 mg
Meal Planning: 1 Carbohydrate, 1 Fat

Chunky Zucchini Tomato Sauce

A tasty, aromatic topping for pasta.

1 tablespoon extra virgin olive oil
2 small zucchini, unpeeled, cut into cubes
2 cloves crushed garlic
4 sun-dried tomatoes, rehydrated and chopped
1 can (28-ounce) kitchen-cut tomatoes
1 teaspoon dried rosemary [or 1 tablespoon fresh chopped]
1 teaspoon dried oregano [or 1 tablespoon fresh chopped]
1 tablespoon balsamic vinegar
1 teaspoon granulated sugar

Coat a large skillet with nonstick cooking spray. Heat skillet over medium heat. Add oil, zucchini and garlic and sauté for 1 minute. Cover and steam for 3 to 4 minutes.

Stir in sun-dried and kitchen-cut tomatoes, rosemary and oregano. Simmer for 15 to 20 minutes, until sauce thickens. Stir in vinegar and sugar.

Serve over whole wheat pasta and sprinkle with freshly grated Parmesan cheese, if desired. Makes 4 servings (approximately 1 cup per serving).

Nutrition Facts: Calories 110, Protein 4.6 gm, Carbohydrate 17.3 gm, Dietary Fiber 4.7 gm, Fat 4.2 gm, Saturated Fat 0.6 gm, Sodium 400 mg
Meal Plannning: 1 Carbohydrate

Recipe Tip: To rehydrate sun-dried tomatoes, place tomatoes in a bowl and cover with hot or boiling water. Soak for 5 to 10 minutes or until soft.

Vegetable Chop Suey

Chock full of vegetables with the refreshing taste of gingerroot.

1 tablespoon low sodium soy sauce
1 tablespoon cornstarch
2 tablespoons dry white wine [or 2 tablespoons gingerale]
1/2 cup water
1 packet low sodium vegetable-flavor instant bouillon
1 tablespoon peanut oil
1 tablespoon minced gingerroot
1 large red bell pepper, seeded and sliced
1 head bok choy or nappa, coarsely shredded
6 green onions, chopped
2 celery ribs, sliced
3 cups sliced fresh mushrooms
3 cups fresh bean sprouts
2 cups cooked brown rice

In a small bowl, combine soy sauce, cornstarch, wine, water and vegetable bouillon. Set aside.

Wash, drain and prepare all vegetables.

Coat a wok or large skillet with nonstick cooking spray. Heat wok over high heat. Add oil and heat oil. Add gingerroot; stir-fry for 30 seconds.

Add red pepper, bok choy, green onions and celery and stir-fry for 3 minutes. Add mushrooms and continue stir-frying for 2 minutes.

Add bean sprouts and sauce mixture. Cook and stir until sprouts soften slightly, about 2 minutes. Serve over 1/2 cup rice per serving. Makes 4 servings (approximately 2 cups per serving).

Nutrition Facts: Calories 211, Protein 7.7 gm, Carbohydrate 36.5 gm, Dietary Fiber 4.4 gm, Fat 4.8 gm, Saturated Fat 0.6 gm, Sodium 192 mg
Meal Planning: 1 Lean Meat/Protein, 1 Carbohydrate, 3 Vegetable

Twice-Cooked Noodles

Ideal for leftover spaghetti– save time with pre-prepped vegetables.

2 cups cooked rice noodles or thin spaghetti
1 tablepoon peanut oil
1 clove crushed garlic
1 medium onion, sliced
2 cups chopped fresh broccoli
2 cups sliced fresh mushrooms
1 cup shredded carrot
3 cups coarsely shredded cabbage
3 tablespoons low sodium soy sauce
1 teaspoon cornstarch
1/3 cup cold water
1/4 teaspoon fresh ground black pepper
1/2 teaspoon curry powder

Coat a wok or large skillet with nonstick cooking spray. Heat over high heat. Add oil and heat. Add noodles and stir-fry for 5 to 6 minutes or until lightly browned. Push up on sides of wok.

Add garlic and stir-fry for 30 seconds. Add onions and broccoli; stir-fry for 2 minutes. Add mushrooms, carrot and cabbage and stir-fry for 2 minutes.

In a small bowl, combine soy sauce, cornstarch, water, black pepper and curry and stir into wok mixture. Cook and stir until thickened and bubbly.

Stir down noodles and mix to combine. Stir-fry for 1 to 2 minutes more to heat through. Makes 4 servings (approximately 2 cups per serving).

Nutrition Facts: Calories 187, Protein 7.3 gm, Carbohydrate 31.6 gm, Dietary Fiber 5.2 gm, Fat 4.4 gm, Saturated Fat 0.7 gm, Sodium 532 mg
Meal Planning: 2 Carbohydrate, 2 Vegetable, 1 Fat

Vegetable-Stuffed Potato Skins

Jazz up a boring baked potato with this vegetable-laden version.

Juice of 2 limes
1 tablespoon extra virgin olive oil
4 cloves garlic, very thinly sliced
1/2 teaspoon ground cumin
1/2 teaspoon fresh ground black pepper
1/4 cup fresh snipped cilantro [or 2 tablespoons dried]
2 small zucchini squash, julienned
1 large red bell pepper, seeded and thickly sliced
1 large yellow bell pepper, seeded and thickly sliced
2 medium vidalia onions, julienned
1/2 cup nonfat sour cream
1/4 teaspoon lemon pepper seasoning
1/4 cup fresh chopped chives [or 2 tablespoons dried]
4 large Russet baking potatoes
1/2 cup shredded lowfat extra sharp Cheddar cheese

Combine lime juice, oil, garlic, cumin, black pepper and cilantro in a recloseable plastic bag. Add zucchini, bell peppers and onions. Seal bag and turn until vegetables are coated. Refrigerate for at least 2 hours to marinade. In a small bowl, whisk sour cream, lemon pepper and chives. Cover and chill until ready to serve.

Scrub and pierce potatoes. Remove any blemishes. Bake potatoes at 400 degrees F until tender, about 40 minutes. (Or microwave for 8 to 10 minutes, turning after 4 minutes.) Cool the potatoes slightly and cut in half lengthwise. Scoop flesh from each potato and reserve for another use.

Coat both sides of skins with nonstick cooking spray. Grill or broil potato skins, turning occasionally, until crisp, about 5 minutes. Drain vegetables from marinade and sauté in a large skillet coated with nonstick cooking spray until tender crisp. Spoon sautéed vegetables into potato skins. Top with sour cream sauce and shredded cheese. Makes 4 servings.

Nutrition Facts: Calories 175, Protein 9.3 gm, Carbohydrate 20.9 gm, Dietary Fiber 4.1 gm, Fat 6.4 gm, Saturated Fat 2.1 gm, Sodium 426 mg
Meal Planning: 1 Lean Meat/Protein, 1/2 Carbohydrate, 2 Vegetable

Fall Fruit Crisp

This dessert will impress any guest.

4 Golden Delicious or Gala apples, unpeeled, cored and diced
4 Bartlett pears, unpeeled, cored and diced
1/2 cup dried cranberries
1 teaspoon ground cinnamon
1 teaspoon ground nutmeg
1 tablespoon all-purpose flour
1/4 cup Splenda® sugar substitute
1 cup old-fashioned rolled oats
1/2 cup all-purpose flour
1/2 cup whole wheat pastry flour
1/3 cup brown sugar
1/3 cup Splenda® sugar substitute
1/4 cup walnuts, finely chopped
4 tablespoons Promise® stick margarine, melted
Nonstick cooking spray

Coat a deep 9 x 13-inch baking pan with nonstick cooking spray. Spread fruit evenly in the bottom of dish.

In a small bowl, combine cinnamon, nutmeg, 1 tablespoon all-purpose flour and 1/4 cup Splenda; sprinkle evenly over fruit. Set aside.

In a medium bowl, combine rolled oats, 1/2 cup all-purpose flour, whole wheat flour, brown sugar, 1/3 cup Splenda® and walnuts. Add melted margarine and stir with a fork to combine. Sprinkle evenly over prepared fruit.

Spray top with nonstick cooking spray. Bake at 350 degrees F for 40 minutes or until lightly browned. Recoat crumb top with nonstick cooking spray after 15 and 30 minutes of baking. Serve hot over lowfat ice cream, if desired, for a delicious dessert. Serves 16.

Nutrition Facts: Calories 136, Protein 2.1 gm, Carbohydrate 24.4 gm, Dietary Fiber 2.7 gm, Fat 3.9 gm, Saturated Fat 0.6 gm, Sodium 38 mg
Meal Planning: 1½ Carbohydrate, 1/2 Fat

Fruited Trifle

A royal dessert for everyday or a special occasion.

2 small packages sugarfree instant vanilla pudding and pie mix
3½ cups cold 1% milk
2 cans (15-ounce each) tropical fruit cocktail, packed in juice
2 cups fresh strawberries, tops removed
6 kiwi, peeled
1 Angel Food Cake, cut into bite-sized chunks

Combine pudding and milk in a large deep bowl. Prepare according to package directions. Drain fruit cocktail well and fold into prepared pudding. Set aside.

Slice strawberries and kiwi. Line the bottom and sides of a trifle bowl or large deep glass bowl with strawberry and kiwi slices, alternating with rows of strawberries and rows of kiwi.

Next place 1/4 cake chunks in the bottom of the fruit-lined trifle bowl. Top with 1/4 pudding-fruit mixture. Repeat layering three times. Finish with pudding mixture.

Garnish with strawberry and kiwi slices, if desired. Makes 16 servings.

Nutrition Facts: Calories 180, Protein 5.2 gm, Carbohydrate 39.7 gm, Dietary Fiber 2.5 gm, Fat 0.9 gm, Saturated Fat 0.4 gm, Sodium 275 mg
Meal Planning: 2½ Carbohydrate

Doubly-Good Blueberry Pie

An updated recipe from an old Farm Journal cookbook.

6 sheets fresh or frozen (thawed) phyllo dough
1/3 cup granulated sugar
3 tablespoons cornstarch
1/8 teaspoon salt
1/4 cup 100% white grape juice
4 cups blueberries, divided
1/3 cup Splenda® sugar substitute
1 tablespoon margarine
1 tablespoon lemon juice

Coat a 9-inch pie plate with nonstick cooking spray. Place 1 sheet of phyllo in pie plate, pressing it lightly into bottom and side (edges will overhang). Lightly spray entire sheet with cooking spray. Repeat to make 5 more layers, crisscrossing each layer so edges are distributed around pie plate. (Do not allow phyllo dough to dry out; keep dough moist by covering sheets with a damp cloth while preparing the crust.) Twist the overhanging edges under to form a rim. Bake at 350 degrees F for about 10 minutes or until golden. Set aside to cool.

Combine sugar, cornstarch and salt in a saucepan. Add juice and 2 cups blueberries. Cook over medium heat, stirring constantly, until mixture comes to a boil and is thickened and clear. Remove from heat, and stir in Splenda, margarine and lemon juice. Let cool.

Place remaining 2 cups blueberries in prepared baked pie shell. Pour cooked blueberry mixture over top. Chill. Makes 8 servings.

Nutrition Facts: Calories 133, Protein 1.6 gm, Carbohydrate 27.2 gm, Dietary Fiber 1.9 gm, Fat 2.6 gm, Saturated Fat 0.4 gm, Sodium 123 mg
Meal Planning: 2 Carbohydrate, 1/2 Fat

Recipe Variation: Place 2 tablespoons graham cracker crumbs in the bottom of 8 custard cups. Prepare blueberry mixture as directed and make individual desserts.

Half a loaf is better than no bread.
Irish Proverb

Man cannot live by bread alone.
The Bible

The rung of a ladder was never meant to rest upon,
but only to hold a man's foot long enough
to enable him to put the other somewhat higher.
Thomas Huxly

Be happy while you're living
for you're a long time dead.
Scottish Proverb

My advice to you — grind your own grain.

Azerbaijani Proverb

Healthy people select high fiber foods and prepare recipes with whole grains and other minimally-processed foods.

- Read labels carefully. Choose foods with 3 or more grams of dietary fiber per serving.
- Select foods with 1 or more grams of soluble fiber per serving.
- Choose unrefined or minimally-processed grains and starches. Minimally-processed means close to its natural state and retaining its whole grain kernal, skin or seeds.
- Look for foods that list the word "whole" as the first ingredient.
- Leave the skins on potatoes, fruits and vegetables during preparation whenever possible.
- Select hot or cold breakfast cereals that are minimally-processed without large amounts of added sugar, salt or fat.
- Add dried, canned or cooked beans, peas and lentils to recipes to increase dietary fiber.
- Add wheat, rice or oat bran to bread, muffin, cooked cereals and other recipes.
- Add ground flax seed, nuts and other seeds to pasta, rice and other grain dishes for extra flavor and fiber.
- Add 1/3 cup ground flax seed to recipes such as muffins, biscuits, breads and other baked goods to increase fiber. For dry doughs and batters, decrease the flour content by 1/4 cup.
- Use combinations of whole grain flours, such as oat flour, whole wheat flour, soy flour and rye flour, instead of solely all-purpose flour.
- If a whole grain flavor or texture is not desired, use a combination of 50% all-purpose flour, 25% oat flour and 25% soy flour.
- Consider taking a soluble fiber supplement to help achieve certain health goals such as lowering cholesterol or blood sugar levels.

Whole Wheat Waffles

A nutty flavor for a breakfast tradition– serve with pure maple syrup!

2 eggs [or 1/2 cup egg substitute]
2 cups fat-free or 1% milk
3 tablespoons canola oil
1 tablespoon honey [or 1 tablespoon pure maple syrup]
1 teaspoon pure vanilla extract
1 cup plus 2 tablespoons whole wheat pastry flour
1/2 cup all-purpose flour
1/2 cup toasted wheat germ
3 tablespoons ground flax seed
1 teaspoon fresh ground nutmeg
2 teaspoons baking powder
Dash salt
Nonstick cooking spray

In a large bowl, beat eggs at high speed of an electric mixer for 4 minutes.

Add milk, oil, honey and vanilla; beat until blended. Add flours, wheat germ, flax, nutmeg, baking powder and salt. Beat at low speed until smooth.

Coat a waffle iron with nonstick cooking spray, and allow waffle iron to preheat. Pour 1/4 cup batter per waffle onto hot waffle iron. Bake for 5 minutes or until steaming stops. Recoat waffle iron with nonstick cooking spray between each batch. Makes 16 waffles.

Nutrition Facts: Calories 95, Protein 3.6 gm, Carbohydrate 12.1 gm, Dietary Fiber 1.2 gm, Fat 3.7 gm, Saturated Fat 0.4 gm, Sodium 85 mg
Meal Planning: 1 Carbohydrate

Cinnamon Sweet Rolls

The incredible aroma of cinnamon rolls often greeted us after school.

1/3 cup warm water (115 to 120 degrees F)
1 teaspoon granulated sugar
1/2 teaspoon salt
2 packages rapid-rise dry yeast
2 to 2½ cups all-purpose flour
1 cup **each** whole wheat flour and whole wheat pastry flour
1 cup lowfat buttermilk
2 tablespoons Promise® stick margarine
1 egg, lightly beaten
2/3 cup dark raisins
1/4 cup ground flax seed
1/4 cup dark brown sugar
1 to 2 tablespoons ground cinnamon

In a large bowl, combine water, granulated sugar and salt. Sprinkle yeast over water mixture, and stir to dissolve. Let stand until mixture bubbles. Add 1 cup all-purpose flour, 1 cup whole wheat flour, buttermilk, margarine and egg to yeast mixture. Beat with an electric mixer at high speed for 3 minutes. Stir in remaining flour, adding enough flour to make a moderately stiff dough. Turn dough out onto a lightly floured surface. Knead for 8 minutes or until smooth and elastic. (Or use a dough hook attachment for food processor and process for 2 minutes.) Place dough in a large bowl coated with nonstick cooking spray, turning to coat. Cover and let rise in a warm place until doubled in bulk, about 30 minutes.

Punch dough down and divide in half. Roll out each piece into an 18-inch rectangle. Sprinkle evenly with raisins, flax, brown sugar and cinnamon. Beginning at the short end, roll up tightly like a jellyroll. Place on a baking sheet coated with nonstick cooking spray. Score every 1-inch with a knife, then bend into a horseshoe-shape. Let rise again until doubled in bulk, about 30 minutes. Bake at 350 degree F for 20 minutes or until golden. Makes 2 loaves or 18 servings.

Nutrition Facts: Calories 167, Protein 6 gm, Carbohydrate 30.5 gm, Dietary Fiber 2.8 gm, Fat 2.5 gm, Saturated Fat 0.5 gm, Sodium 108 mg
Meal Planning: 2 Carbohydrate

Chocolate-Covered Cherry Muffins

The taste of chocolate-covered cherries is always cordial.

3/4 cup all-purpose flour
1 cup whole wheat pastry flour
1/4 cup toasted wheat germ or ground flax seed
1/3 cup unsweetened cocoa powder
Dash salt
1/3 cup granulated sugar
1 tablespoon baking powder
1 cup fat-free or 1% milk
1 egg, lightly beaten [or 1/4 cup egg substitute]
1/3 cup nonfat ricotta cheese
1 teaspoon canola oil
1/4 cup maraschino cherries, chopped [or 1/4 cup dried cherries]

In a large bowl, combine flours, wheat germ, cocoa, sugar and baking powder. Make a well in the center of mixture.

In a blender or food processor, combine milk, egg, ricotta cheese, and oil; process until smooth. Fold in cherries by hand. Add mixture to dry ingredients, stirring with a flat wooden spoon just until combined.

Spoon or scoop batter into muffin cup pans coated with nonstick cooking spray. *Do not use paper liners.* Bake at 400 degrees F for 20 minutes or until wooden toothpick inserted in center comes out clean. Let cool for 5 minutes, then remove from pan and cool on wire racks. Makes 12 muffins.

Nutrition Facts: Calories 124, Protein 6 gm, Carbohydrate 22 gm, Dietary Fiber 2.1 gm, Fat 2.3 gm, Saturated Fat 0.5 gm, Sodium 145 mg
Meal Planning: 1 Carbohydrate, 1/2 Fat

Orange Cranberry Muffins

A cool, fruity flavor for an energizing breakfast.

1 cup chopped fresh cranberries [or 1 cup frozen, thawed]
1/4 cup Splenda® sugar substitute
1/4 cup granulated sugar
1 cup all-purpose flour
3/4 cup whole wheat pastry flour
2 teaspoons baking powder
3/4 cup fat-free or 1% milk
1 egg, lightly beaten
1/4 cup nonfat ricotta cheese
1 teaspoon grated orange peel
1 tablespoon margarine, melted
1/2 teaspoon ground cinnamon

In a small bowl, combine cranberries and Splenda; let stand for 5 minutes.

In a large bowl, combine sugar, flour and baking powder. Make a well in the center of mixture. Set aside.

In a blender or food processor, combine milk, egg, orange peel and ricotta cheese. Process until smooth. Stir in cranberries and melted margarine by hand.

Add cranberry-milk mixture to flour mixture, stirring with a flat wooden spoon just until combined. Do not overmix.

Spoon or scoop batter into muffin cup pans coated with nonstick cooking spray. *Do not use paper liners.* Bake at 400 degrees F for 20 to 25 minutes or until done. Make 12 muffins.

Nutrition Facts: Calories 115, Protein 4 gm, Carbohydrate 21.7 gm,
Dietary Fiber 1.3 gm, Fat 1.6 gm, Saturated Fat 0.3 gm, Sodium 125 mg
Meal Planning: 1½ Carbohydrate

Hearty Raisin Bran Muffins

The full-bodied flavor of molasses allows you to use less sugar.

2 cups raisin bran cereal
1¼ cups lowfat buttermilk
1/4 cup molasses
1/3 cup nonfat ricotta cheese
1 teaspoon canola oil
1 egg [or 1/4 cup egg substitute]
1 cup all-purpose flour
1/3 cup ground flax seed
1/4 cup brown sugar substitute [or 1/4 cup brown sugar]
2 teaspoons baking powder
1 teaspoon baking soda
Pinch salt
1 teaspoon ground cinnamon
1/4 teaspoon ground nutmeg
1/4 teaspoons ground cloves
1/3 cup finely ground walnuts

In a large bowl, combine cereal and buttermilk. Let stand for a few minutes until cereal softens. Whisk in molasses.

In a blender or food processor, combine ricotta cheese, oil and egg. Process until smooth and well combined. Stir into bran-molasses mixture.

In a medium bowl, combine remaining dry ingredients. Add dry ingredients to bran-milk mixture, stirring with a flat wooden spoon just until combined. Do not overmix.

Spoon or scoop batter into muffin cup pans coated with nonstick cooking spray. *Do not use paper liners.* Bake at 400 degrees F for 15 to 20 minutes or until golden brown. Let cool in pans for 2 to 3 minutes, then remove to a wire rack to cool. Makes 12 muffins.

Nutrition Facts: Calories 136, Protein 5.1 gm, Carbohydrate 23.3 gm,
Dietary Fiber 1.3 gm, Fat 2.8 gm, Saturated Fat 0.4 gm, Sodium 379 mg
Meal Planning: 1½ Carbohydrate, 1/2 Fat

Favorite Pumpkin Muffins

My pantry is always stocked with pumpkin to whip up this treat.

3/4 cups all-purpose flour
3/4 cup whole wheat pastry flour
1/2 cup soy flour
1/2 cup Fiber One® or other bran cereal
1/3 cup granulated sugar
1/3 cup Splenda® sugar substitute
1 heaping tablespoon baking powder
Pinch salt
1/3 cup dark raisins
1/4 cup miniature chocolate chips
1 teaspoon ground cinnamon
1 cup fat-free or 1% milk [or 1 cup water]
1/3 cup nonfat ricotta cheese
1 egg, lightly beaten
1 cup unsweetened canned pumpkin puree
1 teaspoon canola oil

In a large bowl, combine flours, bran, sugar, Splenda, baking powder, salt, raisins, chocolate chips and cinnamon. Stir to combine. Make a well in the center of mixture. Set aside.

In a blender or food processor, combine remaining ingredients. Process until smooth. Add to dry ingredients, mixing with a flat wooden spoon just until combined. Do not overmix.

Spoon or scoop batter into muffin cup pans coated with nonstick cooking spray. *Do not use paper liners.* Bake at 400 degrees F for 20 to 25 minutes or until very lightly brown on top. Do not overbake. Let cool for 2 minutes; remove from pan and cool on wire racks. Makes 12 large muffins.

Nutrition Facts: Calories 153, Protein 5.9 gm, Carbohydrate 28.9 gm, Dietary Fiber 4 gm, Fat 2.9 gm, Saturated Fat 1.0 gm, Sodium 155 mg
Meal Planning: 1½ Carbohydrate, 1/2 Fat

Date-Nut Bread

This bread is so good it tastes like dessert.

2/3 cup water
2/3 cup unsweetened orange juice
1/3 cup Promise® stick margarine, melted
2 eggs, lightly beaten [or 1/2 cup egg substitute]
1/3 cup honey
2 cups all-purpose flour
1 cup whole wheat flour
1 cup chopped dates, dusted in flour
Pinch salt
1/3 cup finely chopped pecans
1½ teaspoons baking soda
1/2 teaspoon baking powder

Combine water, juice, margarine, eggs and honey in a small bowl. Whisk together and set aside.

Combine remaining ingredients in a large bowl; make a well in center of dry ingredients. Add orange juice mixture all at once; stir with a fork just until dry ingredients are moistened. Pour into two 9 x 5-inch loaf pans coated with nonstick cooking spray. Bake at 350 degrees F for 50 minutes.

Cool in pans for 10 minutes. Remove from pans. Cool completely on a wire rack. Makes 2 loaves or 24 servings.

Nutrition Facts: Calories 126, Protein 2.5 gm, Carbohydrate 22 gm, Dietary Fiber 1.3 gm, Fat 3.7 gm, Saturated Fat 0.6 gm, Sodium 127 mg
Meal Planning: 1½ Carbohydrate, 1/2 Fat

Prune & Nut Bread

I often enjoyed this bread while having lunch with my Grandmother.

1 cup sour milk – *See directions below*
1 tablespoon canola oil
1/2 cup granulated sugar
1/2 cup Splenda® sugar substitute
1 egg, lightly beaten
1/2 cup prune juice
2 cups cooked, chopped prunes
2 cups whole wheat flour
1 cup all-purpose flour
1/2 teaspoon salt
5 teaspoons baking powder
1/2 teaspoon baking soda
1 cup chopped walnuts

To make make sour milk, place 1 tablespoon lemon juice in a glass measure. Add enough fat-free milk to make 1 cup. Let stand for 5 minutes.

In a food processor or blender, combine oil, sugar, Splenda, egg, prune juice and sour milk. Process until well combined. Stir in prunes by hand. Set aside.

In a large bowl, combine flours, salt, baking powder, baking soda and walnuts. Make a well in center of dry ingredients. Add prune mixture all at once; stir with a wooden spoon just until dry ingredients are moistened. Pour into two 9 x 5-inch loaf pans coated with nonstick cooking spray (pans should be 2/3 full). Bake at 350 degrees F for 50 minutes or until toothpick inserted in center comes out clean. Cool in pans for 10 minutes. Remove from pans. Cool completely on a wire rack. Makes 2 loaves or 24 servings.

Nutrition Facts: Calories 119, Protein 2.9 gm, Carbohydrate 24.8 gm, Dietary Fiber 2.2 gm, Fat 1.7 gm, Saturated Fat 0.2 gm, Sodium 158 mg
Meal Planning: 1½ Carbohydrate

Original Prune Bread recipe from my grandmother La Vera Beckstine from Greenville, Pennsylvania

Lemon-Blueberry Bread

A nice combination of refreshing flavors.

3/4 cup all-purpose flour
1 cup whole wheat pastry flour
1/3 cup ground flax seed, optional
2 teaspoons baking powder
1/4 teaspoon salt
2 tablespoons Promise® stick margarine, softened
2 tablespoons lowfat buttermilk
1/4 cup plus 2 tablespoons brown sugar
2 eggs, lightly beaten [or 1/2 cup egg substitute]
1/2 cup fat-free or 1% milk
1 cup fresh blueberries
1½ tablespoons grated lemon rind

Combine flours, baking powder and salt in a medium bowl. Set aside.

Cream margarine and buttermilk in a large bowl. Gradually add sugar, beating until light and fluffy. Add eggs, one at a time, beating well after each addition.

Add flour mixture alternately with 1/2 cup fat-free milk. Mix just until blended after each addition. Stir in blueberries and lemon rind. Pour batter into a 9 x 5-inch loaf pan coated with nonstick cooking spray.

Bake at 350 degrees F for 40 to 45 minutes or until a wooden pick inserted in center comes out clean. Cool bread in pan for 10 minutes. Remove from pan and cool completely. Makes 1 loaf or 12 servings.

Nutrition Facts: Calories 182, Protein 5.8 gm, Carbohydrate 30.6 gm, Dietary Fiber 2.0 gm, Fat 3.9 gm, Saturated Fat 0.6 gm, Sodium 147 mg
Meal Planning: 2 Carbohydrate, 1 Fat

Squash Butterhorn Rolls

A great recipe that everyone will be talking about.

1 cup fat-free or 1% milk
1/3 cup granulated sugar
2 tablespoons Promise® stick margarine
1/2 teaspoon salt
1 package rapid-rise dry yeast
1/4 cup warm water (105 to 115 degrees F)
1 package (10-ounce) or 1 cup mashed winter squash, thawed
2 to 2½ cups all-purpose flour
2 to 2½ cups whole wheat flour

In a saucepan or microwave, heat milk, sugar, margarine and salt until margarine melts. Cool to lukewarm – 105 to 115 degrees F.

Dissolve yeast in warm water in a large bowl. Stir in milk mixture, squash and 1 cup of each flour. Beat until smooth. Stir in enough remaining flour to make dough easy to handle.

Turn dough onto a lightly floured surface. Knead about 5 minutes or until smooth and elastic. (Or use a dough hook attachment for food processor and process for 2 minutes.) Place in a bowl coated with nonstick cooking spray; turn coated side up. Cover and let rise in a warm place about 1 hour or until doubled in bulk.

Punch down dough and divide in half. Let rest for a few minutes.

Roll dough out on a lightly floured surface into a 16-inch circle. Using a pizza cutter, cut each circle into 12 wedges. To shape rolls, begin at wide end of wedge and roll toward point. Place point side down on baking sheets coated with nonstick cooking spray. Cover and let rise in a warm place for 30 minutes or until doubled in bulk. Bake at 400 degrees F for 15 to 20 minutes or until golden brown. Makes 24 rolls.

Nutrition Facts: Calories 96, Protein 2.9 gm, Carbohydrate 18.8 gm,
Dietary Fiber 1.3 gm, Fat 1.3 gm, Saturated Fat 0.2 gm, Sodium 62 mg
Meal Planning: 1 Carbohydrate

Potato Crescent Rolls

A mild, light roll sure to impress a crowd.

1 cup fat-free or 1% milk
1/4 cup Promise® stick margarine
1 cup cooked instant mashed potatoes [or 1 cup homemade]
2 tablespoons brown sugar
1 package rapid-rise dry yeast
1/2 teaspoon salt
1 egg
1 cup all-purpose flour
1 cup whole wheat flour
1 cup whole wheat pastry flour
1/3 cup ground flax seed

In a saucepan or microwave, heat milk and margarine until margarine melts. Let cool to lukewarm - 115 to 120 degrees F.

In a large bowl, combine milk mixture, potatoes, sugar, yeast, salt, egg, 1/2 cup all-purpose flour and 1/2 cup whole wheat flour. Beat at low speed with an electric mixer for 30 seconds, scraping bowl constantly. Beat for 3 minutes at medium speed. Stir in the rest of flours, whole wheat pastry flour and flax seed to make a soft dough. Turn dough onto a lightly floured surface. Knead about 8 minutes or until smooth and elastic. (Or use a dough hook attachment for food processor and process for 2 minutes.) Place in a bowl coated with nonstick cooking spray; turn coated side up. Cover and let rise in a warm place about 45 minutes or until doubled in bulk.

Punch down dough. Let rest for a few minutes. On a lightly floured surface, roll dough out into a 16-inch circle. Cut into 20 wedges. Roll up each wedge tightly, starting at wide end and rolling toward point. Place point side down on baking sheets coated with nonstick cooking spray. Cover and let rise in a warm place for 30 minutes or until doubled in bulk. Bake at 400 degrees F for 15 to 18 minutes or until golden brown. Makes 20 rolls.

Nutrition Facts: Calories 115, Protein 3.8 gm, Carbohydrate 17.2 gm, Dietary Fiber 2 gm, Fat 3.5 gm, Saturated Fat 0.6 gm, Sodium 119 mg
Meal Planning: 1 Carbohydrate, 1/2 Fat

English Muffin Bread

A light and airy bread that makes great toast in the morning.

1 to 1½ cups all-purpose flour
1 cup whole wheat flour
1/2 cup whole wheat pastry flour
1/3 cup ground flax seed
1 package active dry yeast
1¼ cups water
3/4 teaspoon salt
1 tablespoon granulated sugar
Cornmeal

In a large bowl, combine 1/2 cup all-purpose flour, 1/2 cup whole wheat flour and yeast.

In a saucepan or in microwave, heat water, salt and sugar until warm – 115 to 120 degrees F. Add to flour mixture. Beat at low speed with an electric mixer for 30 seconds, scraping bowl constantly. Beat for 3 minutes at high speed. Stir in the rest of whole wheat flour, whole wheat pastry flour, flax seed and enough remaining all-purpose flour to make a soft dough. Shape into a ball. Place in a bowl coated with nonstick cooking spray; turn coated side up. Cover and let rise in a warm place for 1 hour or until doubled in bulk.

Punch down dough. Cover and let rest for 10 minutes. Coat a 1-quart casserole with nonstick cooking spray and sprinkle with cornmeal. Place rested dough in casserole. Cover and let rise until doubled in bulk , about 30 to 45 minutes.

Bake at 400 degrees F for 40 to 45 minutes. Cover with foil if top browns too quickly. Remove from pan and cool. Makes 1 loaf or 16 slices.

Nutrition Facts: Calories 96, Protein 3.4 gm, Carbohydrate 18.2 gm, Dietary Fiber 2.3 gm, Fat 0.9 gm, Saturated Fat 0.1 gm, Sodium 101 mg
Meal Planning: 1 Carbohydrate

Multi-Grain Biscuits

Serve with your favorite lowfat gravy or fresh strawberry jam.

1 cup whole wheat pastry flour
3/4 cup all-purpose flour
1/4 cup toasted wheat germ
1/2 teaspoon salt
1 tablespoon baking powder
3 tablespoons chilled Promise® stick margarine
3/4 cup plus 1 tablespoon fat-free or 1% milk

In a large bowl, combine flour, wheat germ, salt and baking powder. Add margarine and cut into dry ingredients with a pastry blender or 2 knives, until the mixture is the consistency of coarse cornmeal. Make a well in the center.

Add milk all at once. Stir until the dough is fairly free from the sides of the bowl. Turn the dough onto a lightly floured board. Knead gently and quickly, making about 8 to 10 folds.

Gently roll with a lightly floured rolling pin to 1/2-inch thickness. Cut with a biscuit cutter dipped lightly in flour.

Place on a baking sheet coated with nonstick cooking spray. Bake at 450 degree F until lightly browned, about 12 to 15 minutes. Makes about 12 biscuits.

Nutrition Facts: Calories 103, Protein 3.5 gm, Carbohydrate 15.5 gm,
Dietary Fiber 1.5 gm, Fat 3.4 gm, Saturated Fat 0.6 gm, Sodium 222 mg
Meal Planning: 1 Carbohydrate, 1/2 Fat

Whole Grain Pita Bread

A wonder to watch puff up in the oven— great fun for kids.

2½ cups all-purpose flour
2 cups whole wheat or other whole grain flour
2 packages active dry yeast
2 cups fat-free or 1% milk
3 tablespoons granulated sugar
2 tablespoons Promise® stick margarine
1 teaspoon salt

In a large mixing bowl, combine 1 cup of each flour and yeast.

Heat milk, sugar, margarine and salt in a saucepan or microwave just until warm (115 to 120 degrees F), stirring to melt margarine. Add to dry mixture. Beat at low speed with an electric mixer for 30 seconds, scraping bowl. Beat 3 minutes at high speed. By hand or food processor, stir in enough remaining flour to make a moderately stiff dough.

Knead on floured surface until smooth. (Or use a dough hook attachment for food processor and process for 2 minutes.) Place in a bowl coated with nonstick cooking spray; turn coated side up. Cover and let rise in a warm place about 40 to 45 minutes or until doubled in bulk. Punch down; cover and let rest for 10 minutes. Form into balls, 1½-inches in diameter.

Place on ungreased baking sheets; roll each into a 4-inch circle. Bake at 400 degrees F until puffed, about 7 to 9 minutes. Cool on cloth-covered surface. Makes about 32 pitas.

Nutrition Facts: Calories 74, Protein 3 gm, Carbohydrate 15 gm, Dietary Fiber 1.1 gm, Fat 1 gm, Saturated Fat 0.2 gm, Sodium 84 mg
Meal Planning: 1 Carbohydrate

Lower Fat Pie Pastry

This recipe takes a little practice but it's worth the 50% savings in fat.

3/4 cup pastry (cake) flour
3/4 cup whole wheat pastry flour
1/4 teaspoon salt
3 tablespoons Promise® stick margarine
2 tablespoons fat-free cream cheese
4 to 5 tablespoons water

In a medium bowl, combine flours and salt. Using a pastry blender, cut in margarine and cream cheese until pieces are the size of small peas.

Sprinkle 1 tablespoon water over part of mixture then toss with a fork. Push moistened dough to side of bowl. Repeat, using 1 tablespoon water at time until dough is moist. Form dough into a ball. Wrap in plastic wrap and chill for 1 hour.

On a lightly floured surface, flatten dough and lightly roll out to form a 12-inch circle. Do not over-roll. Carefully transfer to a 9-inch pie plate coated with nonstick cooking spray. Using a sharp knife, trim pastry around the edge of the pie plate and flute edges. Makes 1 (9-inch) pie pastry or 8 servings. *This recipe may take several tries before mastering the technique of making a tender lower fat pie pastry. Use club soda in place of the water for a flakier crust.*

Nutrition Facts: Calories 125, Protein 3.4 gm, Carbohydrate 17.4 gm, Dietary Fiber 1.4 gm, Fat 4.8 gm, Saturated Fat 0.8 gm, Sodium 142 mg
Meal Planning: 1 Carbohydrate, 2 Fat

Pizza Roll

Using frozen bread dough saves time but offers a great homemade taste.

1 loaf frozen whole wheat bread dough, thawed
1 cup sliced fresh mushrooms
1 medium onion, chopped
1 clove crushed garlic
1 teaspoon extra virgin olive oil
1 box (10-ounce) frozen chopped spinach, thawed and well-drained
1 egg, lightly beaten
2 tablespoons freshly grated Romano cheese
1/2 teaspoon dried oregano
1 tablespoon dried parsley
1/4 teaspoon salt
1/2 teaspoon fresh ground black pepper
1 cup shredded part-skim mozzarella cheese
1/2 cup shredded nonfat mozzarella cheese
2 egg whites, lightly beaten

For crust, follow package directions and allow bread to rise until doubled in bulk. Punch down and let dough rest for a few minutes. On a lightly floured surface, roll dough into a large rectangle. Set aside.

To make filling, sauté mushrooms, onion and garlic in olive oil in a small skillet.

In a medium bowl, combine spinach, sautéed onion/garlic, egg, Romano cheese, oregano, parsley, salt and pepper. Spread over prepared crust. Top with mozzarella cheese.

Starting at short end, roll up like a jellyroll, sealing the seam well. (Lightly brush 1 egg white on inside of seam to help seal.) Place pizza roll, seam side down, on a baking sheet coated with nonstick cooking spray. Brush with egg white. Bake at 350 degrees F for 30 minutes or until lightly browned. Let cool for 10 minutes before slicing. Serve with marinara sauce for dipping, if desired. Makes 12 servings.

Nutrition Facts: Calories 169, Protein 10.3 gm, Carbohydrate 25.2 gm, Dietary Fiber 3.9 gm, Fat 3.9 gm, Saturated Fat 1.6 gm, Sodium 405 mg
Meal Planning: 1 Carbohydrate, 1/2 Fat

Baked Potato Chips

You'll feel like you are eating "junk food."

6 medium red skin or Yukan gold potatoes
Olive oil nonstick cooking spray
2 teaspoons extra virgin olive oil
1/2 teaspoon salt, optional
1/2 teaspoon fresh ground black pepper
1/2 teaspoon paprika

Preheat oven to 500 degrees F. Brush 2 baking sheets with olive oil. Set aside.

Wash and scrub potatoes. Remove any blemishes. Dry potatoes with a cotton or paper towel.

Using a very sharp knife or slicer attachment of food processor, slice potatoes as thinly as possible.

Lay potato chips in a single layer on prepared baking sheets coated with nonstick cooking spray. Coat top of potato chips with nonstick cooking spray and lightly season with salt, pepper and paprika.

Bake at 500 degrees for 20 minutes or until tops begin to brown. Remove from oven and turn each potato chip over to brown the other side. Coat second side of potato chips with nonstick cooking spray. Lightly season with salt, pepper and paprika, if desired. Return to oven and bake for 10 more minutes or until top browns. (Second side browns very quickly.) Season with vinegar, if desired. Makes 4 servings (approximately 15 to 20 chips per serving, depending on thickness).

Nutrition Facts: Calories 119, Protein 2.6 gm, Carbohydrate 22.6 gm,
Dietary Fiber 5.1 gm, Fat 2.4 gm, Saturated Fat 0.3 gm, Sodium 274 mg
Meal Planning: 1 Carbohydrate, 1/2 Fat

*Recipe Variation: Use sweet potatoes or yams in place
of white potatoes. Sweet potatoes are a good source
of vitamin A while yams provide none.*

Spicy Tortilla Chips

Serve with your favorite chunky salsa for a spicy treat.

3 tablespoons peanut oil
1 tablespoon water
3 cloves crushed garlic
1/2 teaspoon dried oregano
1/2 teaspoon ground cumin
1/2 teaspoon paprika
1/2 teaspoon salt
1/2 teaspoon fresh ground black pepper
1/2 teaspoon ground white pepper
1/8 teaspoon ground red pepper
4 (6-inch) white or yellow corn tortillas
4 (6-inch) whole wheat tortillas
4 (6-inch) spinach tortillas

In a food processor or blender, combine oil, garlic, oregano, cumin, paprika, salt and peppers. Process for 1 to 2 minutes or until pureed.

Brush both sides of all tortillas with pureed spice mixture. (Use 12 of any variety of lowfat tortillas. Read labels carefully. Some tortillas are high in fat and/or contain lard.)

Stack tortillas and cut into 8 wedges. Arrange wedges in a single layer on baking pans coated with nonstick cooking spray. Bake at 400 degrees F for 10 minutes or until crisp and lightly browned. Serve warm with your favorite salsa. Makes 12 servings (8 chips per serving).

Nutrition Facts: Calories 117, Protein 2.7 gm, Carbohydrate 15.7 gm, Dietary Fiber 2.7 gm, Fat 5 gm, Saturated Fat 0.9 gm, Sodium 220 mg
Meal Planning: 1 Carbohydrate, 1/2 Fat

Lite Potato Salad

A lightened up version of an American classic.

2 pounds potatoes (about 6 medium), unpeeled
4 celery ribs, finely chopped
1 small sweet onion, finely chopped
1/2 cup sweet pickles, finely chopped
2 hard-cooked eggs, coarsely chopped
1/4 cup lite mayonnaise
1/4 cup Miracle Whip® Free® Nonfat Dressing
2 teaspoons honey mustard
1/4 teaspoon salt
1/4 teaspoon fresh ground black pepper
1/4 teaspoon ground white pepper
1 teaspoon paprika

In a large saucepot, bring 2 inches of water to a boil. Add potatoes. Return to boiling; reduce heat and cover. Cook until tender, about 30 to 40 minutes. Drain and cool.

Cut cooked potatoes into cubes. Do not peel. Place in a large bowl. Add celery, onion, sweet pickles and chopped eggs.

In a small bowl, combine mayonnaise, Miracle Whip, mustard, salt and peppers. Pour over potatoes and fold gently to combine. Adjust seasonings. Garnish with paprika. Makes 10 servings.

Nutrition Facts: Calories 99, Protein 2.5 gm, Carbohydrate 16 gm,
Dietary Fiber 1.4 gm, Fat 3.1 gm, Saturated Fat 0.7 gm, Sodium 353 mg
Meal Planning: 1 Carbohydrate, 1/2 Fat

Northern Corn Pudding

An old family recipe that takes corn from bland to brilliant.

2 cups yellow corn [fresh or frozen]
2 cups white shoepeg corn [fresh or frozen]
2 heaping tablespoons all-purpose flour
1 tablespoon granulated sugar
1/2 teaspoon salt
1½ cups fat-free or 1% milk
2 eggs, lightly beaten [or 1/2 cup egg substitute]
2 tablespoons lite whipped butter, melted
1/8 teaspoon fresh ground black pepper

Place corn (total of 4 cups) in a 2-quart casserole coated with nonstick cooking spray.

Sprinkle flour, sugar and salt over corn and stir to combine.

In a small bowl, combine milk and eggs and pour slowly into corn mixture. Stir to combine.

Stir melted butter into corn. Season with black pepper. Bake at 325 degrees F for 1 hour or until knife inserted into center comes out clean. Makes 8 servings (approximately 3/4 cup per serving).

Nutrition Facts: Calories 120, Protein 5.6 gm, Carbohydrate 20.1 gm, Dietary Fiber 2.1 gm, Fat 3 gm, Saturated Fat 1.1 gm, Sodium 196 mg
Meal Planning: 1 Carbohydrate, 1/2 Fat

Cheese Garden Casserole

An interesting combination of textures and flavors from the garden.

1 tablespoon lite tub margarine
1/4 cup slivered almonds
2 cups cooked brown rice
1/4 cup fresh chopped parsley
2 tablespoons low sodium soy sauce
2 cups fresh broccoli, chopped
2 cups matchstick or coarsely shredded carrots
1 medium zucchini squash, unpeeled and cut into julienne strips
1 cup cut green beans
1 cup cauliflower florets
2 cups marinara or tomato sauce
1/2 cup shredded lowfat extra sharp Cheddar cheese
1/2 cup shredded lowfat Monterey Jack cheese

Coat a medium skillet with nonstick cooking spray; heat over medium-high heat. Add margarine and melt; add almonds and sauté until lightly golden. Stir in rice, parsley and soy sauce. Spread rice mixture in the bottom of a 9 x 13-inch baking pan coated with nonstick cooking spray.

Combine all vegetables in a steamer and steam until crisp-tender, about 5 to 7 minutes. Drain vegetables thoroughly and spoon over rice mixture. Pour marinara sauce evenly over top. Cover and bake at 375 degrees F until heated through, about 30 minutes.

Combine cheeses and sprinkle over casserole. Return pan to oven, and bake, uncovered, until cheese melts. Makes 10 servings (approximately 1 cup per serving).

Nutrition Facts: Calories 165, Protein 7.4 gm, Carbohydrate 21.5 gm, Dietary Fiber 2.9 gm, Fat 5.5 gm, Saturated Fat 1.1 gm, Sodium 513 mg
Meal Planning: 1/2 Lean Meat/Protein, 1 Carbohydrate, 1 Vegetable

Recipe Time Saver: Use frozen chopped broccoli, cauliflower and green beans— thaw before using in recipe.

Green Rice Pilaf

Mild and spicy at the same time.

2 tablespoons lite tub margarine
1 cup quick-cooking brown rice
1 small sweet onion, finely chopped
1 can (6-ounce) diced green chilies
6 green onions, chopped
1 clove crushed garlic
1/4 teaspoon salt
1/4 teaspoon ground cumin
1½ cups low sodium vegetable broth
1 cup shredded lowfat Monterey Jack cheese
1/3 cup fresh chopped cilantro [or 2 tablespoons dried]

Melt margarine in a large skillet coated with nonstick cooking spray. Add rice. Spray lightly with nonstick cooking spray. Cook and stir for 2 minutes or until rice turns opaque.

Add onion; cook and stir for 1 minute. Stir in chilies, green onions, garlic, salt and cumin; cook and stir to combine. Add broth. Bring to a boil over high heat; reduce heat to low. Cover and simmer for 5 minutes or until rice is almost tender. Remove from heat.

Add cheese and chopped cilantro; toss lightly to combine. Cover until cheese is melted. Makes 6 servings.

Nutrition Facts: Calories 166, Protein 7.1 gm, Carbohydrate 32.7 gm, Dietary Fiber 3.8 gm, Fat 2.8 gm, Saturated Fat 0.7 gm, Sodium 266 mg
Meal Planning: 2 Carbohydrate

Great Grain Bake

A hearty blend of barley and beans.

1/4 cup slivered almonds
1 tablespoon extra virgin olive oil
1 pound sliced fresh mushrooms
1 cup finely chopped celery
1 cup finely chopped green onion
1 cup quick-cooking barley
2 cups low sodium vegetable broth
1 can (15-ounce) black-eyed peas, drained and rinsed
1 can (15-ounce) black beans, drained and rinsed
1/2 cup fresh chopped parsley [or 1/4 cup dried]
1/4 teaspoon salt
1/8 teaspoon fresh ground black pepper

Coat a large cast iron or oven-safe skillet with nonstick cooking spray. Place on medium heat. Add almonds and toast almonds by stirring constantly over medium heat until golden, about 1 to 2 minutes. Remove from skillet and set aside.

Add oil to skillet. Heat oil. Add mushrooms, celery and onion. Sauté over medium heat until vegetables are tender.

Add barley; cook and stir for 2 to 3 minutes or until barley is golden. Add broth, black-eyed peas, black beans, parsley, salt and pepper. Cover with an oven-safe lid and bake at 350 degrees F for 50 to 60 minutes or until the barley is tender and liquid is absorbed. Remove from oven and stir in almonds. Makes 8 servings.

Nutrition Facts: Calories 217, Protein 11.6 gm, Carbohydrate 46.3 gm, Dietary Fiber 11.2 gm, Fat 2.8 gm, Saturated Fat 0.4 gm, Sodium 233 mg
Meal Planning: 1 Lean Meat/Protein, 2 Carbohydrate, 1 Vegetable

Recipe Tip: Rinsing canned beans and vegetables reduces the sodium content by approximately 40 percent.

Bulgur-Chickpea Pilaf

The nutty flavor of sesame oil adds pizzazz to this pilaf.

1 cup medium-grain bulgur
1 cup boiling water
2 teaspoons sesame oil
1 medium onion, finely chopped
1 clove crushed garlic
1 teaspoon ground cumin
1 can (15-ounce) chickpeas [garbanzo beans], drained and rinsed
1 cup low sodium vegetable broth
1/2 teaspoon salt
1/4 teaspoon ground black pepper

Place bulgur in a medium bowl and cover with boiling water. Let stand for 10 minutes to soften.

Meanwhile, coat a deep skillet with nonstick cooking spray. Add oil and heat. Add onion, garlic and cumin and sauté over medium heat for 5 minutes, or until the onion is softened but not browned.

Stir in chickpeas, mashing slightly. Add bulgur and broth, mixing well. Bring to a boil. Reduce heat to low, cover and simmer over low heat for about 10 minutes, or until liquid is absorbed.

If bulgur seems too wet, uncover skillet and cook over medium heat until liquid is absorbed. Fluff with a fork, season with salt and pepper. Makes 6 servings.

Nutrition Facts: Calories 160, Protein 7.1 gm, Carbohydrate 30.4 gm, Dietary Fiber 7.3 gm, Fat 2.4 gm, Saturated Fat 0.3 gm, Sodium 466 mg
Meal Planning: 1½ Carbohydrate, 1/2 Fat

Seafood Pasta Salad

Serve this luscious dish for your next luncheon or picnic.

1½ cups tri-colored corkscrew pasta
1½ cups whole wheat corkscrew pasta
1/3 cup red wine vinegar
2 tablespoons extra virgin olive oil
2 tablespoons water
2 cloves crushed garlic
1/2 teaspoon salt
1/4 teaspoon ground white pepper
1/4 teaspoon fresh ground black pepper
2 teaspoons honey
1/4 teaspoon **each** dried thyme, oregano and basil
1 pounds assorted cooked seafood - salad shrimp, lump crabmeat,
    imitation crab, etc.
2 cups fresh broccoli florets
2 large tomatoes, unpeeled and chopped
1 medium sweet onion, finely chopped
1 cup coarsely chopped cabbage
1/4 cup sliced black olives
3 cups mixed lettuce greens

In a large stockpot, cook pasta in a large amount of water for 8 minutes or until al dente. *Do not add salt or oil.* Stir occasionally while boiling. Drain and rinse briefly with cold water and toss.

In a large bowl, combine vinegar, oil, water, garlic, salt, pepper, honey, thyme, oregano and basil. Mix with a whisk to combine. Add cooked pasta, seafood, broccoli, tomatoes, onion, cabbage and olives; toss to coat. Cover and refrigerate for 4 to 24 hours, stirring occasionally. Toss in mixed greens before serving. Makes 10 servings (approximately 1½ to 2 cups per serving).

Nutrition Facts: Calories 207, Protein 11.3 gm, Carbohydrate 31.5 gm,
Dietary Fiber 3.5 gm, Fat 4.8 gm, Saturated Fat 0.6 gm, Sodium 375 mg
Meal Planning: 1 Lean Meat/Protein, 1 Carbohydrate, 2 Vegetable, 1 Fat

Penne Salad With Spring Peas

This unique dressing gives this salad a wonderful light appeal.

8 ounces penne pasta
8 ounces whole wheat penne pasta
1½ cups frozen spring peas, thawed
1/2 cup sliced green onions
1 large red bell pepper, seeded and sliced
1 cup fat-free or 1% milk
1/2 cup red wine vinegar
1/2 cup nonfat mayonnaise or mayonnaise-type salad dressing
1/4 cup fresh minced parsley [or 2 tablespoons dried]
1/4 cup Splenda® sugar substitute
1/2 teaspoon salt
1/4 teaspoon fresh ground black pepper

In a large stockpot, cook pasta in a large amount of water for 8 minutes or until al dente. *Do not add salt or oil.* Stir occasionally while boiling. Drain and rinse briefly with cold water and toss.

In a large bowl, combine cooked pasta, peas, green onions and red pepper.

In a small bowl, combine milk, vinegar, mayonnaise, parsley and Splenda. Whip with a wire whisk to combine. Pour dressing over salad and toss. Season to taste with salt and pepper. Makes 12 servings (approximately 1 cup per serving).

Nutrition Facts: Calories 177, Protein 6.4 gm, Carbohydrate 35.3 gm, Dietary Fiber 2.7 gm, Fat 1.7 gm, Saturated Fat 0.1 gm, Sodium 249 mg
Meal Planning: 2 Carbohydrate, 1 Vegetable

Linguine With Greens

Broccoli rabe adds great flavor, texture and color to any dish.

8 ounces whole wheat linguine or spaghetti
2 bunches kale or collard greens
1 bunch broccoli rabe
1 tablespoon extra virgin olive oil
2 cloves crushed garlic
1/2 teaspoon salt
1/4 teaspoon fresh ground black pepper
1½ cups low sodium vegetable or chicken broth
1/4 teaspoon crushed red pepper
1/4 cup toasted pine (pignolia) nuts
1/2 cup freshly grated Romano or Asiago cheese

In a large saucepot, cook linguine in a large amount of water for 6 minutes or until al dente. *Do not add salt or oil.* Stir occasionally while boiling. Drain and return to saucepot. Set aside.

Meanwhile, discard tough stems from greens and broccoli rabe. Rinse and drain well.

Coat a large skillet with nonstick cooking spray. Add oil and garlic and cook until garlic is lightly golden, about 30 to 45 seconds. Add greens, broccoli rabe and salt. Cook, stirring frequently, just until greens wilt.

Stir broth into reserved cooked linguine. Bring to a boil. Add greens and broccoli rabe to linguine; gently toss to mix well. Sprinkle with crushed red pepper and Romano cheese. Makes 8 servings (approximately 3/4 cup per serving).

Nutrition Facts: Calories 172, Protein 9 gm, Carbohydrate 29 gm, Dietary Fiber 2 gm, Fat 6 gm, Saturated Fat 1.8 gm, Sodium 322 mg
Meal Planning: 2 Carbohydrate, 1 Fat

Angel Hair With Rosa Sauce

Blending tomato and milk products creates a mellow flavor.

8 ounces whole wheat angel hair pasta
1 tablespoon extra virgin olive oil
2 cloves crushed garlic
1 can (28-ounce) kitchen cut tomatoes
1 cup sliced fresh mushrooms
1/2 teaspoon salt
1/4 teaspoon fresh ground black pepper
1/8 teaspoon fennel seed
3 tablespoons fresh chopped basil [or 1½ teaspoons dried]
1 cup nonfat ricotta cheese [or 1 cup fat-free half and half]
1/4 cup freshly grated Parmesan cheese

In a large stockpot, cook linguine in a large amount of water for 6 minutes or until al dente. *Do not add salt or oil.* Stir occasionally while boiling. Drain. Set aside.

Meanwhile, coat a large skillet with nonstick cooking spray. Add oil and garlic and sauté garlic over medium heat until golden, about 30 to 45 seconds. Add remaining ingredients, except ricotta and Parmesan cheeses. Reduce heat and simmer for 10 minutes while pasta is cooking.

Puree ricotta cheese in a food processor or whip with a wire whisk until smooth. Stir ricotta cheese into tomato sauce until well blended. Heat through and let reduce slightly.

Place cooked pasta on a serving platter. Top with sauce and sprinkle with Parmesan cheese; toss to mix. Makes 4 main-dish servings (approximately 1½ cups per serving).

Nutrition Facts: Calories 339, Protein 21.6 gm, Carbohydrate 55.1 gm, Dietary Fiber 2.2 gm, Fat 6.2 gm Saturated Fat 1.6 gm, Sodium 808 mg
Meal Planning: 2 Lean Meat/Protein, 3 Carbohydrate, 2 Vegetable

Four-Pepper Pasta

The blend of sweet, sour and herbs will make this a frequent recipe.

8 ounces whole wheat mostaccioli or penne pasta
1/2 teaspoon salt
1 to 2 large red bell peppers, seeded
1 to 2 large yellow bell peppers, seeded
1 large green bell pepper, seeded
1/2 teaspoon fresh ground black pepper
1 large sweet onion
2 tablespoons extra virgin olive oil
1 tablespoon granulated sugar
3 tablespoons balsamic vinegar
1 teaspoon dried basil leaves [or 2 tablespoons fresh chopped]

In a large saucepot, cook linguine in a large amount of water for 8 minutes or until al dente. *Do not add salt or oil.* Stir occasionally while boiling. Drain. Set aside.

Meanwhile, cut peppers and onion into 1/2-inch strips.

Coat a large skillet with nonstick cooking spray. Add oil, peppers, black pepper, onion and salt. Cook until vegetables are tender, about 15 minutes.

Stir sugar, vinegar and basil into pepper mixture; heat through. Add cooked pasta to pepper mixture and toss. Makes 8 servings (approximately 3/4 cup per serving).

Nutrition Facts: Calories 159, Protein 3.7 gm, Carbohydrate 26 gm, Dietary Fiber 2.4 gm, Fat 5.2 gm, Saturated Fat 0.5 gm, Sodium 203 mg
Meal Planning: 3 Carbohydrate, 2 vegetable

Recipe Time Saver: Use 1 pound frozen Birds Eye® Pepper Stir-Fry instead of fresh bell peppers and onion; thaw before using.

Green Pizza

It might not be easy being green but this green pizza goes down easy.

1 Hearty Wheat Pizza Crust (*Recipe on Page 98*) [or 1 loaf flat bread]
Cornmeal
2 teaspoons extra virgin olive oil, divided
2 cloves crushed garlic
2 cup coarsely chopped fresh spinach
1 cup pepperocini rings
1/4 cup sliced green olives
1 cup sliced fresh mushrooms
1 cup shredded part-skim mozzarella cheese
1/4 cup freshly grated Parmesan cheese
1 tablespoon fresh chopped basil [or 1 teaspoon dried]

Place pizza crust or flat bread on a large pizza pan coated with nonstick cooking spray and sprinkled lightly with cornmeal. Brush 1 teaspoon olive oil over dough.

Layer remaining ingredients in order listed and drizzle with remaining 1 teaspoon olive oil.

Bake at 500° for 15 minutes or until crust is golden brown. Makes 1 large pizza or 8 slices.

Nutrition Facts: Calories 205, Protein 10.4 gm, Carbohydrate 26.4 gm, Dietary Fiber 2.6 gm, Fat 7.3 gm, Saturated Fat 3 gm, Sodium 385 mg
Meal Planning: 1 Lean Meat/Protein, 1 Carbohydrate, 2 Vegetable, 1/2 Fat

Hearty Wheat Pizza Crust

It's worth the extra effort to enjoy a homemade pizza crust.

1 cup water
2 teaspoons extra virgin olive oil
2 teaspoons granulated sugar
1½ cups whole wheat flour
1/2 cup whole wheat pastry flour
1 cup all-purpose flour
1 package rapid-rise dry yeast
1/2 teaspoon salt
3 tablespoons cornmeal

In a small saucepan, combine water, oil and sugar and heat until 115 to 120 degrees F.

In a large bowl, combine flours, yeast and salt. Add hot water mixture and stir with a wooden spoon until combined. Turn out onto a lightly floured board and knead 10 times.

Place dough in a bowl coated with nonstick cooking spray, turning to coat. Cover and let rise in a warm place for 30 minutes or until doubled in bulk.

Punch dough down. Let dough rest for a few minutes. Press dough out onto 2 large pizza pans coated with nonstick cooking spray and sprinkled lightly with cornmeal. Cover with a towel and let rest for 10 minutes.

Bake at 500 degrees F for 5 minutes. Top one crust with your favorite pizza toppings and bake for 15 to 20 minutes. Freeze second crust for later use. Makes 2 large pizza crusts or 8 slices each (1 slice per serving).

Nutrition Facts: Calories 88, Protein 2.8 gm, Carbohydrate 17.6 gm, Dietary Fiber 1.4 gm, Fat 0.9 gm, Saturated Fat 0.1 gm, Sodium 67 mg
Meal Planning: 1 Carbohydrate

Hummus Pizza

The sweetness of Jarlsberg mingles with vidalia for a great pizza.

1 Potato Pizza Crust (*Recipe on Page 100*)
1 tablespoon extra virgin olive oil
2 cups thinly sliced vidalia onion, separated into rings
1/2 cup prepared hummus
3/4 cup fresh chopped spinach
1 teaspoon balsamic vinegar
1/2 cup shredded lowfat Jarlsberg cheese
2 tablespoons crumbled lowfat Feta cheese
3 tablespoons fresh shaved Parmesan cheese

Coat a large skillet with nonstick cooking spray. Add oil and heat. Add onion; cover and cook for 15 minutes or until deep golden, stirring frequently.

Spread hummus over crust. Sprinkle spinach with vinegar and spread over hummus; top with cooked onion. Sprinkle with cheese. Bake at 500 degrees F for 15 minutes or until crust is crisp. Makes 1 large pizza or 8 slices (1 slice per serving).

Nutrition Facts: Calories 149, Protein 6.7 gm, Carbohydrate 22.3 gm, Dietary Fiber 2.7 gm, Fat 3.3 gm, Saturated Fat 1.3 gm, Sodium 335 mg
Meal Planning: 1/2 Lean Meat/Protein, 1 Carbohydrate, 1 Vegetable

Potato Pizza Crust

A mild light crust that will have them asking for more.

2/3 cup water
1/4 cup fat-free or 1% milk
2/3 cup instant mashed potato flakes [or 1 cup mashed potatoes]
1 cup very warm water (120 to 130 degrees F)
1 tablespoon honey
2 cups all-purpose flour
1 package rapid-rise dry yeast
1 cup whole wheat flour
1 cup whole wheat pastry flour
1/2 teaspoon salt
1 teaspoon extra virgin olive oil
3 tablespoons cornmeal

In a small microwave-safe bowl, combine 2/3 cup water and milk. Microwave on HIGH for 1½ minutes or until hot. Stir in potato flakes to moisten. Let stand until liquid is absorbed. Fluff with a fork. In a large bowl, combine prepared mashed potatoes, 1 cup warm water and honey. Combine 1/2 cup all-purpose flour and yeast and stir into potato mixture. Let stand for 10 minutes.

In a large bowl, combine remaining flours and salt. Add potato-yeast mixture and oil. Stir with a wooden spoon until well combined and dough leaves the sides of the bowl, forming a ball. Knead several times in the bowl. (Or use food processor.) Place dough in a large bowl coated with nonstick cooking spray, turning to coat. Cover and let rise in a warm place for 30 to 40 minutes or until doubled in bulk.

Punch dough down and turn out onto a lightly floured surface; knead 3 or 4 times. With floured hands, divide dough and form into 3 balls. Cover dough and let rest for 15 minutes. Pat balls onto 3 large pizza pans coated with nonstick cooking spray and sprinkled lightly with cornmeal. Add favorite pizza toppings. Makes 3 large pizza crusts or 8 slices each (1 slice per serving).

Nutrition Facts: Calories 82, Protein 2.7 gm, Carbohydrate 17.2 gm, Dietary Fiber 1.3 gm, Fat 0.5 gm, Saturated Fat 0.1 gm, Sodium 48 mg
Meal Planning: 1 Carbohydrate

May the plates of lentils and pasta line up all the way to the house's door.

Lebanese Proverb

Healthy people select more plant-based meals including more soy products, legumes and other vegetarian meals.

- Eat legumes (dried beans, peas, lentils, peanuts and soybeans) at least five times per week, optimally once or twice daily.
- Eat legumes or soy products in place of meat or poultry for excellent sources of protein. Substitute 3 cups (cooked) brown, black or French lentils in place of 1 pound ground meat.
- Add black-eyed peas, kidney or garbanzo beans to salads.
- Add black beans or lentils to rice and other grain recipes.
- Save time by using canned beans. Drain and rinse with water to reduce the sodium content by 40%.
- Look for organic, no salt added canned beans available in many health food, specialty and grocery stores.
- Take advantage of commercially prepared soy meat-alternative foods such as deli meats, burgers, hotdogs, bacon and sausage.
- Use soy ground meat substitute or texturized soy protein instead of ground meat.
- Substitute 1/4 cup soft or silken tofu for 1 whole egg in baking.
- Substitute firm or extra firm tofu for eggs in stir-frys.
- Freeze and thaw tofu for a chewier texture and darker color.
- Treat tofu like meat— brown and sear it in oil before adding other ingredients.
- Snack on soynuts or use crushed soynuts in recipes.
- Use lentil, soy and other bean pastas available at health food, specialty and many grocery stores— an excellent source of fiber and protein without refined flours.
- Gradually add legumes to the diet to allow the digestive tract to adjust and tolerate without gastrointestinal distress.

Hot & Sour Soup

I've been told restaurants can't compete with this Hot & Sour Soup.

5 cups low sodium vegetable or chicken broth
3 tablespoons rice vinegar
1 tablespoon dry sherry
2 teaspoons soy sauce
1 clove crushed garlic
1/2 teaspoon minced gingerroot
5 dried Chinese mushrooms, soaked in hot water for 20 minutes
1 cup matchstick carrots
1 can (3-ounce) bamboo shoots, drained and rinsed
1/2 teaspoon hot pepper or chili sauce
2 tablespoons cornstarch
3 tablespoons water
4 ounces extra firm tofu, cut into thin strips
2 green onions, shredded

Bring broth to a boil in a large saucepot. Stir vinegar, sherry, soy sauce, garlic and gingerroot into broth.

Remove stems from mushrooms and slice mushrooms. Slice bamboo shoots into very thin slices. Add mushrooms, carrot, bamboo shoots and hot-pepper sauce to soup. Bring to a boil then simmer for 10 minutes.

In a small bowl, blend cornstarch and water. Stir cornstarch-water mixture and tofu into soup. Simmer for 2 minutes or until slightly thickened. Sprinkle with green onions. Makes 6 servings (approximately 1 cup per serving).

Nutrition Facts: Calories 78, Protein 4.7 gm, Carbohydrate 12.7 gm, Dietary Fiber 1.4 gm, Fat 1.2 gm, Saturated Fat 0.2 gm, Sodium 243 mg
Meal Planning: 1 Carbohydrate

Quick Minestrone Soup

An Italian tradition with less fat but all the flavor.

1 cup matchstick carrots
1 cup chopped celery
1 cup sliced zucchini squash, unpeeled
2/3 cup chopped onion
1 can (15-ounce) dark red kidney beans, drained and rinsed
1 can (15-ounce) garbanzo beans, drained and rinsed
4 cups low sodium vegetable broth
1 cup water
2/3 cup lentil, bean or soy orzo pasta
1 can (14-ounce) whole tomatoes, cut up
Herb Pistou - *See recipe below*

Coat a large saucepot with nonstick cooking spray. Heat pot over medium heat. Add carrots, celery, zucchini and onion and sauté for 1 to 2 minutes. Cover and cook for 8 minutes.

Stir in beans, broth and water. Bring to a boil. Reduce heat and simmer for 15 minutes. Stir in pasta. Cook for 5 to 7 minutes, or until pasta is al dente. Stir in tomatoes and Herb Pistou. Heat through. Makes 4 servings (approximately 2 cups per serving).

To make Herb Pistou: In a small bowl, combine *2 teaspoons dried basil, 1/2 teaspoon dried rosemary, 2 cloves crushed garlic, 1/4 teaspoon fresh ground black pepper and 1/8 teaspoon salt.* Stir in *1 teaspoon extra virgin olive oil* to make a paste.

Nutrition Facts: Calories 318, Protein 21.2 gm, Carbohydrate 53.5 gm, Dietary Fiber 9.1 gm, Fat 3.3 gm, Sat Fat 0.4 gm, Sodium 755 mg
Meal Planning: 2 Lean Meat/Protein, 2 Carbohydrate, 3 Vegetable

Tortellini Soup

The easiest soup recipe you'll ever try— and one of the best.

1 can (28-ounce) Italian-style diced tomatoes, undrained
1 can (28-ounce) crushed tomatoes
1 can (15-ounce) condensed tomato soup
1/2 cup water
1 cup canned cannellini (white kidney) beans, drained and rinsed
1 cup matchstick carrots
1 cup diced onion (fresh or frozen)
1 cup diced green bell pepper (fresh or frozen)
1 tablespoon dried basil
1 tablespoon dried cilantro
1 tablespoon granulated sugar
1 teaspoon garlic powder
1/2 teaspoon fresh ground black pepper
1/2 teaspoon salt
8 ounces frozen cheese tortellini

Place all ingredients except tortellini in a large crockpot. Stir to combine.
Turn temperature to HIGH and let cook for at least 3½ to 4 hours or
until bubbly. Add tortellini 20 minutes before serving.

Optional Preparation: Place all ingredients except tortellini in a large
saucepot. Cover and bring to a slow boil. Reduce heat to simmer. Cover
and cook for 30 minutes. Add tortellini and cook for 15 to 20 more
minutes. Makes 10 servings (approximately 1 to 1½ cups serving).

Nutrition Facts: Calories 217, Protein 10 gm, Carbohydrate 38 gm,
Dietary Fiber 5 gm, Fat 3.5 gm, Saturated Fat 1.2 gm, Sodium 757 mg
Meal Planning: 1 Lean Meat/Protein, 2 Carbohydrate

*Original Tortellini Soup recipe by my friend
Robin Nagle from North East, Pennsylvania*

Curried Lentil Vegetable Soup

A sweet surprise– try different varieties of lentils.

1 cup dried lentils – brown, red, yellow, black or French
5 cups low sodium vegetable broth
1 cup chopped, peeled parsnips
1 cup matchstick carrots
1 large vidalia onion, sliced
1 cup cauliflower florets
1 small zucchini, unpeeled and sliced
1 cup shredded cabbage
2 teaspoons curry powder
1/2 teaspoon salt
1/4 teaspoon crushed red pepper
2 cloves crushed garlic

Rinse, sort and drain lentils.

Place lentils and broth in a large stockpot. Bring to a boil; reduce heat. Cover and simmer for 20 minutes.

Stir in parsnips, carrots, onion, cauliflower, zucchini, cabbage, curry, salt, red pepper and garlic. Return to a boil; reduce heat.

Cover and simmer for 10 to 15 minutes more or until lentils and vegetables are tender. Makes 4 servings (approximately 2 to 2½ cups per serving).

Nutrition Facts: Calories 254, Protein 18.4 gm, Carbohydrate 46.5 gm, Dietary Fiber 19.6 gm, Fat 0.9 gm, Saturated Fat 0.1 gm, Sodium 502 mg
Meal Planning: 2 Lean Meat/Protein, 2 Carbohydrate

Tofu Vegetable Stir-Fry

A wonderful way to experience tofu– freeze tofu for better texture.

1 pound extra firm tofu, drained
1 tablespoon cornstarch
2 tablespoons low sodium soy sauce
1/2 teaspoon brown sugar
1/2 cup cold water
1/4 cup broken walnuts
1 tablespoon peanut oil
1 tablespoon minced gingerroot
2 cloves crushed garlic
1 head bok choy, coarsely chopped
2 cups matchstick or sliced carrots
2 cups sliced fresh mushrooms
2 cups fresh broccoli, cut into florets
2 cups cooked brown rice

Press tofu to remove excess water; cut into 1/4-inch strips. Set aside. In a small bowl, stir cornstarch into soy sauce; stir in sugar and water. Set aside.

Coat wok or large skillet with nonstick cooking spray. Place over high heat. Add walnuts and toast, stirring constantly, for 1 to 2 minutes or until toasted. Remove from wok and set aside.

Add oil to wok and heat. Add gingerroot and garlic and stir-fry for 30 seconds. Add tofu and stir-fry for 3 to 5 minutes or until golden. Do not cover while stir-frying tofu.

Add bok choy, carrots, mushrooms and broccoli and stir-fry for 5 minutes. Cover for 1 to 2 minutes to steam. Stir in soy sauce mixture and toasted walnuts. Cook and stir until thickened and bubbly. Serve over brown rice. Makes 4 servings (1/2 cup rice and approximately 2 cups stir-fry per serving).

Nutrition Facts: Calories 290, Protein 15.5 gm, Carbohydrate 36.1 gm, Dietary Fiber 5.2 gm, Fat 11 gm, Saturated Fat 1.7 gm, Sodium 311 mg
Meal Planning: 2 Lean Meat/Protein, 2 Carbohydrate, 1 Vegetable

I Can't Believe It's Not Egg Salad

You really won't believe how good this recipe is— give it a try.

1 pound extra firm tofu, previously frozen and thawed
1 hard boiled egg
1/4 cup lite mayonnaise
1/4 cup Miracle Whip® Free® nonfat dressing
1 teaspoon prepared yellow mustard
1 tablespoon sweet relish
1/4 cup chopped green olives
1/4 cup chopped sweet onion
1/4 cup chopped red bell pepper or pimiento
1/4 cup finely shredded carrots
1/2 teaspoon salt
1/4 teaspoon ground white pepper
1/4 teaspoon fresh ground black pepper
1/4 teaspoon paprika
Dash ground tumeric, optional

Press tofu with paper towels to remove excess water. (For complete pressing, place several layers of paper towels on a cutting board surface. Lay tofu on top of towels. Cover with several more layers of paper towels and place a heavy object on top of paper towels. Let press for 10 minutes. Remove paper towels and proceed with recipe.)

Using a fork, mash pressed tofu and hard boiled egg in a large bowl, incorporating egg into tofu. Add remaining ingredients and mix well to combine. Refrigerate for 1 hour before serving. For a balanced meal, serve with lettuce and tomato in a whole wheat pita with a fresh fruit salad. Makes 6 servings (approximately 3/4 cup).

Nutrition Facts: Calories 172, Protein 12.5 gm, Carbohydrate 10.8 gm, Dietary Fiber 1.9 gm, Fat 9.5 gm, Saturated Fat 2.0 gm, Sodium 490 mg
Meal Planning: 2 Lean Meat/Protein, 1 Vegetable, 1/2 Fat

Sweet & Sour Tofu

Not the deep-fried, fat-laden version that you are used to.

1 pound extra firm tofu, previously frozen, thawed and drained
1 tablespoon peanut oil
2 cloves crushed garlic
2 cups assorted bell pepper strips – red, green, yellow and orange
2 celery ribs, diagonally sliced
3 cups matchstick carrots
1 tablespoon cornstarch
1/4 cup low sodium soy sauce
1 can (8-ounce) chunk pineapple, in juice, undrained
3 tablespoons apple cider vinegar
1 tablespoon brown sugar
2 tablespoons Splenda® sugar substitute
1/2 teaspoon ground ginger

Press tofu to remove excess water; cut into 1/2-inch cubes. Set aside.

Coat a wok or large skillet with nonstick cooking spray. Add oil and heat. Add garlic and tofu and stir-fry until golden brown. Do not cover while stir-frying tofu.

Add peppers, celery and carrot. Cook and stir-fry for 2 to 3 minutes or until tender-crisp.

In a medium bowl, combine cornstarch, soy sauce, undrained pineapple, vinegar, brown sugar, Splenda and ginger. Add to tofu mixture. Bring to a full boil and cook until thick. Serve over brown rice, if desired. Makes 4 (approximately 2 cups per serving).

Nutrition Facts: Calories 232, Protein 11.5 gm, Carbohydrate 30.7 gm, Dietary Fiber 5.3 gm, Fat 9.1 gm, Saturated Fat 1.4 gm, Sodium 547 mg
Meal Planning: 1 Lean Meat/Protein, 1 Carbohydrate, 2 Vegetable, 1 Fat

Fried Rice & Tofu

A good first way to try tofu— you can fool the family with this one.

1 tablespoon peanut oil
1/2 cup egg substitute [or 2 eggs, lightly beaten]
1 pound extra firm tofu, drained, pressed and crumbled
1 cup sliced fresh mushrooms
2 celery ribs, chopped
2 cups fresh bean sprouts
3 green onions, chopped
2 cups cooked brown rice
1 cup petite green peas, frozen
3 tablespoons low sodium soy sauce
1/4 teaspoon fresh ground black pepper

Coat a wok or large skillet with nonstick cooking spray. Add oil and heat over medium heat. Add egg substitute and tofu. Stir-fry lightly until eggs are almost set; remove from pan and set aside.

In the same pan, add mushrooms, celery, bean sprouts and green onions. Stir-fry for about 2 minutes.

Continue stir-frying and add peas, rice and reserved egg-tofu mixture. Gradually add soy sauce and black pepper. Cover to heat through. Makes 4 servings.

Nutrition Facts: Calories 339, Protein 20 gm, Carbohydrate 38.8 gm, Dietary Fiber 5.4 gm, Fat 13.3 gm, Saturated Fat 2.2 gm, Sodium 505 mg
Meal Planning: 3 Lean Meat/Protein, 2 Carbohydrate, 1 Vegetable

Tofu Peasant Salad

This recipe will become a frequent dinner guest– it's scrumptious.

1/4 cup extra virgin olive oil
1/3 cup red wine vinegar
1/3 cup water
1/4 cup fresh chopped basil leaves
2 tablespoons capers, drained
1/2 teaspoon salt
1/4 teaspoon fresh ground black pepper
1 clove crushed garlic
1 pound extra firm tofu, drained and pressed
4 medium tomatoes
2 medium English cucumbers, unpeeled
1 large yellow bell pepper, seeded
1 medium red onion
1 loaf (12-ounces) Italian bread [whole wheat, if available]
10 kalamata or Greek-style olives, pitted and sliced
4 ounces lowfat feta cheese, crumbled

In a large bowl, whisk together oil, vinegar, water, basil, capers, salt, pepper and garlic.

Cut tofu, tomatoes, cucumber, bell pepper and onion into bite-size pieces. Add to bowl with dressing; toss well. Cover and refrigerate until ready to serve.

Cut bread into 1-inch chunks. Just before serving, add bread to vegetable mixture; toss gently to coat with dressing. Top salad with olives and feta cheese. Makes 10 servings (approximately 1 cup per serving).

Nutrition Facts: Calories 239, Protein 10.9 gm, Carbohydrate 23.5 gm, Dietary Fiber 3 gm, Fat 11.9 gm, Saturated Fat 2.7 gm, Sodium 469 mg
Meal Planning: 1 Lean Meat/Protein, 1 Carbohydrate, 1 Vegetable, 1 Fat

Lentils & Pasta with Vegetables

Lentils provide a mild flavor unlike any other legume.

3/4 cup elbow macaroni
3/4 cup whole wheat elbow macaroni
1 cup low sodium vegetable broth
1/2 cup lentils, rinsed, drained and sorted
1/2 cup chopped onion
1 teaspoon dried thyme
1/2 teaspoon salt
1/4 teaspoon fresh ground black pepper
1/4 teaspoon ground white pepper
2 cups diced carrots (fresh or frozen)
1 box (10-ounce) frozen chopped spinach, thawed and well-drained
1 cup chopped fresh tomato (about 1 large)
2 tablespoons freshly grated Parmesan cheese

In a large stockpot, cook both pastas in a large amount of boiling water according to package directions. *Do not add salt or oil.* Stir occasionally while boiling. Drain and reserve.

In same stockpot, combine broth, lentils, onion, thyme, salt and peppers. Bring to a boil; reduce heat. Cover and simmer for 20 minutes. Add carrots. Simmer for 10 additional minutes or until carrots and lentils are tender. Add cooked pasta, spinach and tomato. Heat through.

To serve, sprinkle with Parmesan cheese. Makes 4 servings (approximately 2 cups per serving).

Nutrition Facts: Calories 300, Protein 16.2 gm, Carbohydrate 55.5 gm, Dietary Fiber 13.3 gm, Fat 3 gm, Saturated Fat 0.6 gm, Sodium 432 mg
Meal Planning: 2 Lean Meat/Protein, 2 Carbohydrate, 2 Vegetable

Vegetarian Tacos

A quick meal that tastes just like the original– minus the fat.

1 teaspoon extra virgin olive oil
1 medium onion, finely chopped
1 pound frozen soy ground meat crumbles, 3 cups cooked lentils
    or 3 cups canned black beans, drained and rinsed
1 package reduced sodium taco seasoning mix
1/2 cup chunky salsa
1/3 cup water
1 can (4-ounce) diced green chilies
12 white or yellow corn taco shells
2 cups coarsely shredded lettuce
1 cup chopped tomatoes
1 cup shredded lowfat extra sharp Cheddar cheese
Taco sauce

Coat a large skillet with nonstick cooking spray. Add oil and heat over medium-high heat. Add onion and sauté until opaque.

Add soy ground meat, lentils or black beans. Stir in taco seasoning, salsa, water and chilies. Bring to a boil over medium-high heat. Reduce heat, cover and simmer for 15 minutes.

To assemble tacos, place 3 to 4 tablespoons of taco mixture in each taco shell. Top with shredded lettuce, chopped tomatoes, cheese and taco sauce. For a balanced meal, serve with a side dish of refried beans and sliced papaya and kiwi. Makes 12 tacos.

Nutrition Facts: Calories 153, Protein 8.5 gm, Carbohydrate 19.9 gm, Dietary Fiber 5.4 gm, Fat 4.9 gm, Saturated Fat 1.5 gm, Sodium 169 mg
Meal Planning: 1 Lean Meat/Protein, 1 Carbohydrate, 1 Vegetable

Lentil Rigatoni

Save loads of calories and tons of fat with this meatless version.

1 tablespoon extra virgin olive oil
1 clove crushed garlic
1 medium onion, chopped
1 can (28-ounce) crushed tomatoes
1 can (6-ounce) tomato paste
1 cup sliced fresh mushrooms
1 tablespoon molasses
1 teaspoon dried basil [or 1 tablespoon fresh chopped]
1 teaspoon dried oregano [or 1 tablespoon fresh chopped]
2 tablespoons dried parsley [or 1/4 cup fresh chopped]
1/8 teaspoon ground allspice
1/2 teaspoon salt
1/4 teaspoon fresh ground black pepper
1/4 teaspoon ground white pepper
3 cups cooked lentils [or 3 cups canned lentils, drained and rinsed]
6 ounces whole wheat rigatoni

Coat a large saucepot with nonstick cooking spray. Add oil and heat over high heat. Add garlic and cook for 30 seconds until golden. Add onions and cook until opaque.

Add remaining ingredients, except rigatoni, stirring well. Bring to a boil. Reduce heat to low and simmer for 30 to 45 minutes. Adjust seasonings.

In a large stockpot, cook rigatoni in a large amount of boiling water according to package directions. *Do not add salt or oil.* Stir occasionally while boiling. Drain well and toss. Add to sauce just before serving. Makes 6 servings (approximately 1½ cups per serving).

Nutrition Facts: Calories 387, Protein 15.7 gm, Carbohydrate 49.6 gm, Dietary Fiber 13.3 gm, Fat 3.7 gm, Saturated Fat 0.9 gm, Sodium 504 mg
Meal Planning: 2 Lean Meat/Protein, 2 Carbohydrate, 1 Vegetable

Favorite Baked Beans

A little time-consuming but so much better than buying canned.

1 pound assorted dried beans (Great Northern, Navy, Lima, etc.)
Water
1/2 cup ketchup
1 can (6-ounce) tomato paste
1 teaspoon salt
1/2 teaspoon fresh ground black pepper
1/2 teaspoon fresh ground white pepper
3 tablespoons molasses
2 tablespoons brown sugar [or 2 tablespoons brown sugar substitute]
1/3 cup dry sherry, optional

Rinse, drain and sort beans. In a large stockpot, combine beans and 6 cups water. Place over high heat and bring to a boil. Reduce heat slightly and boil for 2 minutes. Remove from heat and let stand for 1 hour.

After 1 hour, drain and rinse beans. (This quick-soak method removes many of the gas-forming oligosaccharides in the beans.) Return to stockpot and add 6 cups fresh water. Place over high heat and bring to a boil. Reduce heat, cover and simmer for 1 to 1½ hours or until beans are tender. Drain beans, reserving cook water.

Return beans to saucepot. Stir in ketchup, tomato paste, salt, peppers, molasses, brown sugar and sherry. Add enough reserved cook water until desired consistency.

Serve immediately. Or place in a casserole coated with nonstick cooking spray and bake for 30 to 45 minutes or until bubbly and crusty on top. Makes 8 servings.

Nutrition Facts: Calories 184, Protein 13.7 gm, Carbohydrate 50.4 gm, Dietary Fiber 21.6 gm, Fat 0.3 gm, Saturated Fat 0 gm, Sodium 494 mg
Meal Planning: 2 Lean Meat/Protein, 2 Carbohydrate

Baked Lentils

Lentils are a surprisingly fast-cooking legume requiring no soaking.

2 cups dried lentils
1 tablespoon extra virgin olive oil
Olive oil nonstick cooking spray
1/2 cup chopped onions
1/2 cup diced celery
1/2 cup diced carrots
1/2 cup chopped fresh mushrooms
3 tablespoons all-purpose flour
1½ cups low sodium vegetable broth
1/2 cup vegetable juice cocktail [regular or spicy]
1/2 teaspoon salt
1/4 teaspoon fresh ground black pepper
1/4 teaspoon dried basil
1/4 teaspoon ground thyme
1 tablespoon dried parsley [or 2 tablespoons fresh chopped]
1/4 cup dry whole wheat bread crumbs

Rinse, sort and drain lentils. In a large stockpot, combine lentils and 6 cups water. Place over high heat and bring to a boil. Reduce heat; cover and simmer for 30 minutes. Drain.

While lentils are cooking, coat a large deep skillet with nonstick cooking spray. Add oil and heat. Add celery, carrots and mushrooms and sauté over medium heat until tender. Stir in flour and cook for 1 minute stirring constantly. Whisk in vegetable broth and juice. Bring to a boil. Remove from heat and season with salt, pepper and herbs. Stir cooked lentils into vegetable sauce.

Spread in a 9 x 13-inch baking pan coated with nonstick cooking spray. Sprinkle with bread crumbs. Coat bread crumbs with nonstick cooking spray. Bake at 375 degrees F for 40 minutes. Makes 8 servings (approximately 1 cup per serving).

Nutrition Facts: Calories 215, Protein 15 gm, Carbohydrate 35.2 gm, Dietary Fiber 15.7 gm, Fat 2.5 gm, Saturated Fat 0.3 gm, Sodium 261 mg
Meal Planning: 2 Lean Meat/Protein, 1 Carbohydrate, 1 Vegetable

Sloppy Joe Pizza

An unusual union of food and flavors.

1/2 cup ketchup
2 tablespoons tomato paste
2 tablespoons apple cider vinegar
1 tablespoon prepared yellow mustard
2 tablespoons molasses
1 tablespoon brown sugar
1/2 teaspoon fresh ground black pepper
1 can (15-ounce) lentils, well-drained and rinsed
1 can (15-ounce) black beans, well-drained and rinsed
3/4 cup yellow corn
1/2 cup sliced green onions
1 large (12-inch) whole wheat flat bread or prepared pizza crust
1 cup shredded lowfat extra sharp Cheddar cheese
1/2 cup shredded nonfat mozzarella cheese

In a small bowl, combine ketchup, tomato paste, vinegar, mustard, molasses, brown sugar and pepper. Mix well. Set aside. (Substitute 3/4 cup prepared barbecue sauce for this step if desired.)

Coat a large skillet with nonstick cooking spray. Add lentils, beans, corn, onions and prepared sauce. Simmer over medium heat until heated thoroughly.

Place flat bread on a baking sheet. Spoon lentil mixture over top; sprinkle with cheeses. Bake at 425 degrees F for 12 to 15 minutes or until cheese is melted; cut into 8 wedges. Makes 8 servings.

Nutrition Facts: Calories 294, Protein 17.5 gm, Carbohydrate 47.8 gm, Dietary Fiber 9.1 gm, Fat 4.8 gm, Saturated Fat 2 gm, Sodium 680 mg
Meal Planning: 2 Lean Meat/Protein, 2 Carbohydrate, 1 Vegetable

Homestyle Refried Beans

Once you make homemade, you'll hate to open a can.

1½ cups dried pinto, pink or anasazi beans
Water
1 medium onion, coarsely chopped
1 teaspoon salt
2 tablespoons peanut oil
2 clove crushed garlic
1 tablespoon molasses
1/2 teasoon fresh ground black pepper
1/2 teaspoon ground white pepper

Rinse and sort beans. In a large stockpot, combine beans, 4½ cups water and onion. Place over high heat and bring to a boil. Reduce heat slightly and boil for 2 minutes. Remove from heat and let stand for 1 hour.

After 1 hour, drain and rinse beans. Return to stockpot and add 4½ cups fresh water and salt. Place over high heat and bring to a boil. Reduce heat, cover and simmer for 1 hour or until beans are tender but not soft. **Do not drain.**

Coat a large deep heavy skillet with nonstick cooking spray. Add oil and heat over medium heat. Add garlic and sauté for 30 seconds.

Increase heat to high and add 1 cup undrained beans, molasses and peppers. Cook and stir, mashing beans with a potato masher. As beans begin to dry, add another 1 cup undrained beans. Cook and stir, mashing beans. Repeat until all beans and cooking liquid have been added and beans form a thick puree. Adjust heat, as needed, to prevent beans from sticking and burning. Total cooking time is about 20 minutes. Serve immediately, or refrigerate for 1 day and reheat in a baking dish at 350 degrees F for 30 minutes. Makes about 4½ cups (1/2 cup per serving).

Nutrition Facts: Calories 142, Protein 6.7 gm, Carbohydrate 22 gm, Dietary Fiber 7.9 gm, Fat 3.4 gm, Saturated Fat 0.6 gm, Sodium 241 mg
Meal Planning: 1 Lean Meat/Protein, 1 Carbohydrate

Hoppin' John

A healthy version of a Southern tradition.

1/4 cup long-grain rice
1/2 cup brown, black or Japonica rice
1 tablespoon extra virgin olive oil
2 cloves crushed garlic
4 soy link sausage, thawed and coarsely chopped
1 large green bell pepper, seeded and chopped
1 large red bell pepper, seeded and chopped
1 large yellow bell pepper, seeded and chopped
1 cup matchstick carrots
1 cup yellow corn [fresh or frozen]
1 small onion, finely chopped
1 can (15-ounce) black-eyed peas, drained and rinsed
1 can (15-ounce) black beans, drained and rinsed
1 cup fresh chopped tomatoes (about 1 large)
2 tablespoons fresh minced parsley [or 1 tablespoon dried]
1 tablespoon fresh minced thyme [or 1 teaspoon dried]
1/2 teaspoon salt
1/4 teaspoon cayenne pepper flakes
1/8 teaspoon fresh ground black pepper

Cook rice according to package directions. Set aside.

Coat a large skillet with nonstick cooking spray. Heat skillet. Add oil and heat over high heat. Add garlic, sausage, peppers, carrots, corn and onion. Cover and cook for 6 to 8 minutes or until tender-crisp, stirring once or twice.

Add black-eyed peas, black beans, cooked rice and tomatoes; stir gently to combine. Cover and cook over low heat for 5 minutes or until heated through, stirring occasionally. Add herbs and seasonings. Makes 6 servings (approximately 1½ cup per serving).

Nutrition Facts: Calories 272, Protein 14 gm, Carbohydrate 49.7 gm, Dietary Fiber 9.6 gm, Fat 2 gm, Saturated Fat 0.3 gm, Sodium 690 mg
Menu Planning: 1 Lean Meat/Protein, 2 Carbohydrate, 2 Vegetable

Calico Beans

One of my family's favorite recipes— not your ordinary baked beans.

1 large onion, chopped
2/3 cup ketchup
2 tablespoons dark brown sugar
1/3 to 1/2 cup Splenda® sugar substitute, to taste
1½ tablespoons prepared yellow mustard
3 tablespoons apple cider vinegar
1/2 teaspoon salt
1/4 teaspoon fresh ground black pepper
1 can (15-ounce) butter beans, drained and rinsed
1 package (10-ounce) frozen lima beans, thawed
1 can (15-ounce) dark red kidney beans, drained and rinsed
1 can (27-ounce) vegetarian-style baked beans, undrained
1 package (10-ounce) cut green beans, thawed

Coat a large casserole or 9 x 13-inch deep baking pan with nonstick cooking spray.

Combine all ingredients in baking pan; stir to thoroughly combine. Cover with foil and bake at 350 degrees F for 45 minutes to 1 hour, or until bubbly.

Remove foil during last 20 minutes of baking. Stir beans during baking if top becomes dry. Makes 12 servings (approximately 1 cup per serving).

Nutrition Facts: Calories 164, Protein 9 gm, Carbohydrate 34 gm, Dietary Fiber 6.5 gm, Fat 0.7 gm, Saturated Fat 0.1 gm, Sodium 684 mg
Meal Planning: 1/2 Lean Meat/Protein, 1 Carbohydrate, 2 Vegetable

Vegetarian Taco Salad

Quick and easy– ready in no time at all.

3 teaspoons extra virgin olive oil, divided
1/2 pound soy ground meat crumbles
3 cloves crushed garlic
1 large onion, chopped
1 can (4-ounce) chopped green chilies
1/2 cup prepared salsa
1/4 teaspoon fresh ground black pepper
4 yellow or white corn tortillas, cut into 1/4-inch strips
2 cups coarsely chopped Romaine lettuce
1 cup canned black beans, drained and rinsed
1 cup coarsely chopped tomatoes
1/2 cup shredded lowfat extra sharp Cheddar cheese, optional
1/4 cup chopped avocado
Calypso Dressing – *1/2 cup lowfat Ranch dressing* mixed with
    1 teaspoon reduced sodium taco seasoning mix

Coat a large skillet with nonstick cooking spray. Add 1 teaspoon oil, and heat over medium heat. Add meat substitute, garlic, onion and chilies. Sauté until onions are opaque. Stir in salsa. Season with peppers. Cover and reduce heat to simmer.

Coat a medium skillet with nonstick cooking spray. Add 2 teaspoons olive oil and heat. Add tortilla strips and brown over medium-high heat until golden. Remove to a paper towel to cool. (Lowfat or baked tortilla chips may be substituted.)

To assemble layered taco salad, place tortillas strips or chips on each plate. Top with lettuce, taco mixture, beans, tomatoes, cheese and avocado. Top with Calypso Dressing or other favorite lowfat or fat-free dressing. Vegetarian Taco Salad is a complete balanced meal– serve with sliced mango or papaya if desired. Makes 4 servings.

Nutrition Facts: Calories 300, Protein 20.9 gm, Carbohydrate 35.4 gm, Dietary Fiber 8.8 gm, Fat 6.9 gm, Saturated Fat 1.5 gm, Sodium 910 mg
Meal Planning: 3 Lean Meat/Protein, 2 Carbohydrate, 1 Vegetable

Black Bean & Rice Burgers

A great fusion of herbs, spices and textures.

1½ cups canned black beans, drained and rinsed
1 cup cooked brown rice
1 teaspoon extra virgin olive oil
1 small onion, finely chopped
1 small red bell pepper, seeded and finely chopped
1 teaspoon dried cumin
2 cloves crushed garlic
2 tablespoons fresh chopped parsley [or 1 tablespoon dried]
2 tablespoons tomato paste
1/2 teaspoon salt
1/4 teaspoon fresh ground black pepper
2 tablespoons extra virgin olive oil

In a medium bowl, combine beans and rice. Mash with a potato masher. Set aside.

Heat 1 teaspoon oil in a large skillet coated with nonstick cooking spray. Add onion, red pepper, cumin and garlic. Sauté until onion is tender. Add sautéed vegetables, parsley, tomato paste, salt and pepper to mashed bean mixture. Mix well. Form into 6 patties.

Recoat skillet with nonstick cooking spray. Add 1 tablespoon oil and heat over medium heat. Place patties in hot skillet and cook until lightly browned on both sides. Recoat skillet with nonstick cooking spray and add remaining 1 tablespoon oil before turning to brown second side. Serve in a whole wheat pita with lettuce, alfalfa sprouts and tomato slices. For a balanced meal, serve with fresh fruit salad and lowfat cottage cheese. Makes 6 patties.

Nutrition Facts: Calories 175, Protein 6.6 gm, Carbohydrate 24.3 gm, Dietary Fiber 5.7 gm, Fat 5.6 gm, Saturated Fat 0.8 gm, Sodium 473 mg
Meal Planning: 1 Lean Meat/Protein, 1 Carbohydrate, 2 Vegetable

Garbanzo-Corn Fritters

A delicious burger alternative or side dish.

2 teaspoons sesame oil
1 medium vidalia onion, finely chopped
1½ cups white shoepeg or yellow corn
1 can (15-ounce) garbanzo beans, drained and rinsed
2 tablespoons fresh chopped parsley [or 1 tablespoon dried]
1/4 teaspoon dried thyme
1/2 cup fresh whole wheat bread crumbs
2 tablespoons yellow cornmeal
1/2 teaspoon salt
1/4 teaspoon fresh ground black pepper
1/4 teaspoon ground white pepper
1 tablespoon sesame oil

Heat 1 teaspoon sesame oil in a large skillet coated with nonstick cooking spray. Add onion, corn, parsley and thyme. Sauté over medium heat until onion is tender.

In a large bowl, combine sautéed onion mixture, 1 teaspoon sesame oil, garbanzo beans, breadcrumbs, cornmeal, salt and pepper. Use a pastry blender or potato masher to work mixture into a chunky blend. (Or place in food processor and pulse several times until combined and chunky.) Form into 8 patties pressing firmly with your hands.

Recoat skillet with nonstick cooking spray. Add 1 tablespoon sesame oil and heat over medium heat. Place fritters in hot skillet and cook until lightly browned on both sides. Recoat skillet with nonstick cooking spray before turning to brown second side. For a balanced meal, serve with stir-fried vegetables, fresh fruit salad and fat-free milk. Makes 8 fritters (2 fritters per serving).

Nutrition Facts: Calories 170, Protein 6.7 gm, Carbohydrate 28.3 gm, Dietary Fiber 6.2 gm, Fat 4.7 gm, Saturated Fat 0.7 gm, Sodium 363 mg
Meal Planning: 1 Lean Meat/Protein, 1 Carbohydrate, 1 Vegetable

Vegetarian Stuffed Peppers

A re-creation of a familiar banquet tradition.

1 cup texturized soy protein, soaked in 7/8 cup boiling water
    [or 2 cups soy ground meat crumbles]
1 tablespoon extra virgin olive oil
1 medium onion, chopped
2 cloves crushed garlic
1 cup cooked long-grain brown rice
1 can (8-ounce) crushed or diced tomatoes
1 teaspoon granulated sugar
1/4 cup chopped walnuts
1/4 teaspoon salt
1/4 teaspoon fresh ground black pepper
4 large green bell peppers
2 cups low sodium vegetable broth

Coat a medium skillet with nonstick cooking spray. Heat over high heat. Add oil and heat. Add onion and garlic and sauté until onion is opaque.

Fluff softened soy protein with a fork. In a large bowl, combine soy protein, sautéed onions, rice, crushed tomatoes, sugar, walnuts, salt and black pepper. Set aside.

Cut tops from peppers and remove seeds. Stuff each pepper with the vegetable mixture. Place stuffed peppers in a baking pan and pour vegetable stock around the base of the peppers. Cover and bake at 350 degrees F for 30 minutes or until peppers are tender. Makes 4 servings.

Nutrition Facts: Calories 294, Protein 26.9 gm, Carbohydrate 35.6 gm, Dietary Fiber 5.1 gm, Fat 5.9 gm, Saturated Fat 0.7 gm, Sodium 633 mg
Meal Planning: 3 Lean Meat/Protein, 1 Carbohydrate, 3 Vegetable

The Best Bean Chili

A bit unorthodox but truly delicious.

1 tablespoon canola or extra virgin olive oil
1 large onion, diced [or 1 cup frozen diced]
3 cloves crushed garlic
1 large green bell pepper, seeded and diced [or 1 cup frozen diced]
1 can (4-ounce) diced green chilies
1 can (15-ounce) black beans, drained and rinsed
1 can (15-ounce) cannellini (white kidney) beans, drained and rinsed
1 can (28-ounce) crushed tomatoes
1 can (6-ounce) tomato paste
1/2 cup water
1/2 cup frozen white shoepeg corn
1 teaspoon ground cumin
2 tablespoons molasses
2 tablespoons unsweetened cocoa powder
1/2 teaspoon salt
1/4 teaspoon fresh ground black pepper

Coat a large saucepot or deep skillet with nonstick cooking spray. Heat skillet. Add oil and heat. Add onions, garlic, bell pepper and chilies and sauté over medium heat. Add remaining ingredients and simmer for 30 minutes.

Garnish with chopped green onions, nonfat sour cream and lowfat extra sharp cheddar cheese, if desired. For a balanced meal, serve with corn bread and mixed greens tossed salad. Makes 8 servings (1½ to 2 cups per serving).

Nutrition Facts: Calories 365, Protein 16 gm, Carbohydrate 48 gm, Dietary Fiber 14.5 gm, Fat 3 gm, Saturated Fat 0.5 gm, Sodium 244 mg
Meal Planning: 2 Lean Meat/Protein, 2 Carbohydrate

Quick Bean & Rice Casserole

Super quick and super good.

3 cups cooked instant brown rice
2 cans (15-ounce each) black beans, drained & rinsed
1 can (4-ounce) diced green chilies
1½ cups chunky salsa
1 teaspoon ground cumin
1 teaspoon dried cilantro [or 1 tablespoon fresh chopped]
1/4 teaspoon salt
1/4 teaspoon fresh ground black pepper

Combine all ingredients in a large bowl. Adjust seasonings.

Transfer to a covered microwave-safe casserole coated with nonstick cooking spray.

Cover and microwave on HIGH for 3 to 4 minutes or until hot. Stir 1 to 2 times while cooking to distribute heat. Makes 12 servings (approximately 1/2 cup per serving).

Nutrition Facts: Calories 127, Protein 5.3 gm, Carbohydrate 24.6 gm, Dietary Fiber 3.1 gm, Fat 0.4 gm, Saturated Fat 0.1 gm, Sodium 415 mg
Meal Planning: 1 Carbohydrate, 2 Vegetable

Minestrone-In-Minutes

Cannellini beans blend beautifully with pasta in this quick dish.

8 ounces whole wheat penne
1 tablespoon extra virgin olive oil
2 cloves crushed garlic
1 can (28-ounces) Roma tomatoes, coarsely chopped
2 cups sliced fresh mushrooms
1 teaspoon granulated sugar
1 tablespoon fresh chopped basil [or 1 teaspoon dried]
1/4 teaspoon salt
1/8 teaspoon fresh ground black pepper
1 can (15-ounce) cannellini (white kidney) beans, drained and rinsed
1/2 cup freshly grated Parmesan cheese

In a large stockpot, cook pasta in a large amount of boiling water according to package directions. *Do not add salt or oil.* Stir occasionally during boiling. Drain.

Meanwhile, coat a large deep skillet with nonstick cooking spray. Add oil and heat over medium heat. Add garlic and sauté until golden, about 30 seconds.

Add tomatoes, mushrooms, sugar, basil, salt and pepper and stir to combine. Cover and cook for 5 minutes or until mushrooms soften. Uncover and stir in cannellini beans. Reduce heat to simmer.

To serve, combine cooked pasta and sauce in a large pasta bowl. Sprinkle with Parmesan cheese. Makes 6 servings (approximately 1 cup per serving).

Nutrition Facts: Calories 266, Protein 14.2 gm, Carbohydrate 40.3 gm, Dietary Fiber 7.9 gm, Fat 5.4 gm, Saturated Fat 2.3 gm, Sodium 663 mg
Meal Planning: 2 Lean Meat/Protein, 2 Carbohydrate, 1 Vegetable

Black Bean & Couscous Salad

Lime juice makes this couscous salad light and refreshing.

1¼ cups water
1 teaspoon onion powder
2 cloves crushed garlic
1½ cups medium-grain couscous
1 can (15-ounce) black beans, drained and rinsed
1 large tomato, chopped
2 green onions, sliced
1/4 cup lime juice
2 tablespoons water
2 tablespoons extra virgin olive oil
1 teaspoon granulated sugar
1/4 cup fresh chopped cilantro
1/2 teaspoon salt
1/4 teaspoon fresh ground black pepper
1/4 teaspoon ground cumin
1/4 teaspoon ground red pepper

Combine 1¼ cups water, onion powder and garlic in a medium saucepan. Bring to a boil. Stir in couscous and remove from heat. Cover with a tight-fitting lid and let stand for 5 minutes.

Uncover couscous and fluff with a fork. Stir in beans, tomatoes and green onions. Set aside.

Combine lime juice, 2 tablespoons water, oil, sugar, cilantro, salt, black pepper, cumin and red pepper in a jar with a screw-top lid. Cover tightly and shake vigorously. Pour over couscous mixture. Stir to combine. Cover and refrigerate for at least 8 hours, stirring occasionally. Makes 8 servings (approximately 3/4 cup per serving).

Nutrition Facts: Calories 211, Protein 7.6 gm, Carbohydrate 36.2 gm, Dietary Fiber 4.3 gm, Fat 3.7 gm, Saturated Fat 0.5 gm, Sodium 251 mg
Meal Planning: 2 Carbohydrate, 1 Vegetable, 1/2 Fat

Sweet 4 Bean Salad

Only 25% of the fat & sugar of the original recipe but 100% of the taste.

1/4 cup extra virgin olive oil
3/4 cup white balsamic vinegar
1/4 cup water
1/3 cup granulated sugar
1/3 cup Splenda® sugar substitute
1/2 teaspoon fresh ground black pepper
1/2 teaspoon celery seed, optional
1 package (16-ounce) cut green beans, thawed
1 package (16-ounce) cut yellow beans, thawed
1 can (15-ounce) dark red kidney beans, drained and rinsed
1 can (15-ounce) garbanzo beans, drained and rinsed
1 medium sweet onion, finely chopped
1 medium green bell pepper, seeded and finely chopped
1 medium red bell pepper, seeded and finely chopped

Combine oil, vinegar, water, sugar, Splenda, black pepper and celery seed in a jar with a screw-top lid. Cover tightly and shake vigorously to mix well. Set aside.

In a large bowl, combine all beans, onion and chopped peppers. Pour dressing over mixture and stir to combine.

Cover and refrigerate for several hours or overnight to blend flavors. Makes 12 servings (approximately 3/4 to 1 cup per serving).

Nutrition Facts: Calories 173, Protein 6.5 gm, Carbohydrate 25.3 gm, Dietary Fiber 4.6 gm, Fat 6.1 gm, Saturated Fat 0.9 gm, Sodium 121 mg
Meal Planning: 1 Carbohydrate, 2 Vegetable, 1 Fat

Bean Burritos

A great idea for a last-minute meal.

8 large whole wheat tortillas
1 can (15-ounce) pinto beans, drained and rinsed
1 can (15-ounce) black beans, drained and rinsed
1 can (4-ounce) diced green chilies
1/2 cup sliced green onions
1/4 cup shredded lowfat Monterey Jack cheese
1/4 cup shredded lowfat extra sharp Cheddar cheese
1/2 cup salsa
1/4 cup nonfat sour cream
2 cups coarsely shredded Romaine lettuce
1 cup chopped tomatoes

Wrap tortillas in a clean damp lint-free towel. Microwave on HIGH for 45 seconds to warm.

Place beans in a large bowl and mash beans with a potato masher. Stir in chilies.

To assemble burritos, place 1/8 of beans, green onions and cheeses on each tortilla. Fold in 2 sides, then roll up.

Arrange burritos, seam side down, in a 9 x 13-inch baking pan. Bake at 350 degrees F for 15 minutes or until heated through.

To serve burritos, top with salsa and sour cream. Serve with coarsely shredded lettuce and chopped tomatoes. For a balanced meal, serve with mixed greens tossed salad and fresh fruit salad. Makes 8 burritos.

Nutrition Facts: Calories 221, Protein 11 gm, Carbohydrate 36.6 gm, Dietary Fiber 7.4 gm, Fat 3.5 gm, Saturated Fat 1.3 gm, Sodium 523 mg
Meal Planning: 1 Lean Meat/Protein, 2 Carbohydrate

Spaghetti with Nuts & Raisins
If you're tired of the same old pasta, try this nutty recipe.

1/3 cup raisins
2 tablespoons extra virgin olive oil
3 cloves crushed garlic
2 cans (15-ounce) black-eyed peas, drained and rinsed
1 bunch escarole, trimmed and shredded
1/2 teaspoon salt
1/4 teaspoon fresh ground black pepper
6 ounces whole wheat spaghetti
6 tablespoons toasted pine nuts (pignolia)

In a small bowl, soak raisins in enough lukewarm water to cover for about 30 minutes. Drain and set aside.

Coat a large skillet with nonstick cooking spray. Add oil and heat over low heat. Add garlic and sauté, stirring frequently until golden. Add black-eyed peas and escarole, stirring to coat well with oil. Season to taste with salt and pepper. Cover and continue cooking over low heat for 10 minutes, stirring occasionally.

Meanwhile, bring a large amount of water to a boil in a large stockpot. Cook spaghetti in boiling water until al dente, about 5 minutes. Drain pasta and stir into bean-escarole mixture. Add the softened raisins and cook over low heat, stirring frequently, about 2 minutes.

Arrange the pasta on a platter. Sprinkle with pine nuts and serve hot. For a balanced meal, serve with mixed greens tossed salad, fresh strawberries and fat-free milk. Makes 6 servings (approximately 1½ cups per serving).

Nutrition Facts: Calories 304, Protein 13 gm, Carbohydrate 47 gm, Dietary Fiber 4.6 gm, Fat 9.5 gm, Saturated Fat 1.5 gm, Sodium 407 mg
Meal Planning: 2 Lean Meat/Protein, 2 Carbohydrate, 2 Vegetable

Black Bean Hummus

Serve up this mild hummus with pita bread or a tortilla wrap.

2 cans (15-ounce each) black beans, drained and rinsed
1/4 cup toasted almond slivers
1/4 cup fresh lemon juice
1 tablespoon sesame oil
2 cloves crushed garlic
1/2 teaspoon ground cumin
1/4 teaspoon salt
1/2 teaspoon fresh ground black pepper
1 can (4-ounce) diced green chilies

In a food processor or blender, combine beans, almonds, lemon juice, oil, garlic, cumin, salt, pepper and chilies. Process until desired (spreadable) consistency. Cover and chill to blend flavors. Serve with with whole wheat pita, flat bread or lowfat tortilla chips. Or spread on a sun-dried tomato or spinach wrap and top with favorite vegetables. Roll up and serve with Black Bean Relish. Makes about 3 cups hummus (1/4 cup per serving).

Nutrition Facts: Calories 92, Protein 4.8 gm, Carbohydrate 12.1 gm, Dietary Fiber 3.3 gm, Fat 2.7 gm, Saturated Fat 0.3 gm, Sodium 195 mg
Meal Planning: 1/2 Lean Meat/Protein, 1/2 Carbohydrate, 1/2 Fat

Black Bean Relish

So good it's hard to believe how it's made— it doesn't get any easier.

2 cans (15-ounce each) black soy beans, drained and rinsed
1 jar (9.5-ounce) Nance's® Corn Relish

Combine ingredients in a medium bowl. Stir to combine. Serve at room temperature. Store in refrigerator and use in your favorite recipes. Makes about 4 cups (1/4 cup per serving).

Nutrition Facts: Calories 43, Protein 2.4 gm, Carbohydrate 6.8 gm, Dietary Fiber 1.5 gm, Fat 1.3 gm, Saturated Fat 0.2 gm, Sodium 82 mg
Meal Planning: 1 Vegetable

Hummus

You'll be the hit of the party with this delicious recipe.

1 large onion, finely chopped
2 cloves crushed garlic
1½ teaspoons sesame oil, divided
1 teaspoon fresh lemon juice
2 tablespoons water
1/4 cup finely ground sesame seeds
2 cups garbanzo beans, drained and rinsed
1/2 cup fresh lemon juice
1 tablespoon reduced sodium soy sauce
1/2 teaspoon salt

In a small skillet, sauté onion and garlic in 1 teaspoon sesame oil until soft. Set aside.

In a food processor or blender, combine 1 teaspoon lemon juice, remaining 1/2 teaspoon sesame oil, water and sesame seeds. Process on low speed to puree.

Add garbanzo beans, sautéed onion, 1/2 cup lemon juice, soy sauce and salt to sesame mixture. Process on low speed and puree until smooth. Serve the hummus with whole wheat pita or flat bread or with fresh vegetables. Makes 2 cups hummus (1/4 cup per serving).

Nutrition Facts: Calories 115, Protein 4.5 gm, Carbohydrate 16.2 gm, Dietary Fiber 3 gm, Fat 4.1 gm, Saturated Fat 0.6 gm, Sodium 329 mg
Meal Planning: 1/2 Lean Meat/Protein, 1 Carbohydrate, 1/2 Fat

A word of kindness
is better than a fat pie.
Russian Proverb

Healthy people choose foods and recipes low in saturated fats and other processed fats such as trans fats.

- Choose lowfat foods with 3 or less grams of total fat per serving. Look for 1 or less grams of saturated fat per serving.
- Strive for more poultry and fish meals. Limit red meat intake to a few (2 to 3) times per week. Select only very lean meats and limit or exclude fatty or marbled meats.
- Trim fat from meats and remove poultry skin before cooking.
- Reduce meat portion sizes to 3 to 4 ounces — about the size of a deck of cards. Limit to 5 to 6 ounces daily.
- Portion your plate with only 1/4 filled with meat/protein.
- Cut the fat in lean ground beef by combining extra lean (93% lean or greater) ground beef with ground turkey breast.
- Consider meat from non-domesticated animals such as venison and other wild game. Try buffalo or ostrich meat for a lean beef-taste alternative.
- Use lowfat cooking and preparation methods — bake, broil, roast, grill, steam and sauté. Limit or exclude deep-fried foods.
- Select lowfat [1%] or fat-free milk and milk products.
- Try new designer foods such as fat-free half and half and "choice" fat-free milk designed to taste like 2% milk.
- For quicker meal preparation, choose lowfat convenience food ingredients — 3 or less grams of total fat per serving.
- Substitute lowfat ingredients for high fat ingredients.
- Use lite tub or trans fat free margarines rather than butter or stick margarine. Cooking for the Health of It recipes use Promise® stick margarine– the only trans fat free stick margarine currently on the market. When possible, substitute liquid plant oils (preferably olive, canola or peanut oils) for solid fats such as lard, butter, shortening and bacon fat. Use lite whipped butter when butter is a must-have.

133

Orange Ginger Chicken

An easy flavor-filled way to serve chicken.

2 pounds boneless, skinless chicken breasts
2 tablespoons olive oil tub margarine
2 cups 100% country-style orange juice
2 tablespoons Dijon mustard
2 teaspoons ground ginger

Cut chicken into 1½-inch strips.

Coat a large skillet with nonstick cooking spray. Add margarine and melt. Add chicken strips and sauté lightly over medium heat.

In a small bowl, combine 1½ cups orange juice, mustard and ginger.

Pour orange sauce over chicken. Turn chicken pieces frequently to ensure even cooking. Sauce will thicken and reduce.

Add remaining 1/2 cup orange juice immediately before serving. For a balanced meal, serve with red skin potatoes, fresh spinach salad and sliced pears and apples. Makes 8 servings.

Nutrition Facts: Calories 180, Protein 27 gm, Carbohydrate 6.7 gm, Dietary Fiber 0.2 gm, Fat 4.2 gm, Saturated Fat 0.8 gm, Sodium 149 mg
Meal Planning: 4 Lean Meat/Protein

Chicken Stew with Tortellini

Practically a balanced meal in one pot.

1 medium zucchini or yellow summer squash, unpeeled
2 cups low sodium chicken broth
2 cups water
1 large red bell pepper, seeded and diced
1 large green bell pepper, seeded and diced
1 medium onion, cut into wedges
6 cups torn spinach (fresh or frozen)
2 cups sliced carrots (fresh or frozen)
1 cup cheese tortellini (fresh, frozen or dried)
1 teaspoon dried basil [or 1 tablespoon fresh chopped]
1/2 teaspoon dried oregano [or 1 teaspoon fresh chopped]
1/2 teaspoon salt
1/4 teaspoon fresh ground black pepper
2 cups chopped cooked chicken

Halve squash lengthwise and cut into 1/2-inch slices.

In a large saucepot, bring broth and water to a boil. Add squash, peppers, onion, spinach, carrots, tortellini and seasonings. Reduce heat. Simmer, covered, about 15 minutes or until tortellini and vegetables are nearly tender.

Stir in cooked chicken. Cover and cook for 5 minutes more or until pasta and vegetables are tender. For a balanced meal, serve with wholegrain cornbread and yogurt with fresh fruit topping. Makes 6 servings (approximately 2 cups per serving).

Nutrition Facts: Calories 209, Protein 27 gm, Carbohydrate 14.4 gm, Dietary Fiber 3.4 gm, Fat 6 gm, Saturated Fat 1.8 gm, Sodium 595 mg
Meal Planning: 3 Lean Meat/Protein, 1 Carbohydrate

Chicken-Walnut Stir-Fry

Toasted walnuts add a great flavor to this easy stir-fry.

1 tablespoon peanut oil
1/4 cup chopped walnuts
2 cloves crushed garlic
1 tablespoon minced gingerroot
4 boneless, skinless chicken breasts, cut into thin strips
3 cups sliced fresh mushrooms
2 large red bell peppers, seeded and cut into thin strips
1 large green bell pepper, seeded and cut into thin strips
6 green onions, sliced diagonally
1 pound sugarsnap peas (fresh or frozen)
1/2 cup water
1/4 cup low sodium soy sauce
2 tablespoons dry sherry, optional
4 teaspoons cornstarch
2 cups fresh bean sprouts, rinsed and drained

Coat a wok or large skillet with nonstick cooking spray. Add oil and heat. Add walnuts and cook over medium heat for 2 to 3 minutes or until walnuts are lightly toasted. Remove walnuts and set aside.

Increase heat to high. Add garlic and gingerroot to wok and sauté for 30 to 45 seconds until golden brown. Add chicken and cook for 4 to 5 minutes or until chicken is no longer pink. Push chicken up sides of wok. Add mushrooms, peppers, onions and sugarsnap peas. Cook for 2 minutes or until vegetables are tender-crisp.

In a small bowl, combine water, soy sauce, sherry, cornstarch and ginger, stirring until smooth. Add to chicken mixture and cook until thick and bubbly. Stir in reserved toasted walnuts and bean sprouts; heat through. For a balanced meal, serve with brown rice and fresh fruit salad. Makes 4 servings.

Nutrition Facts: Calories 342, Protein 37.6 gm, Carbohydrate 35 gm, Dietary Fiber 11 gm, Fat 7.3 gm, Saturated Fat 1.3 gm, Sodium 606 mg
Meal Planning: 4 Lean Meat/Protein, 1 Carbohydrate, 3 Vegetable

Sweet & Sour Chicken

So much better for you than the deep-fried version— and so good tasting!

1 pound boneless, skinless chicken breasts
1 tablespoon peanut oil
1 large green bell pepper, seeded and cut into strips
2 large red bell peppers, seeded and cut into strips
3 cups matchstick carrots
1 clove crushed garlic
1 tablespoon cornstarch
1/4 cup low sodium soy sauce
1 can (8-ounce) chunk pineapple, in juice, undrained
3 tablespoons apple cider vinegar
3 tablespoons brown sugar [or Sugar Twin® brown substitute]
1/2 teaspoon ground ginger
3 cups cooked brown rice

Cut chicken into strips.

Coat a large skillet with nonstick cooking spray. Add oil and heat. Add chicken and stir-fry in hot oil until browned.

Add peppers, carrots and garlic. Stir-fry for 1 to 2 minutes or until tender-crisp and chicken is thoroughly cooked and no longer pink.

In a small bowl, combine cornstarch and soy sauce. Add cornstarch mixture, pineapple in juice, vinegar, sugar and ginger to chicken mixture. Bring to a full boil and cook until thick. Serve over brown rice. Makes 6 servings.

Nutrition Facts: Calories 292, Protein 21.3 gm, Carbohydrate 41.8 gm, Dietary Fiber 2.5, Fat 4.5 gm, Saturated Fat 0.9 gm, Sodium 395 mg
Meal Planning: 2 Lean Meat/Protein, 2 Carbohydrate, 2 Vegetable

Miso Chicken

Quick, easy and simply delicious.

4 boneless, skinless chicken breasts
4 teaspoons extra virgin olive oil
4 cloves crushed garlic
1/2 cup prepared Miso dressing or marinade
2 teaspoons dried parsley [or 2 tablespoons fresh chopped]

Pound chicken breasts with a metal mallet to tenderize and flatten.

Coat a skillet liberally with nonstick cooking spray. Place on high heat. Add olive oil and garlic to hot skillet. Sauté until garlic is golden, about 30 to 45 seconds. Add chicken and brown on one side for 3 minutes; turn and brown second side for 3 minutes.

Pour 1 tablespoon Miso sauce on each chicken breast. Cover, reduce heat to medium and continue cooking for 6 to 8 minutes or until chicken reaches an internal temperature of 170 degrees.

Pour 1 additional tablespoon Miso sauce over each chicken breast and sprinkle with parsley. Reduce heat to low; cover and cook an additional 1 minute to heat sauce. For a balanced meal, serve with baked sweet potatoes and mixed greens tossed salad. For recipe variation, substitute salmon for chicken. Makes 4 servings.

Nutrition Facts: Calories 229, Protein 27.3 gm, Carbohydrate 6 gm, Dietary Fiber 0, Fat 9.9 gm, Saturated Fat 2.1 gm, Sodium 347 mg
Meal Planning: 4 Lean Meat/Protein

Marsala Chicken

One client couldn't believe this recipe was "allowed" on a healthy diet.

8 boneless, skinless, chicken breasts
1/2 cup all-purpose flour
1/4 teaspoon salt
1/4 teaspoon fresh ground black pepper
Nonstick cooking spray
1 tablespoon olive oil tub margarine
1 can Campbell's® Condensed Golden Mushroom Soup
5 ounces (1/2 can) Marsala wine, optional

Pound chicken breasts with a metal mallet.

Combine flour, salt and pepper in a pie pan. Dredge chicken breasts in flour mixture coating all sides.

Coat a large skillet with nonstick cooking spray. Add margarine and melt over medium heat. Add chicken breasts. Cook chicken for several minutes, turning when lightly browned.

Pour soup over chicken. Fill soup can 1/2 full with Marsala wine and incorporate any soup sticking to side of can. Mix wine into soup, stirring to combine. (If not using wine, use water.) Cook until heated through and bubbly. For a balanced meal, serve with brown rice, sautéed whole green beans and fresh fruit salad. Makes 8 servings.

Nutrition Facts: Calories 226, Protein 28.1 gm, Carbohydrate 10.6 gm, Dietary Fiber 0.5 gm, Fat 5.3 gm, Saturated Fat 1.2 gm Sodium 583 mg
Meal Planning: 4 Lean Meat/Protein, <1 Carbohydrate

Original Chicken Marsala recipe from my sister
Jeanne Livingston Roper from Phoenix, Arizona

Chicken Spareribs

A great alternative to chicken wings.

2 pounds boneless, skinless chicken breasts
Nonstick olive oil cooking spray
1 tablespoon extra virgin olive oil
1/2 cup water
1/3 cup low sodium soy sauce
3 tablespoons dark brown sugar
1/4 cup 100% apple juice
2 tablespoons ketchup
1 tablespoon cider vinegar
1 clove crushed garlic
1/4 teaspoon crushed red pepper
1/4 teaspoon ground ginger
2 tablespoons cornstarch
2 tablespoons water

Cut chicken breasts into 1-inch strips. Coat a large skillet with nonstick cooking spray. Add oil and heat over medium-high heat. Add chicken and lightly brown on all sides, recoating with nonstick cooking spray as needed. Turn frequently and continue browning for about 6 to 7 minutes.

Combine next 9 ingredients in a bowl; pour over chicken. Bring to a boil, cover, reduce heat and simmer for 10 minutes.

In a small bowl, blend cornstarch and water. Add to chicken and cook until sauce thickens and glazes chicken pieces. For a balanced meal, serve with homemade baked potato chips, mixed greens tossed salad and sliced apples. Makes 8 servings.

Nutrition Facts: Calories 163, Protein 27 gm, Carbohydrate 4.4 gm, Dietary Fiber 0.1 gm, Fat 3.6 gm, Saturated Fat 0.7 gm, Sodium 444 mg
Meal Planning: 4 Lean Meat/Protein

Recipe Variation: Substitute pre-frozen extra firm tofu for chicken. Cut tofu into 1-inch strips.

Chicken Fingers

The illusion of fried chicken nuggets– kids will love them.

Nonstick cooking spray
2 tablespoons olive oil tub margarine
1 cup finely crushed cornflake cereal
3 tablespoons freshly grated Parmesan cheese
1/4 teaspoon salt
1/8 teaspoon fresh ground black pepper
1/4 teaspoon paprika
1 pound boneless, skinless chicken breasts
1 egg white plus 1/4 cup fat-free milk

Preheat oven to 425 degrees F. Coat a 9 x 9-inch baking dish with nonstick cooking spray. Place margarine in baking dish and place in hot oven to melt.

Meanwhile, combine corn flakes, Parmesan cheese, salt and pepper in a pie or flat pan. Set aside.

Slice chicken breasts into 1½-inch strips. Dip in egg-milk mixture then dredge in corn flake mixture. Place in baking dish over melted margarine.

Bake at 425 degrees F for 15 to 20 minutes. For a balanced meal, serve with lowfat steak fries, assorted raw vegetables with lowfat dip and fresh fruit salad. Makes 4 servings.

Nutrition Facts: Calories 218, Protein 30 gm, Carbohydrate 6 gm,
Dietary Fiber 0.1 gm, Fat 7.0 gm, Saturated Fat 1.7 gm, Sodium 405 mg
Meal Planning: 4 Lean Meat/Protein

Chicken Gravy with Biscuits

A quick-prep version of your grandmother's chicken and biscuits.

4 boneless, skinless chicken breasts
2 cups water
1 low sodium chicken bouillon cube or instant granules
2 cups diced onion (fresh or frozen)
2 cups diced celery
2 cups diced carrot (fresh or frozen)
1/4 teaspoon ground white pepper
1/8 teaspoon fresh ground black pepper
1 can Campbell's® Healthy Request® Cream of Chicken Soup
2 tablespoons water
1 tablespoon cornstarch
Multi-Grain Biscuits (*See Recipe on Page 80*)

In a medium saucepot, combine chicken, water, bouillon cube, onion, celery, carrot, salt and pepper. Bring to a boil over high heat. Reduce heat, cover, and simmer for 20 minutes or until chicken is no longer pink.

Remove from heat. With 2 forks, shred chicken into bite-size pieces. Stir in soup. Return to heat and bring to a slow boil.

In a small bowl, combine water and cornstarch. Gradually stir into chicken mixture. Cook over low heat until desired thickness. Serve over whole wheat biscuits or noodles. For a balanced meal, serve with steamed broccoli and sliced peaches. Makes 4 servings.

Nutrition Facts: Calories 239, Protein 33 gm, Carbohydrate 22 gm, Dietary Fiber 4.4 gm, Fat 3.4 gm, Saturated Fat 1.2 gm, Sodium 606 mg
Meal Planning: 4 Lean Meat/Protein, 1 Carbohydrate, 1 Vegetable

Chicken Crepes

I love to serve this recipe for luncheons, showers and other parties.

8 crepes – *See recipe below*
1 tablespoon extra virgin olive oil
1 small onion, chopped
1 can Campbell's® Healthy Request® Cream of Chicken Soup
1/3 cup 1% milk
1/2 cup nonfat sour cream
2 cups shredded or finely chopped, cooked chicken
1/4 teaspoon dried rosemary
1/8 teaspoon fresh ground black pepper
1/4 cup freshly grated Parmesan cheese

To make Crepes: In a food processor or blender, combine 1 cup all-purpose flour, 1 cup fat-free milk and 1 egg and process on low until well mixed. Heat a 10-inch skillet coated with nonstick cooking spray over medium heat. Remove skillet from heat and spoon in a scant 1/4 cup of batter. Lift and tilt skillet to evenly spread batter. Return to heat; brown crepe on one side only. Invert skillet over paper towels. Remove crepe. Repeat to make 8 crepes, recoating skillet with nonstick cooking spray each time.

Coat a small skillet with nonstick cooking spray. Add oil and heat; add onion and sauté until opaque. Add remaining ingredients, except Parmesan cheese. Cook over medium heat, stirring, until mixture bubbles and thickens.

Evenly divide filling among 8 crepes, spooning across lower third of each crepe and roll to enclose. Place filled crepes, seam side down, in a 9 x 13-inch baking pan coated with nonstick cooking spray. Cover and bake at 375 degrees F for about 20 minutes.

Remove cover and sprinkle with Parmesan cheese and serve. For a balanced meal, serve with mixed greens tossed salad and marinated vegetable salad. Makes 8 crepes.

Nutrition Facts: Calories 228, Protein 19 gm, Carbohydrate 20.6 gm, Dietary Fiber 0.4 gm, Fat 6.9 gm, Saturated Fat 1.9 gm, Sodium 253 mg
Meal Planning: 2 Lean Meat/Protein, 1 Carbohydrate

Honey Mustard Chicken

Add some tang to a chicken breast sandwich.

4 boneless, skinless chicken breasts
1/4 cup dry sherry
2 tablespoons Dijon mustard
2 tablespoons honey
2 tablespoons tomato paste
1 tablespoon low sodium soy sauce

Pound chicken breasts with a metal mallet until flat– about 1/4-inch thick. Place in a 9 x 13-inch pan.

In a small bowl, combine sherry, mustard, honey, tomato paste, and soy sauce. Stir to combine. Pour over chicken and marinate for 30 minutes.

Place chicken on a broiler pan or grill coated with nonstick cooking spray. Broil or grill for 3 minutes. Turn and brush with marinade. Broil 2 to 3 more minutes or until chicken is no longer pink or reaches an internal temperature of 170 degrees F. Discard any remaining marinade.

For a delicious sandwich, serve on a whole grain bun with lettuce and tomato. Makes 4 servings.

Nutrition Facts: Calories 193, Protein 27.3 gm, Carbohydrate 11.3 gm, Dietary Fiber 0.6 gm, Fat 2.3 gm, Saturated Fat 0.5 gm, Sodium 299 mg
Meal Planning: 4 Lean Meat/Protein, <1 Carbohydrate

Recipe Variation: For a unique flavor, try different varieties of mustards such as stadium, raspberry, tarragon, garlic or horseradish mustard.

Chicken Veronique

Not your ordinary chicken stir-fry.

4 boneless, skinless chicken breasts
2 tablespoons olive oil tub margarine
1 cup sliced fresh mushrooms
6 green onions, chopped
1/3 cup chicken broth
1 tablespoon all-purpose flour
1 cup seedless green grapes, cut in half
1/4 cup dry white wine [or 1/4 cup nonalcoholic white wine}

Cut chicken breasts into 1-inch strips; set aside.

Coat a wok or large skillet with nonstick cooking spray. Add margarine and melt over medium-high heat. Stir-fry mushrooms and onions in margarine for 2 minutes or until soft. Add chicken pieces and stir-fry for 5 minutes or until chicken is done and no longer pink.

In a small bowl, blend chicken broth and flour. Add to chicken mixture. Cook and stir until thickened and bubbly.

Cook and stir 1 additional minute. Stir in grapes and wine; heat through. For a balanced meal, serve with steamed baby carrots and lowfat waldorf salad. Serve over brown rice. Makes 4 servings.

Nutrition Facts: Calories 292, Protein 32.1 gm, Carbohydrate 25.3 gm, Dietary Fiber 6.4 gm, Fat 6.8 gm, Saturated Fat 1.2 gm, Sodium 292 mg
Meal Planning: 4 Lean Meat/Protein, 1 Carbohydrate, 2 Vegetable

Sunny Chicken & Fruit Grill

A deliteful combination of poultry and fruit– a great summer grill.

1/4 cup 100% pineapple juice
1/4 cup low sodium teriyaki sauce
4 boneless, skinless chicken breasts
1 fresh peach, pitted and cut in half
1/2 fresh golden pineapple, skinned, cored and sliced lengthwise
1 fresh Bartlett pear, cored and cut in half
1 fresh mango, peeled, pitted and sliced
1 fresh banana, peeled and sliced

In a small bowl, combine pineapple juice and teriyaki sauce.

Grill chicken over medium-hot coals until almost done, basting with pineapple juice and teriyaki sauce mixture.

Divide chicken breasts between 2 medium pieces of foil. Divide fruit and place on top of chicken. Seal foil tightly.

Place foil packets on a medium-hot grill and turn often to cook fruit lightly, approximately 15 minutes. For a balanced meal, serve with brown rice pilaf and mixed greens tossed salad. Makes 4 servings.

Nutrition Facts: Calories 253, Protein 28.1 gm, Carbohydrate 30.8 gm, Dietary Fiber 3.8 gm, Fat 2.6 gm, Saturated Fat 0.6 gm, Sodium 562 mg
Meal Planning: 3 Lean Meat/Protein, 2 Carbohydrate

English Chicken

An old recipe from my Grandmother– but she was French-Dutch.

1 whole chicken
5 cups water
1 loaf oatmeal bread, cut into cubes
2 eggs, lightly beaten [or 1/2 cup egg substitute]
1 tablespoon olive oil tub margarine
3 tablespoons chopped celery leaves
2 teaspoons ground sage
1 small onion, chopped
1 tablespoon dried parsley [or 2 tablespoons fresh chopped]
1/2 teaspoon salt
1/4 teaspoon fresh ground black pepper

In a large stockpot, combine chicken and water. Bring to a boil. Reduce heat and cook until chicken is very tender and falls off bones, about 1½ hours. Remove chicken from stock and debone, discarding skin. Refrigerate chicken stock overnight. Skim off and discard any hardened fat. Reserve stock.

Place bread cubes in a large bowl. Moisten bread with eggs and 3 cups of reserved (defatted) chicken stock.

Coat a small skillet with nonstick cooking spray. Add margarine and melt over medium-high heat. Add celery, sage, onion and parsley. Sauté until onion is soft. Add to bread mixture along with cooked chicken, salt and pepper.

Place mixture into a 9 x 13-inch baking pan coated with nonstick cooking spray. Set in a larger pan filled with water. Bake at 375 degrees F for 1 hour. To make a fat-free gravy, thicken the extra chicken stock with cornstarch and serve with English chicken. For a balanced meal, serve with whole green and yellow beans and fresh fruit salad. Makes 10 servings.

Nutrition Facts: Calories 269, Protein 21.8 gm, Carbohydrate 31.7 gm, Dietary Fiber 4.8 gm, Fat 6.7 gm, Saturated Fat 1.6 gm Sodium 591 mg
Meal Planning: 2½ Lean Meat/Protein, 2 Carbohydrate

Chicken Enchilada Casserole

One of those taste-better-than-it-looks recipes!

1 whole chicken
5 cups water
1 tablespoon olive oil tub margarine
1 large onion, chopped
1 can Campbell's® Healthy Request® Cream of Mushroom Soup
1 can Campbell's® Healthy Request® Cream of Chicken Soup
1 can (4-ounce) diced green chilies
6 large flour tortillas
2 cups shredded lowfat extra sharp Cheddar cheese

In a large stockpot, combine chicken and 5 cups water. Bring to a boil, reduce heat and cook until chicken is very tender and falls off bones, about 1½ hours. Remove chicken from stock and debone, discarding skin. Refrigerate chicken stock overnight. Skim off and discard any hardened fat. Reserve 1½ cups stock for use in casserole. Use remainder in another recipe or freeze for later use.

Coat a large skillet with nonstick cooking spray. Add margarine and onion; sauté onion until golden. Add soups, green chilies, 1½ cups reserved (defatted) chicken stock and cooked chicken.

Coat a 9 x 13-inch baking pan with nonstick cooking spray. To assemble casserole, layer 3 torn flour tortillas overlapping edges to cover entire bottom of pan. Next spread 1/2 of chicken mixture over tortillas and top with 1/2 of grated cheese. Layer 3 more torn tortillas, the remainder of chicken mixture and the remainder of grated cheese. Bake at 350 degrees F until bubbly, about 45 to 60 minutes. For a balanced meal, serve with refried beans and mixed greens and sliced tomato and avocado salad. Makes 10 servings.

Nutrition Facts: Calories 265, Protein 22.3 gm, Carbohydrate 20.6 gm, Dietary Fiber 1.6 gm, Fat 7.3 gm, Saturated Fat 2.6 gm, Sodium 617 mg
Meal Planning: 3 Lean Meat/Protein, 1 Carbohydrate

Original Chicken Enchilada Casserole recipe from my sister Jeanne Livingston Roper from Phoenix, Arizona

Chicken Baked Taco

A great alternative to shake and bake-type coatings.

2 cups dry whole wheat bread crumbs
1 packet reduced sodium taco seasoning mix
8 boneless, skinless chicken breasts
1 egg white plus 1/2 cup fat-free milk
Olive oil nonstick cooking spray

Combine bread crumbs and taco seasoning in a large pie or flat pan. Mix well.

Dip chicken breasts in egg-milk mixture then dredge in bread crumbs, coating thoroughly.

Place prepared chicken on a baking sheet coated with nonstick cooking spray. Coat tops of chicken lightly with nonstick cooking spray.

Bake at 425 degrees F for 20 to 25 minutes or until chicken reaches an internal temperature of 170 degrees F. (Chicken parts may also be used, but remove skin first. Bake for 45 to 60 minutes.) After 10 minutes of baking, recoat tops with nonstick cooking spray. For a balanced meal, serve with red beans and rice and steamed California-blend vegetables. Makes 8 servings.

Nutrition Facts: Calories 242, Protein 31.1 gm, Carbohydrate 20.7 gm, Dietary Fiber 2.9 gm, Fat 3.7 gm, Saturated Fat 0.9 gm, Sodium 404 mg
Meal Planning: 4 Lean Meat/Protein, 1 Carbohydrate

Peppered Chicken Fajitas

Full of flavor with a south-of-the-border flare.

1 pound boneless, skinless chicken breasts
1 tablespoon extra virgin olive oil
2 cloves crushed garlic
1 large vidalia onion, sliced
1 large red bell pepper, seeded and sliced
1 large green bell pepper, seeded and sliced
1 large yellow bell pepper, seeded and sliced
1 fresh lemon
1/2 teaspoon ground cumin
1/4 teaspoon salt
1/4 teaspoon fresh ground black pepper
1/2 cup picante sauce or salsa
4 fajita-style flour or spinach tortillas

Cut chicken into 1/2-inch strips. Coat a large skillet with nonstick cooking spray. Heat over high heat; add oil and heat. Add garlic and sauté for 30 seconds until golden. Add chicken strips and sauté for 1 minute. Add sliced onions and peppers and continue sautéing.

Roll lemon on countertop surface and break up pulp; cut in half and squeeze lemon over top of chicken. Cover and reduce heat.

Continue cooking for 2 to 3 additional minutes; add cumin, salt and black pepper. Add salsa and stir to thoroughly coat.

To serve, place chicken-vegetable mixture on lower half of tortilla. Top with coarsely chopped lettuce and chopped tomatoes, if desired. Fold up bottom of tortilla; fold in both sides and roll up. For a balanced meal, serve with lard-free refried beans and sliced mango. Makes 4 servings.

Nutrition Facts: Calories 308, Protein 30.3 gm, Carbohydrate 25.2 gm, Dietary Fiber 2.7 gm, Fat 9.1 gm, Saturated Fat 1.6 gm, Sodium 540 mg
Meal Planning: 4 Lean Meat/Protein, 1 Carbohydrate, 1 Vegetable

Baked Chicken Parmesan

Just as good as the deep-fried original but better for you.

4 boneless, skinless chicken breasts
1/2 cup dry whole wheat bread crumbs
1/8 teaspoon salt
1/4 teaspoon fresh ground black pepper
1/2 teaspoon Italian herb seasonings
Nonstick cooking spray
1 tablespoon olive oil tub margarine
1 tablespoon extra virgin olive oil
4 thin slices lowfat Provolone or part-skim mozzarella cheese
2 cups prepared [lowfat] marinara sauce

Pound chicken breast with a metal mallet until 1/4-inch thick.

Combine bread crumbs, salt, pepper and Parmesan cheese in a pie or flat pan. Dredge chicken breasts in crumb mixture, pressing crumbs onto chicken to coat completely.

Coat a large skillet with nonstick cooking spray. Add margarine and oil and heat over medium heat until margarine melts. Brown chicken breasts on each side for 4 minutes. Coat top of chicken with nonstick cooking spray before turning to cook second side. Cook until no longer pink or until chicken reaches an internal temperature of 170 degrees F.

Place 1 cheese slice on each chicken breast; cover and continue cooking for 1 minute or until cheese melts. Top with marinara sauce and cover until sauce is heated. For a balanced meal, serve with whole wheat pasta and Romaine lettuce salad with tomato and cucumber slices. Makes 4 servings.

Nutrition Facts: Calories 316.5, Protein 34.2 gm, Carbohydrate 20.3 gm, Dietary Fiber 4.1 gm, Fat 11 gm, Saturated Fat 3 gm, Sodium 687 mg
Meal Planning: 4 Lean Meat/Protein, 1 Carbohydrate

Recipe Variation: *Substitute lean veal cutlets for chicken breasts.*

Beef Stroganoff

Given to my sister by her mother-in-law Libby Lewin.

1/2 pound extra lean beef tenderloin fillet, well-trimmed
1 to 2 large vidalia or other sweet onions, chopped
1 to 2 cloves crushed garlic
1 to 2 tablespoons all-purpose flour
1 container (16-ounce) nonfat or lite sour cream
About 1/2 cup water
2 packages (8-ounce each) sliced fresh mushrooms
1/2 cup white or red wine [according to taste preference]
1/2 teaspoon salt
1/4 teaspoon fresh ground black pepper
2 to 3 teaspoons ketchup
1/2 to 1 teaspoon prepared yellow mustard
2 cups cooked long-grain or brown rice

Pound fillet with a metal mallet and thinly slice into 1/2-inch strips. (Fillet is easier to slice thinly if it is slightly frozen.)

Coat a large skillet with nonstick cooking spray. Place over medium-high heat. Add onions and garlic and sauté until golden. Add sliced fillet and brown over medium-high heat. Drain off any fat. Reduce heat to medium-low. Sprinkle flour over onion-meat mixture, adding enough flour to coat the meat. Stir in sour cream and deglaze the pan. Add enough water until desired consistency, stirring well. Add mushrooms and stir to combine.

Cook stroganoff for a few minutes. Add wine, salt and pepper. Add mustard and ketchup, just for coloring. Simmer until time to serve. Do not allow to boil. Adjust seasonings. Serve over rice. For a balanced meal, serve with whole green beans and sliced kiwi and red grape salad. Makes 4 servings.

Nutrition Facts: Calories 414, Protein 20.3 gm, Carbohydrate 52.6 gm, Dietary Fiber 5.3 gm, Fat 9.4 gm, Saturated Fat 3.4 gm, Sodium 755 mg
Meal Planning: 2 Lean Meat/Protein, 3 Carbohydrate, 1 Vegetable

*Original Beef Stroganoff recipe from my sister
Jamie Livingston Lewin from San Francisco, California*

Apache Indian Chili Stew

A comfort food recipe for a cold winter day.

1½ pounds venison or extra lean beef stew meat, cut into cubes
1/2 cup all-purpose flour
1 tablespoon extra virgin olive oil
1 clove crushed garlic
1/4 teaspoon salt
1/2 teaspoon fresh ground black pepper
2 tablespoons chili powder
1 can (16-ounce) stewed tomatoes
1 can (16-ounce) tomato sauce
2 large onions, cut into chunks
5 large potatoes, unpeeled, cut into quarters

Dredge meat in flour. Coat a large saucepot with nonstick cooking spray. Add oil and brown meat in oil.

Add garlic, salt, pepper, chili powder, stewed tomatoes, tomato sauce and onions. Cook until meat is almost done, about 20 to 30 minutes.

Add potatoes and cook for 30 additional minutes. Add water as needed. For a balanced meal, serve with whole grain bread and fresh fruit salad. Makes 8 servings.

Nutrition Facts: Calories 285.3, Protein 20.4 gm, Carbohydrate 25.4 gm, Dietary Fiber 2.7 gm, Fat 11.7 gm, Saturated Fat 4.3 gm, Sodium 737 mg
Meal Planning: 3 Lean Meat/Protein, 1 Carbohydrate, 1 Fat

Steak Pinwheel & Vegetables

A little extra work but worth the time and effort.

8 ounces sliced fresh mushrooms
2 green onions, chopped
1 teaspoon extra virgin olive oil
1½ pounds extra lean beef flank steak, well-trimmed
1/4 teaspoon salt
1/4 teaspoon fresh ground black pepper
1/4 teaspoon **each** dried marjoram, basil and parsley
1/2 cup soft whole wheat bread crumbs
1 tablespoon extra virgin olive oil
2 tablespoons Worcestershire sauce
6 large carrots, peeled and cut into 2-inch pieces
6 celery ribs, cut into 2-inch pieces
6 potatoes, unpeeled, cut into wedges

Preheat oven to 425 degrees F. Coat a deep roasting pan with nonstick cooking spray. Place mushrooms, onions and 1 teaspoon olive oil in pan. Place in preheated oven for 10 minutes.

Meanwhile, pound steak to 1/4-inch thickness. Sprinkle lightly with salt and pepper. Rub marjoram, basil and parsley on 1 side of the meat. Top with cooked mushroom-onion mixture to within 1 inch of edges. Sprinkle with bread crumbs. Roll steak, jellyroll style, starting from short side. Tie with a string.

Place meat, seam side down, on a rack in a roasting pan. Combine 1 tablespoon olive oil and Worcestershire sauce and brush mixture over steak. Arrange carrots, celery and potatoes around steak.

Bake at 425° for 45 to 60 minutes or until meat is tender, brushing occasionally with oil-Worcestershire sauce mixture. Remove string and slice to serve. For a balanced meal, serve with a spinach salad and fresh fruit slices. Makes 6 servings.

Nutrition Facts: Calories 369, Protein 27 gm, Carbohydrate 31.5 gm, Dietary Fiber 6.1 gm, Fat 15.6 gm, Saturated Fat 5.6 gm, Sodium 282 mg
Meal Planning: 3 Lean Meat/Protein, 1 Carbohydrate, 1 Vegetable, 1 Fat

Mom's Barbecued Meatballs

A long-time family favorite– the kids will ask for this recipe.

1/2 cup quick-cooking or old-fashioned rolled oats
1 small onion, finely chopped
1 egg, lightly beaten [or 1/4 cup egg substitute]
1/8 teaspoon fresh ground black pepper
1 tablespoon dried parsley
1/4 teaspoon salt
2 tablespoons ketchup
1 pound 95% extra lean ground beef
Easy Barbecue Sauce - *See recipe below*

Combine oatmeal, onion, egg, black pepper, parsley, paprika and salt in a large bowl. Add ground beef and ketchup and mix lightly until just combined. Do not overmix.

Gently shape into 1½-inch balls. Place half of the meatballs in a circle on a microwave-safe meat rack. Cover with wax paper and microwave on HIGH for 3 minutes. Rotate 1/4 turn and microwave 2 more minutes or until done. Place cooked meatballs in a large skillet coated with nonstick cooking spray. Place on stove over low heat to keep warm. Repeat with remaining half. Discard meat drippings.

To make **Easy Barbecue Sauce**, combine *1 cup ketchup, 2 teaspoons prepared yellow mustard, 1/2 teaspoon apple cider vinegar, 1 teaspoon Worcestershire sauce, 1/8 teaspoon fresh ground black pepper, 2 tablespoons molasses or brown sugar and 1/4 cup Splenda® sugar substitute* in a small bowl. Stir to combine. Pour sauce over cooked meatballs. Cook, covered, over medium-low heat for 15 to 20 minutes, stirring occasionally. For a balanced meal, serve with baked potatoes, green beans with almonds and melon slices. Makes 6 servings.

Nutrition Facts: Calories 278, Protein 17 gm, Carbohydrate 21.2 gm, Dietary Fiber 1.3 gm, Fat 14.3 gm, Saturated Fat 5.5 gm, Sodium 685 mg
Meal Planning: 2 Lean Meat/Protein, 1 Carbohydrate, 1 Fat

Beef & Sugar Snap Peas

This is fast and healthy food at its best.

3/4 pound extra lean round steak, well-trimmed
1 teaspoon peanut oil
1 clove crushed garlic
1 tablespoon minced gingerroot
8 ounces sliced fresh mushrooms
1 pound sugarsnap peas (fresh or frozen)
1/2 cup low sodium beef broth
2 teaspoons brown sugar
2 tablespoons dry sherry, optional [or 2 tablespoons Diet Coke®]
2 tablespoons low sodium soy sauce
1 tablespoon cornstarch

Slice steak into very thin strips.

Coat a wok or large skillet with nonstick cooking spray and place on high heat. Add oil and heat. Add garlic and ginger; sauté for 30 to 45 seconds until golden.

Add meat and stir-fry 3 to 4 minutes or until desired doneness. Push meat up sides of wok.

Add mushrooms and sugarsnap peas to wok. Cover and cook for 2 minutes.

Meanwhile, combine hot water, bouillon, sugar and sherry in a small bowl. Pour over beef-vegetable mixture. Bring to a boil. Combine soy sauce and cornstarch and slowly add to stir-fry, stirring until thickened. Serve over brown rice. Makes 4 servings.

Nutrition Facts: Calories 254, Protein 22.4 gm, Carbohydrate 13.4 gm, Dietary Fiber 3.7 gm, Fat 12 gm, Saturated Fat 4.3 gm, Sodium 357 mg
Meal Planning: 3 Lean Meat/Protein, 2 Vegetable, 1/2 Fat

Recipe Tip: As strange as it sounds, Diet Coke makes an almost sodium-free alternative to soy sauce in most stir-fry sauce recipes.

Beef Goulash

One of the first recipes I ever learned how to make.

1 pound 95% extra lean ground beef [or ground venison]
1 large sweet onion, finely chopped
1/2 teaspoon salt
1/4 teaspoon fresh ground black pepper
2 cans (28-ounce each) whole tomatoes
2 teaspoons granulated sugar
4 ounces elbow macaroni
4 ounces whole wheat elbow macaroni

Coat a large saucepot with nonstick cooking spray. Crumble beef into pot. Add onion and brown over medium heat. Drain off and discard any fat. Wipe sides of saucepot with a paper towel.

Add salt, pepper, tomatoes and sugar to cooked meat. Reduce heat to low and simmer.

Meanwhile, in a large stockpot, cook pasta in a large amount of boiling water for 8 minutes or until al dente. *Do not add salt or oil.* Stir occasionally while boiling. Drain well.

Add cooked macaroni to tomato-meat mixture. Stir to combine. Heat through and serve. Adjust seasonings. For a balanced meal, serve with steamed broccoli and fresh fruit salad. Makes 6 servings (approximately 1½ to 2 cups per serving.)

Nutrition Facts: Calories 376, Protein 22 gm, Carbohydrate 42 gm, Dietary Fiber 3.4 gm, Fat 14.1 gm, Saturated Fat 5.3 gm, Sodium 753 mg
Meal Planning: 3 Lean Meat/Protein, 2 Carbohydrate, 2 Vegetable, 1 Fat

Pork Vegetable Stir-Fry

Get the whole family involved in cutting vegetables for stir-frys.

1 teaspoon peanut oil
1 clove crushed garlic
1 tablespoon minced gingerroot
1 pound extra lean pork, well-trimmed and cut into 1/2-inch strips
4 cups sliced stir-fry vegetables (water chestnuts, bok choy, nappa,
    snow peas, etc.) or frozen stir-fry vegetable blend, thawed
1/2 cup sliced green onions
1/2 cup water
1 tablespoon cornstarch
1 tablespoon sherry, optional
1 teaspoon brown sugar
1 teaspoon fresh ground black pepper
1 package low sodium vegetable-flavored bouillon granules

Coat a wok or large skillet with nonstick cooking spray. Place over high heat until hot. Add oil and heat; add garlic and ginger and stir-fry for 30 to 45 seconds until golden.

Add pork strips and stir-fry for 3 to 3½ minutes. Add vegetables and stir-fry for 1 minute.

Add green onions. Cover with lid and steam for 1 minute.

In a small bowl, combine water, cornstarch, sherry, brown sugar, black pepper and bouillon. Add to stir-fry mixture and cook until sauce thickens. For a balanced meal, serve over cooked brown rice and melon slices. Makes 4 servings.

Nutrition Facts: Calories 186, Protein 26.3 gm, Carbohydrate 10.2 gm,
Dietary Fiber 2.1 gm, Fat 5.2 gm, Saturated Fat 1.6, Sodium 200 mg
Meal Planning: 3 Lean Meat/Protein, 2 Vegetable

Pork Piccata

An ideal meal for guests— very elegant.

1 pound extra lean pork sirloin cutlets, well-trimmed, cut 1/2-inch thick
1/4 cup all-purpose flour
1/2 teaspoon salt
1/4 teaspoon fresh ground black pepper
2 tablespoons olive oil tub margarine
1/3 cup dry white wine
2 tablespoons fresh lemon juice

Place each pork cutlet in a heavy plastic storage bag and flatten with a metal mallet to 1/4-inch thickness.

Combine flour, salt and pepper in a pie or flat pan. Dredge cutlets in flour mixture.

Coat a large skillet with nonstick cooking spray. Add margarine and melt. Cook cutlets in margarine over medium-high heat for 5 minutes or until brown on both sides and cooked through to an internal temperature of 160 degrees F. Remove to a platter and keep warm.

Add wine and lemon juice to skillet. Stir to deglaze pan. Heat until liquid is reduced to about 1/2 cup. Pour sauce over cutlets. For a balanced meal, serve with baked potatoes, steamed spinach and assorted apple slices. Makes 4 servings.

Nutrition Facts: Calories 292, Protein 30.1 gm, Carbohydrate 6 gm, Dietary Fiber 0 gm, Fat 13.3 gm, Saturated Fat 3.9, Sodium 366 mg
Meal Planning: 4 Lean Meat/Protein

Recipe Variation: Substitute chicken breasts or veal for pork.

Sweet Zesty Pork Medallions

This recipe works well with almost any type of meat.

1 pound extra lean pork tenderloin, well-trimmed
1/2 cup water
1/3 cup apple cider vinegar
1/4 cup apricot 100% fruit spread
1 tablespoon cornstarch
1 tablespoon granulated sugar
1/2 teaspoon fresh ground black pepper
1 tablespoon dry sherry
1 tablespoon low sodium soy sauce
2 cloves crushed garlic
2 cups cooked mixed brown and wild rice
4 cups steamed broccoli spears

Cut pork tenderloin crosswise into 12 (1-inch thick) medallions. Place each piece in a heavy plastic storage bag and flatten with a metal mallet to 1/4-inch thickness.

In a small bowl, combine water, vinegar, fruit spread, cornstarch, sugar, sherry, soy sauce and garlic. Set aside.

Coat a large skillet with nonstick cooking spray. Heat over medium-high heat. Add pork medallions and brown for 2 to 3 minutes on each side or until cooked through. Remove pork to a platter and keep warm. Add reserved fruit spread mixture to skillet, deglaze skillet and cook for 3 to 4 minutes or until thickened. Add pork medallions, turning to coat.

Combine rice and broccoli. Place on a serving platter. Arrange pork medallions on top. For a balanced meal, serve with fresh melon salad. Makes 4 servings.

Nutrition Facts: Calories 319, Protein 28.5 gm, Carbohydrate 36.5 gm, Dietary Fiber 5.1 gm, Fat 6.6 gm, Saturated Fat 1.7, Sodium 194 mg
Meal Planning: 3 Lean Meat/Protein, 1 Carbohydrate, 3 Vegetable

Black & White Pepper Chops

A sweet-hot flavoring for the mild flavor of pork.

4 (4-ounce each) boneless center loin chops, well-trimmed
2 tablespoons coarsely ground black pepper
1 tablespoon coarsely ground white pepper
Dash salt
2 tablespoons light whipped butter, melted
1/2 tablespoon molasses
1/2 teaspoon freshly squeezed lemon juice

Rub chops on both sides evenly with black and white pepper. Sprinkle lightly with salt. Broil or grill chops over medium hot coals for 12 to 15 minutes, turning once.

Meanwhile, prepare molasses butter by combining butter, molasses and lemon juice. Top each chop with molasses butter and continue cooking for 1 to 2 additional minutes. For a balanced meal, serve with baked sweet potatoes or winter squash, steamed Brussels sprouts and assorted apple slices. Makes 4 servings.

Nutrition Facts: Calories 193, Protein 17 gm, Carbohydrate 3.5 gm, Dietary Fiber 0 gm, Fat 12.4 gm, Saturated Fat 5 gm, Sodium 145 mg
Meal Planning: 3 Lean Meat/Protein, 1 Fat

Frozen Fruited Cream

Inspired from one of my favorite restaurants— The Feedmill.

1 container (16-ounce) lite frozen whipped topping
2 cans (20-ounce each) crushed pineapple, packed in juice
1/2 cup maraschino cherries, chopped
1 can (14-ounce) fat-free sweetened condensed milk

Partially thaw whipped topping.

Drain pineapple well.

In a large bowl, combine whipped topping, pineapple and sweetened condensed milk. Mix with a spoon until well combined. Gently fold in cherries.

Pour mixture into a 9 x 13-inch pan. Smooth top.

Cover loosely with plastic wrap and freeze for 4 hours or until firm. Remove from freezer 5 minutes before cutting into 24 squares. Serve immediately.

This recipe may be made in advance and frozen for up to several days. Cover lightly once completely frozen. Makes 24 servings.

Nutrition Facts: Calories 168, Protein 1.4 gm, Carbohydrate 28 gm,
Dietary Fiber 0.2 gm, Fat 0 gm, Saturated Fat 0 gm, Sodium 83 mg
Meal Planning: 2 Carbohydrate

Chocolate Stuff

Aunt Mary knows how to make great desserts– give this one a try.

1 box Betty Crocker® SuperMoist® Devil's Food cake mix
2 small packages sugarfree instant chocolate fudge pudding mix
3½ cups cold 1% milk
2 cups lite frozen whipped topping, thawed
1 (1-ounce) Heath® Chocolate Bar, finely crushed

In a 9 x 13-inch baking pan coated with nonstick cooking spray, bake devil's food cake according to lowfat, low cholesterol package directions. (*Use 3/4 egg substitute for the 3 eggs. Substitute 1/2 cup nonfat ricotta cheese, silken tofu, nonfat mayonnaise or applesauce for 1/2 cup vegetable oil.*)

Cool baked cake in pan on a cooling rack for 15 minutes. Remove cake from pan and cool completely. When cake is cool, break up into bite-size pieces, placing back into the 9 x 13-inch baking pan. Set aside.

Pour milk into a large deep bowl. Gradually add pudding mix. With a wire whisk or electric mixer, beat at low speed until blended, 1 to 2 minutes. Pour at once over cake, covering entire surface. Let set for 5 minutes.

Top firm cake-pudding mixture with lite whipped topping. Garnish with crushed Heath Bar, if desired. Store in the refrigerator until ready to serve. Makes 16 servings.

Nutrition Facts: Calories 186, Protein 3.9 gm, Carbohydrate 35.4 gm, Dietary Fiber 1.4 gm, Fat 2.6 gm, Saturated Fat 1.2 gm, Sodium 333 mg
Meal Planning: 2 Carbohydrate, 1/2 Fat

Original Chocolate Stuff recipe from my aunt, Mary Livingston Jamison from Zelienople, Pennsylvania

Chocolate Strawberry Tart

The combination of chocolate and strawberries is always a winner.

1 cup lowfat chocolate graham cracker crumbs
2 tablespoons Promise® stick margarine, softened
2½ pints strawberries, tops removed, rinsed and dried
1 tablespoon granulated sugar
1 teaspoon unflavored gelatin
1/4 cup water
2 tablespoons low sugar apple jelly

In a medium bowl, combine chocolate crumbs and margarine. Coat a 9-inch springform pan with nonstick cooking spray. Press crumb mixture firmly onto bottom and slightly up sides. Bake at 375 degrees F for 8 minutes. Cool.

In a food processor or blender, puree enough strawberries to make 1/2 cup puree. Slice remaining strawberries. Set aside.

In a small saucepan, combine pureed strawberries, sugar, gelatin and water. Cook over medium heat until mixture comes to a boil, stirring constantly. Refrigerate until mixture mounds slightly when dropped from a spoon.

Evenly spread strawberry-gelatin mixture into prepared crust. Top with remaining berries.

Melt apple jelly in microwave or in a small saucepan and pour over strawberries. Refrigerate at least 3 hours before serving. To serve, remove springform and slice into 8 slices. Makes 8 servings.

Nutrition Facts: Calories 104, Protein 1.3 gm, Carbohydrate 15.8 gm, Dietary Fiber 2.3 gm, Fat 4.4 gm, Saturated Fat 0.8 gm, Sodium 99 mg
Meal Planning: 1 Carbohydrate, 1 Fat

Broiled Bananas Dessert

A nice mingling of flavors for a light dessert.

4 pitted dates
1/2 cup 100% orange juice concentrate
1 teaspoon almond extract, optional
2 tablespoons lite whipped butter
4 medium ripe bananas, peeled
1/3 cup chopped pecans

In a small food processor or blender, combine orange juice, dates and almond extract. Pulse to chop dates. Set aside.

Coat a baking dish or cast iron skillet with nonstick cooking spray. Add butter and place under broiler until melted.

Cut bananas in half; then split each half lengthwise. Arrange bananas, cut side up, in baking dish over melted butter. Pour orange juice mixture over bananas.

Place bananas under broiler for 4 minutes. Sprinkle pecans over bananas and return to broiler for 1 to 2 additional minutes or until pecans are toasted. Serve plain, garnish with lowfat whipped topping or top with lowfat ice cream. Makes 4 servings.

Nutrition Facts: Calories 194, Protein 2.1 gm, Carbohydrate 37.3 gm, Dietary Fiber 3.0 gm, Fat 5.5 gm, Saturated Fat 1.7 gm, Sodium 30 mg
Meal Planning: 2 Carbohydrate, 1 Fat

A trout in the pot is better than a salmon in sea.
Irish Proverb

Give a man a fish, and he'll eat for a day.
Teach him how to fish, and he'll eat forever.
Chinese Proverb

There's as good fish in the sea as ever came out of it.
Unknown

It is not only what we do but also what we do not do
for which we are accountable.
Jean Moliere

Let your hook be always cast. In the pool where you least expect it, there will be a fish.

Ovid

*Healthy people consume more fish
and other foods rich in omega 3 fatty acids.*

- Strive to eat at least three fish meals per week.
- Prepare fish using lowfat cooking methods— bake, broil, grill, steam, sauté and poach. Do not deep-fry.
- Select white albacore tuna more often than pink tuna for greater amounts of omega 3 fatty acids. Try sardines, mackerel, salmon and other canned fish— all good sources of omega 3 fats.
- Snack on walnuts. Toast walnuts and add different seasonings and spices such as cinnamon or ground red pepper for flavor.
- Add chopped toasted walnuts to baked goods, salads, pasta dishes and other recipes.
- Use two tablespoons ground flax seed daily. Fresh grind whole flax seed in a coffee mill.
- Sprinkle ground flax seed on cold or hot cereal, peanut butter toast, cottage cheese, yogurt and many other favorite foods.
- Use ground flax seed in place of breadcrumbs in meatloaf, meatballs, salmon patties and other recipes. Sprinkle ground flax seed over cooked rice and pasta or stir into marinara sauce.
- Look for commercially available food products made with flax seed such as breads and cereals.
- Discuss the possible benefits of omega 3 fatty acid supplements (liquid flax oil; fish or flax oil capsules) with your health care provider.
- Cook with canola oil in moderation. Use canola oil in recipes in place of regular vegetable oil.
- Use soy foods and soy food products on a regular basis. Look for soy meat alternatives, soybeans and other soy foods.
- Use omega 3-enriched eggs— available at most grocery stores.

Cranberry-Crab Appetizer

A colorful appetizer for the holiday season.

8 ounces fat-free cream cheese
1 can (6-ounce) fancy white crab meat, drained
6 green onions, chopped
45 individual mini fillo dough shells, thawed
1/2 cup whole cranberry sauce

In a food processor or blender, combine cream cheese, crab and onions. Puree until smooth– mixture will turn green. Place fillo shells on a baking sheet or jellyroll pan. Fill each fillo shell with approximately 1 heaping teaspoon of crab-cream cheese mixture. Bake at 375 degrees F for 10 minutes. Remove fillo shells from oven and top with 1/2 teaspoon cranberry sauce. Return to oven for 1 minute. Serve warm. Makes 45 appetizers (3 shells per serving).

Nutrition Facts: Calories 127, Protein 7.2 gm, Carbohydrate 16.3 gm, Dietary Fiber 1.6 gm, Fat 3.3 gm, Saturated Fat 0.1 gm, Sodium 162 mg
Meal Planning: 1 Lean Meat/Protein, 1 Carbohydrate

Crab Pizza Appetizer

Take the ingredients for this recipe with you and assemble at the party.

4 ounces reduced fat cream cheese
4 ounces fat-free cream cheese
3 dashes Worcestershire sauce
3/4 cup cocktail sauce
1/2 pound flaked or shredded crab meat, canned or imitation
1 tablespoon fresh chopped parsley

Place cream cheeses and worcestershire sauce on a 12-inch pizza pan. Work together with a knife and spread out evenly on pan to form the "crust". Spread cocktail sauce over cream cheese, sprinkle with crab and top with parsley. Serve with lowfat whole wheat crackers or melba toast. Makes 12 servings (1/4 cup per serving).

Nutrition Facts: Calories 67, Protein 6.5 gm, Carbohydrate 4.1 gm, Dietary Fiber 0.2 gm, Fat 2.5 gm, Saturated Fat 1.5 gm, Sodium 276 mg
Meal Planning: 1 Lean Meat/Protein

Creamy Crab Salad

A nice variation from tuna salad.

1 pound imitation crab flakes
2 cups shredded cabbage
1 cup coarsely shredded Romaine lettuce
1/2 cup diced sweet onion
1/3 cup lite mayonnaise
1/3 cup Miracle Whip® Free® Nonfat Dressing
1 tablespoon honey mustard
2 tablespoons fresh chopped parsley [or 1 tablespoon dried]
1 teaspoon dried dill [or 1 tablespoon fresh]
1/2 teaspoon old bay seasoning
1/4 teaspoon salt
1/2 teaspoon fresh ground black pepper

Combine crab and vegetables in a large bowl. Toss to combine.

In a small bowl, combine mayonnaise, Miracle Whip, mustard, herbs and seasonings. Add to crab mixture and stir until well combined. Cover and refrigerate for 30 minutes before serving to blend flavors. For a balanced meal, stuff salad in a whole grain pita and serve with fresh fruit. Makes 6 servings (approximately 1 cup per serving).

Nutrition Facts: Calories 115, Protein 13 gm, Carbohydrate 11.8 gm,
Dietary Fiber 1.2 gm, Fat 1.7 gm, Saturated Fat 0.5 gm, Sodium 520 mg
Meal Planning: 2 Lean Meat/Protein, 2 Vegetable

Firecracker Crab Salad

Full of flavor and a little gusto.

3/4 pound cooked lump crabmeat, drained
1/3 cup thinly sliced celery
3 green onions, chopped
2 tablespoons nonfat sour cream
2 tablespoons lite mayonnaise
2 tablespoons canned tomato sauce
1 tablespoon white balsamic vinegar
1/4 teaspoon fresh ground black pepper
1/4 teaspoon hot sauce
Dash salt
1/8 teaspoon ground white pepper
1 clove crushed garlic
2/3 cup diced fresh tomato
2 cups coarsely chopped romaine lettuce

Combine crabmeat, celery and onions in a medium bowl; toss gently and set aside.

In a small bowl, combine sour cream with remaining ingredients except tomato and lettuce. Beat with a wire whisk until smooth.

Add sour cream mixture to crabmeat; stir well. Cover and chill for 1 to 2 hours to blend flavors. To serve, stir in tomato and serve on lettuce-lined plates. For a balanced meal, serve with a whole grain roll and fresh fruit. Makes 4 servings (approximately 3/4 cup per serving).

Nutrition Facts: Calories 141, Protein 19.2 gm, Carbohydrate 13.5 gm,
Dietary Fiber 4.8 gm, Fat 1.8 gm, Saturated Fat 0.5 gm, Sodium 444 mg
Meal Planning: 2 Lean Meat/Protein, 2 Vegetable

Oriental Scallop Salad

An easy salad from the sea prepared mostly in the microwave.

1/4 pound whole wheat angel hair pasta
1 pound bay scallops
2 cups thinly sliced fresh pea pods
1 cup coarsely shredded carrot
1 small onion, thinly sliced
2 cups fresh broccoli florets
1/4 cup white wine vinegar
2 tablespoons low sodium soy sauce
2 tablespoons sesame oil
1 tablespoon honey
1/2 teaspoon grated lemon peel
1/8 teaspoon ground cayenne pepper, optional

Break pasta into 2-inch lengths. In a large stockpot, cook pasta in a large amount of boiling water for 5 minutes or until al dente. *Do not add salt or oil.* Drain and rinse briefly with cold water to prevent sticking; toss. Transfer to a large bowl.

Meanwhile, arrange scallops in single layer in an 8-inch round microwave-safe dish. Cover with wax paper. Microwave on MEDIUM-HIGH (70%) for 5 to 8 minutes or until scallops are opaque; turn once. Let stand for 1 to 2 minutes. Drain and add to reserved pasta.

In a medium microwave-safe casserole, combine pea pods, carrots, onion, broccoli and 1 tablespoon water. Cover and microwave on HIGH for 2 to 4 minutes or until vegetables are tender-crisp, stirring once. Drain and add to reserved pasta mixture.

To make dressing, combine vinegar, soy sauce, oil, honey, lemon peel and cayenne pepper in a small bowl. Mix well and pour over combined salad mixture; toss to coat. Cover and refrigerate at least 4 hours. Makes 6 servings.

Nutrition Facts: Calories 241, Protein 19.2 gm, Carbohydrate 30.6 gm, Dietary Fiber 4.2 gm, Fat 5.7 gm, Saturated Fat 0.8 gm, Sodium 399 mg
Meal Planning: 2 Lean Meat/Protein, 2 Carbohydrate

Crab Pasta Salad

This salad is always a hit– friends will ask for the recipe.

1/4 pound spiral pasta
1/4 pound whole wheat spiral pasta
1 pound cooked crab meat (imitation, canned or lump)
1 medium sweet onion, finely chopped
1 cup coarsely shredded carrot
2 cups cabbage or broccoli coleslaw
1/2 cup lite mayonnaise
1/2 cup Miracle Whip® Free® Nonfat Dressing
2 tablespoons honey mustard
1 teaspoon apple cider vinegar
2 tablespoons Splenda® sugar substitute
    [or 2 tablespoons granulated sugar]
1/4 teaspoon fresh ground black pepper
1/2 teaspoon salt
1/8 teaspoon old bay seasoning

In a large stockpot, cook pasta in a large amount of boiling water for 8 minutes or until al dente. *Do not add salt or oil.* Drain and rinse briefly with cold water to prevent sticking. Transfer cooked pasta to a large bowl. Add crab flakes, onion, carrot and coleslaw, mixing thoroughly. Set aside.

In a small bowl, combine remaining ingredients to make sauce. Blend with a wire whisk. Pour over pasta mixture and mix until well combined. Adjust seasonings. Cover and refrigerate for 1 to 2 hours before serving. Makes 8 servings (approximately 1½ cups per serving).

Nutrition Facts: Calories 210, Protein 13.2 gm, Carbohydrate 33.3 gm, Dietary Fiber 2.2 gm, Fat 2.8 gm, Saturated Fat 0.6 gm, Sodium 554 mg
Meal Planning: 1 Lean Meat/Protein, 2 Carbohydrate

Fresh Tuna Salad Nicoise

The variety of textures, colors and flavors makes this a fabulous salad.

1/2 pound whole tiny new potatoes
1½ cups fresh cut green beans
1 large green bell pepper, seeded and sliced
1 cup cherry or grape tomatoes, cut in half
8 pitted jumbo black olives
3 tablespoons extra virgin olive oil
1/2 cup white wine vinegar
1 tablespoon dry mustard
1 tablespoon capers, drained
1 teaspoon **each** dried basil and oregano
2 cloves crushed garlic
3/4 pound cooked fresh tuna [grilled or broiled]
2 cups **each** torn Romaine and Bibb lettuce

In a medium saucepan, cook potatoes in a small amount of water for 10 minutes. Add beans and continue cooking for 8 minutes or until potatoes are tender and beans are tender-crisp. Drain and rinse briefly with cold water.

Cut potatoes into quarters and transfer quartered potatoes and beans to a large bowl. Add green pepper, tomatoes and olives. Set aside.

Combine 1/2 cup water, oil, vinegar, mustard, capers, basil, oregano and garlic in a screw-top jar. Cover and shake well.

Break tuna into large chunks. Place in a dish large enough to hold fish in a single layer. Pour 1/2 cup prepared dressing over tuna. Pour remaining dressing over reserved vegetable mixture. Cover and marinate separately in refrigerator for approximately 4 hours. To serve, combine lettuces and place lettuce mixture onto 4 large salad plates. Top with marinated tuna, then arrange vegetables around tuna. For a balanced meal, serve with whole grain rolls and fresh fruit. Makes 4 servings.

Nutrition Facts: Calories 266, Protein 23.1 gm, Carbohydrate 17 gm, Dietary Fiber 3.6 gm, Fat 12.6 gm, Saturated Fat 1.8 gm, Sodium 140 mg
Meal Planning: 3 Lean Meat/Protein, 1 Carbohydrate

Maryland Style Crab Cakes

Serve with cornbread and lowfat Caesar salad for a light meal.

1 pound canned lump crab meat
1/3 cup finely chopped sweet onion
2 tablespoons lite mayonnaise
2 tablespoons Miracle Whip® Free® Nonfat Dressing
1 teaspoon old bay seasoning
1/3 cup dry whole wheat bread crumbs
1/4 teaspoon fresh ground black pepper
1 tablespoon extra virgin olive oil
Olive oil nonstick cooking spray

Drain crab reserving liquid. In a medium bowl, combine all ingredients except olive oil and stir lightly to combine. If mixture appears too dry, add reserved crab liquid 1 teaspoon at a time until mixture is desired moisture.

Coat a large skillet with nonstick cooking spray. Add oil and heat over medium-high heat. Gently shape crab mixture into 4 large or 8 small patties. Place in hot oil and flatten slightly with a nonstick spatula. Sauté until bottom is golden brown. Turn to brown second side, recoating skillet with nonstick cooking spray before turning. Cook until second side is golden brown. Makes 4 servings.

Nutrition Facts: Calories 201, Protein 22 gm, Carbohydrate 9.6 gm, Dietary Fiber 1.2 gm, Fat 7.7 gm, Saturated Fat 1.3 gm, Sodium 694 mg
Meal Planning: 3 Lean Meat/Protein, 1/2 Carbohydrate

Recipe Variation: Make Mock Crab Cakes by substituting shredded zucchini for the crab meat. Peel 1 medium zucchini and coarsely shred to make 3 cups. Press between paper towels to remove excess water. Proceed with recipe as directed.

Flounder Grilled In Foil

A great way to prepare any variety of fish.

1 tablespoon olive oil tub margarine
1 leek, cut into matchsticks (julienned)
1 cup matchstick carrots
1 large red bell pepper, seeded and sliced
1 tablespoon fresh lemon juice
2 teaspoons fresh chopped tarragon
4 (4-ounce each) flounder fillets
1/4 teaspoon salt
1/8 teaspoon fresh ground black pepper

Coat a skillet with nonstick cooking spray. Add margarine and place over medium heat until margarine melts. Add leeks, carrots and bell pepper. Sauté for 3 minutes or until crisp-tender. Remove from heat. Stir in lemon juice and tarragon; set aside.

Fold 2 (16 x 12-inch) sheets of heavy-duty aluminum foil in half lengthwise. Open foil and coat inside with nonstick cooking spray. Place 2 fillets on half of each foil sheet. Sprinkle fish with salt and pepper and top with vegetable mixture, evenly distributing between the 2 packets. Coat top of fish with nonstick cooking spray.

Fold foil over fillets; tightly seal edges. Place packets on grill rack over hot coals; cook for 7 minutes. For a balanced meal, serve with baked red skin potatoes and mixed greens tossed salad. Makes 4 servings.

Nutrition Facts: Calories 127, Protein 17.6 gm, Carbohydrate 5.6 gm, Dietary Fiber 1.4 gm, Fat 3.6 gm, Saturated Fat 0.5 gm, Sodium 247 mg
Meal Planning: 3 Lean Meat/Protein, 1 Vegetable

Tuna Burgers

A quick healthy alternative to the drive-thru.

2 cans (6-ounce) albacore tuna in water, drained and rinsed
1/2 cup shredded carrots
1/2 cup chopped green bell pepper
1/2 cup chopped onion
1/2 cup old-fashioned rolled oats
1 egg white, lightly beaten
1/3 cup Miracle Whip® Free® Nonfat Dressing
1 tablespoon sweet relish
2 teaspoons Dijon mustard
1/4 teaspoon garlic powder
1/2 teaspoon fresh ground black pepper
1 tablespoon extra virgin olive oil

In a large bowl, combine flaked tuna, carrots, bell pepper, onion and oats. Mix well.

In a small bowl, combine egg white, Miracle Whip, relish, mustard, garlic powder and black pepper. Combine using a wire whisk. Stir into tuna mixture until well combined. Form into 6 burgers.

Coat a large skillet with nonstick cooking spray. Heat over medium heat. Add oil and heat. Place burgers in hot skillet. Brown both sides until golden. Recoat skillet with nonstick cooking spray before turning to brown second side. Reduce heat to low, cover and cook for 2 minutes to heat through. For a balanced meal, serve on a whole grain bun with lettuce, alfalfa sprouts and tomato and assorted fresh apple slices on the side. Makes 6 burgers.

Nutrition Facts: Calories 149, Protein 17 gm, Carbohydrate 9.8 gm, Dietary Fiber 1.2 gm, Fat 4.0 gm, Saturated Fat 0.8 gm, Sodium 456 mg
Meal Planning: 2 Lean Meat/Protein, 1 Vegetable

Spicy Hot Fillets

Try this zesty recipe with any fresh catch.

1/3 cup all-purpose flour
2 tablespoons cornmeal
1 teaspoon chili powder
1/2 teaspoon ground red pepper
1/2 teaspoon garlic powder
1/2 teaspoon paprika
1/4 teaspoon salt
1/2 teaspoon ground white pepper
1/8 teaspoon fresh ground black pepper
Nonstick cooking spray
1½ pounds firm-textured fillets (catfish, perch, cod, tilapia, etc.)
2 tablespoons peanut oil
2 tablespoons lite tub margarine
Olive oil nonstick cooking spray

In a pie pan or shallow dish, combine flour, cornmeal, chili powder, red pepper, garlic powder, paprika, salt and peppers. Coat fish with non-stick cooking spray and dredge fish in flour mixture.

Coat a large skillet with nonstick cooking spray. Heat over medium heat. Add 1 tablespoon peanut oil and 1 tablespoon margarine and heat to melt margarine. Add half of the coated fish to the skillet in a single layer. Pan-fry 1 side over medium heat for 4 minutes.

Lightly spray top of fillets with nonstick cooking spray. Lift fillets from skillet and recoat skillet with nonstick spray before turning to pan-fry the second side. Pan-fry for an additional 4 to 5 minutes or until fish flakes.

Transfer cooked fish to a serving platter and keep warm. Repeat pan-fry method with remaining oil, margarine and fish. For a balanced meal, serve with cornbread, spinach salad and fresh fruit slices. Makes 6 servings.

Nutrition Facts: Calories 203, Protein 18 gm, Carbohydrate 8 gm, Dietary Fiber 0.5 gm, Fat 9.8 gm, Saturated Fat 1.9 gm, Sodium 193 mg
Meal Planning: 3 Lean Meat/Protein

Seafood Enchiladas

This creamy dish is a quick meal after a long day.

1 pound cooked crab meat (imitation, canned or lump)
1 small onion, finely chopped
3/4 cup nonfat sour cream
2 tablespoons fresh chopped parsley [or 1 tablespoon dried]
Dash salt
Dash fresh ground black pepper
1/2 cup shredded lowfat Monterey Jack cheese
2 tablespoons freshly grated Parmesan cheese
8 (6-inch) whole wheat tortillas

In a large bowl, combine crab, onion, sour cream, parsley, salt and pepper. Mix to combine thoroughly.

To assemble enchiladas, spread about 1/4 cup crab mixture in the center of each tortilla. Fold tortilla in half and roll up.

Place 2 enchiladas on each of 4 microwave-safe plates. Evenly distribute cheeses between enchiladas. Cover loosely with wax paper or micro-wave lid and microwave plated enchiladas on HIGH for 2 to 2½ min-utes. Repeat with remaining plated enchiladas. For a balanced meal, serve with coarsely chopped lettuce, refried beans and sliced mango. Makes 4 servings (2 enchiladas per serving).

Nutrition Facts: Calories 415, Protein 29.6 gm, Carbohydrate 53.3 gm, Dietary Fiber 6.5 gm, Fat 6.8 gm, Saturated Fat 2.3 gm , Sodium 920 mg
Meal Planning: 4 Lean Meat/Protein, 3 Carbohydrate

Orange Steamed Fish

Wok steaming is fun way to prepare any dish.

2 teaspoons peanut oil
1 medium onion, chopped
2 cloves crushed garlic
1 teaspoon grated gingerroot
1/4 cup 100% orange juice concentrate
2 tablespoons fresh chopped parsley [or 1 tablespoon dried]
1 tablespoon low sodium soy sauce
1/8 teaspoon fresh ground black pepper
1 pound orange roughy fillets

Arrange fish in heat-safe serving dish.

Heat wok over high heat. Add oil and heat. Stir-fry onion, garlic and gingerroot in hot oil for 2 minutes. Stir in juice, parsley, soy sauce and pepper and bring to a boil. Pour mixture over fish.

Wipe out wok. Place steamer rack in wok. Add boiling water to reach 1/2-inch below steamer rack. Place heat-safe serving dish with fish on steamer rack. Cover wok and steam for about 10 minutes or until fish flakes with a fork. For a balanced meal, serve with brown rice, steamed sugar snap peas and fresh golden pineapple slices. Makes 4 servings.

Nutrition Facts: Calories 200, Protein 17.6 gm, Carbohydrate 8.6 gm, Dietary Fiber 0.7 gm, Fat 10.3 gm, Saturated Fat 0.5 gm, Sodium 330 mg
Meal Planning: 3 Lean Meat/Protein, 1 Vegetable

Salmon with Orange-Basil Sauce

A great blend of herbs & seasonings– a great source of Omega 3 fats.

1/4 cup 100% orange juice concentrate
1 tablespoon extra virgin olive oil
2 tablespoons fresh chopped basil [or 1 tablespoon dried]
2 tablespoons white balsamic vinegar
1 tablespoon fresh chopped tarragon [or 1 teaspoon dried]
1 tablespoon Worcestershire sauce
2 cloves crushed garlic
1 pound skinless salmon fillets

In a small bowl, combine orange juice concentrate, oil, basil, water, tarragon, Worcestershire sauce and garlic.

Wash salmon and cut salmon into 4-ounce fillets. Place in a large dish in a single layer. Pour juice marinade over salmon. Cover and refrigerate for 1 to 2 hours to marinate. (Other varieties of firm texture fish fillets may be substituted.)

Place marinated salmon fillets under broiler or on hot grill. Broil or grill for 6 to 8 minutes on each side, brushing often with marinade. Cook until color is uniform throughout and salmon flakes. Do not overcook. Discard remaining marinade. For a balanced meal, serve with baked potatoes topped with steamed broccoli and red grape salad. Makes 4 servings.

Nutrition Facts: Calories 194, Protein 23 gm, Carbohydrate 7.9 gm, Dietary Fiber 0.1 gm, Fat 7.3 gm, Saturated Fat 1.1 gm, Sodium 118 mg
Meal Planning: 3 Lean Meat/Protein

Salmon with Monterey Sauce

This recipe was created by "searching" through ingredients on-hand.

1 pound skinless salmon fillets
1 fresh lemon
1/4 cup fat-free Ranch or Bleu Cheese dressing
4 teaspoons Monterey steak seasoning mix

Wash salmon and cut into 4 ounce servings. Roll lemon on countertop surface and break up pulp; cut in half and squeeze over salmon.

Place salmon on hot grill or in hot skillet coated with nonstick cooking spray. Grill or cook (uncovered) on one side until cooked halfway through, about 6 to 7 minutes depending on thickness. Carefully turn salmon over to cook second side. Brush ranch dressing over top of salmon and sprinkle liberally with Monterey steak seasoning, covering entire top of salmon with seasoning mix.

Cover and continue grilling or cooking in skillet until color is uniform throughout and salmon flakes. Do not overcook. For a balanced meal, serve with baked red skin potatoes, sautéed whole green beans and fresh fruit salad. Makes 4 servings.

Nutrition Facts: Calories 148, Protein 22.6 gm, Carbohydrate 3 gm, Dietary Fiber 0 gm, Fat 3.9 gm, Saturated Fat 0.6 gm, Sodium 586 mg
Meal Planning: 3 Lean Meat/Protein

Peppered Fish Fajitas

A bit unorthodox but a wonderful recipe– easy to prepare.

1 tablespoon sesame oil
2 cloves crushed garlic
1 pound Cajun-seasoned fish fillets (fresh or frozen)
1 large vidalia onion, sliced
1 large red bell pepper, seeded and sliced
1 large green bell pepper, seeded and sliced
1 large yellow bell pepper, seeded and sliced
1 fresh lime
1/2 teaspoon ground cumin
1/4 teaspoon fresh ground black pepper
1/2 cup green enchilada sauce
4 fajita-style flour or spinach tortillas

Cut fish into 1/2-inch strips. Coat a large skillet with nonstick cooking spray. Heat over high heat; add oil and heat. Add garlic and sauté for 30 seconds until golden. Add fish and sauté for 1 minute. Add sliced onions and bell peppers and continue sautéing.

Roll lime on countertop surface and break up pulp; cut in half and squeeze lime over top of fish. Cover and reduce heat. Continue cooking for 2 to 3 additional minutes; add cumin and black pepper. Add enchilada sauce and stir to thoroughly coat.

To serve, place fish-vegetable mixture on lower half of tortilla. Top with coarsely chopped lettuce and chopped tomatoes, if desired. Fold up bottom of tortilla; fold in both sides and roll up. For a balanced meal, serve with refried black beans and sliced kiwi. Makes 4 servings.

Nutrition Facts: Calories 279, Protein 24 gm, Carbohydrate 26.6 gm, Dietary Fiber 2.9 gm, Fat 8.3 gm, Saturated Fat 1.9 gm, Sodium 462 mg
Meal Planning: 3 Lean Meat/Protein, 1 Carbohydrate, 2 Vegetable

Pasta Rags & Salmon

An unusual one-of-a-kind salad with wonderful colors and tastes.

4 ounces fresh pasta sheets or dry lasagna noodles
1 tablespoon extra virgin olive oil
1/2 pound skinless salmon fillet, cut into paper-thin slivers
1 fresh lemon
1 cup sun-dried tomatoes, rehydrated and cut into strips
2 small bunches broccoli rabe, trimmed and coarsely chopped
1/4 cup fresh chopped dill [or 2 tablespoons dried]
1/2 teaspoon fresh ground black pepper

Tear or break pasta into irregular pieces. In a large stockpot, cook pasta in a large amount of boiling water according to package directions. *Do not add salt or oil.* Drain. Transfer pasta to a bowl and keep hot.

Meanwhile, coat a large skillet with nonstick cooking spray. Add olive oil and heat over medium heat. Add salmon.

Roll lemon on countertop surface and break up pulp; cut in half and squeeze lemon over top of salmon. Sauté salmon over medium heat until salmon is uniform in color and done (only a few minutes).

Stir in sun-dried tomatoes and broccoli rabe; cover and heat through for 1 to 2 minutes. Add to cooked pasta and stir in dill and black pepper. Serve immediately. For a balanced meal, serve with steamed broccoli and fresh fruit slices. Makes 4 servings.

Nutrition Facts: Calories 247, Protein 21 gm, Carbohydrate 17.8 gm, Dietary Fiber 3 gm, Fat 6.4 gm, Saturated Fat 0.9 gm, Sodium 330 mg
Meal Planning: 3 Lean Meat/Protein, 1 Carbohydrate, 1 Vegetable

Crunch Top Catfish

A great recipe for the not-so-much-of-a-fish-lover.

1 pound catfish fillets (or other fish variety)
1 fresh lemon
1 tablespoon extra virgin olive oil
16 saltine or lowfat butter-flavored crackers, finely crushed
Dash garlic powder
Dash fresh ground black pepper
Dash ground white pepper
Dash salt
Dash paprika
Olive oil nonstick cooking spray

Wash catfish and cut into 4-ounce servings. Place catfish in a 9 x 13-inch baking dish coated with nonstick cooking spray.

Roll lemon on countertop surface and break up pulp; cut in half and squeeze over catfish. Spray top of catfish with nonstick cooking spray.

In a small bowl, combine crushed crackers and seasonings. Sprinkle evenly over top of catfish. Liberally spray nonstick cooking spray over top of crackers to evenly coat. (Pulse spray to prevent crumbs from scattering.)

Bake at 450 degrees F for 15 minutes or until fish is opaque and easily flakes. After 8 minutes, recoat top of crackers with cooking spray. For a balanced meal, serve with baked russet potatoes, sautéed parsley baby carrots and fresh fruit salad. Makes 4 servings.

Nutrition Facts: Calories 190, Protein 19.7 gm, Carbohydrate 8.6 gm, Dietary Fiber 0.3 gm, Fat 8 gm, Saturated Fat 1.5 gm, Sodium 272 mg
Meal Planning: 3 Lean Meat/Protein, 1/2 Carbohydrate

Salmon with Black Bean Relish

An great way to prepare any firm-texture fish.

1 pound skinless salmon (or other firm-texture fish)
1 tablespoon sesame oil
3 tablespoons dry sherry
1 tablespoon teriyaki sauce
1 teaspoon brown sugar
1/2 cup Black Bean Relish (*See Recipe on Page 131*)

Wash salmon and cut into 4-ounce servings. Coat a large skillet with nonstick cooking spray. Place over high heat and heat skillet. Add oil and heat. Add salmon fillets and pan-fry for 6 to 7 minutes or until cooked about half-way.

Turn salmon fillets to cook second side. Cover and reduce heat to medium-high.

In a small bowl, combine dry sherry, teriyaki sauce and brown sugar. Stir well and pour over salmon fillets. Continue cooking salmon for about 5 minutes or until salmon is uniform in color and cooked through. Remove lid and place 2 tablespoons black bean relish across the center of each fillet. Cover and cook for additional minute to heat through.

For a balanced meal, serve with brown rice pilaf, steamed asparagus and red grapes. Makes 4 servings.

Nutrition Facts: Calories 183, Protein 24.1 gm, Carbohydrate 5 gm,
Dietary Fiber 0.8 gm, Fat 5.8 gm, Saturated Fat 0.9 gm, Sodium 291 mg
Meal Planning: 3 Lean Meat/Protein

Scalloped Oysters

Uncle Allen and my mother fought over this recipe every holiday.

1 sleeve (about 20) saltine crackers, finely crushed
1 sleeve (about 20) reduced-fat butter-flavored crackers, finely crushed
1/4 teaspoon fresh ground black pepper
1/8 teaspoon ground white pepper
1 pound fresh oysters, in liquid
1½ cups fat-free or 1% milk
2 eggs, lightly beaten [or 1/2 cup egg substitute]
2 tablespoons lite whipped butter, melted

Coat a 2-quart casserole with nonstick cooking spray. Drain oysters, reserving liquid.

Combine crushed crackers and peppers. Place 1/3 crackers in prepared casserole. Top with 1/3 drained oysters. Repeat layering with 1/3 crackers and 1/3 oysters. Finish with the final 1/3 crackers and 1/3 oysters.

In a small bowl, combine milk, eggs, butter and reserved oyster liquid. Whip with a wire whisk to combine. Pour slowly over oyster-cracker mixture. Do not stir. Add more milk, if necessary, to ensure that crackers are thoroughly soaked.

Bake at 350 degrees F for 45 minutes or until lightly golden, puffy and set. Makes 8 servings (approximately 1/2 cup per serving).

Nutrition Facts: Calories 147, Protein 8.1 gm, Carbohydrate 15.5 gm, Dietary Fiber 0.2 gm, Fat 5.6 gm, Saturated Fat 1.8 gm, Sodium 280 mg
Meal Planning: 1 Carbohydrate, 1/2 Fat

Balsamic-Dill Seafood Sauté with Baby Vegetables

A fabulous recipe sure to please everyone's pallet .

1 tablespoon extra virgin olive oil
4 cloves crushed garlic
1 pound medium shrimp, peeled, deveined and tails removed
1/2 pound bay scallops
1 large sweet onion, sliced
1 pound package Birdseye® Baby Bean and Carrot Blend
2 tablespoons white balsamic vinegar
1 tablespoon lemon juice
1 teaspoon granulated sugar
2 tablespoons dried dill [or 1/4 cup fresh chopped]
1/2 teaspoon fresh ground black pepper
1 tablespoon lite whipped butter

Coat a large skillet with nonstick cooking spray. Place on high heat. Add oil and garlic; sauté for 30 seconds until golden. Add shrimp, scallops and onion; sauté, uncovered for 1 minute. Cover and steam for 2 minutes. Add frozen vegetables; cover and steam for 2 minutes.

Add remaining ingredients, stirring to combine. Reduce heat to medium and continue cooking for an additional 2 to 3 minutes or until sauce reduces slightly, shrimp is pearly opague and scallops are opaque and firm. For a balanced meal, serve with a side of brown rice, whole wheat pasta or new potatoes and mixed greens tossed salad. Makes 4 servings.

Nutrition Facts: Calories 183, Protein 21 gm, Carbohydrate 13 gm, Dietary Fiber 3 gm, Fat 6 gm, Saturated Fat 1.3 gm, Sodium 345 mg
Meal Planning: 3 Lean Meat/Protein, 2 Vegetable

Shrimp with Sun-Dried Tomatoes

Fat-free half & half makes this recipe absolutely delicious & healthy!

1 tablespoon extra virgin olive oil
3 cloves crushed garlic
1 small vidalia onion, chopped
1 pound medium shrimp, peeled, deveined and tails removed
3 to 4 tablespoons dry sherry, optional
10 sun-dried tomatoes, rehydrated and cut into thin strips
2 tablespoons all-purpose flour
1 cup fat-free half and half
1/4 teaspoon salt
1/4 teaspoon fresh ground black pepper
1/4 teaspoon ground white pepper
Pinch ground red pepper
2 cups cooked risotto (arboria rice)
2 tablespoons fresh chopped parsley

Coat a large skillet with nonstick cooking spray. Add olive oil and heat. Add garlic and onion and sauté over medium heat until onion is opaque, about 2 minutes. Add shrimp and cook, stirring constantly for 2 to 3 minutes; shrimp should begin to turn pearly opaque. Add sherry and sun-dried tomatoes and continue cooking for a few minutes.

In a small bowl, combine flour, half and half, salt and peppers. Blend together with a wire whisk to combine. Gradually add half and half mixture to shrimp. Stir constantly until sauce begins to thicken. Cook for 1 more minute or until well blended and heated through. Do not allow to boil.

Cook rice according to package directions. To serve, top risotta with shrimp-tomato mixture. Garnish with parsley, if desired. For a balanced meal, serve with steamed Brussels sprouts and fresh sliced strawberries. Makes 4 servings.

Nutrition Facts: Calories 345, Protein 32.3 gm, Carbohydrate 33.3 gm, Dietary Fiber 5.1 gm, Fat 6.4 gm, Saturated Fat 1.5 gm, Sodium 760 mg
Meal Planning: 4 Lean Meat/Protein, 1 Carbohydrate, 2 Vegetable

Crunchy Baked Fish

Another great recipe for the not-so-much-of-a-fish-lover.

1 tablespoon extra virgin olive oil
1 cup finely crushed cornflake cereal
3 tablespoons freshly grated Parmesan cheese
1/2 teaspoon salt
1/8 teaspoon fresh ground black pepper
1/4 teaspoon paprika
1/4 teaspoon Cajun seasoning, optional
1 pound fish fillets (Cod, Capensis, Walleye, Haddock, etc.)
1 egg white plus 1/4 cup fat-free milk
Nonstick cooking spray

Preheat oven to 450 degrees F. Coat a 9 x 9-inch baking dish with nonstick cooking spray. Place oil in baking dish and place in preheated oven to heat.

Meanwhile, combine cornflakes, Parmesan cheese, salt, pepper, paprika and seasoning in a pie or flat pan. Set aside.

Cut fish fillets into 3-inch pieces. Dip fish pieces in egg-milk mixture, then dredge in crumb mixture. Place in prepared baking dish over hot oil. Coat top with nonstick cooking spray. Bake at 450 degrees F for 20 minutes or until fish flakes. For a balanced meal, serve with homemade baked potato chips, assorted raw vegetables with lowfat dip and fresh fruit slices. Makes 4 servings.

Nutrition Facts: Calories 174, Protein 23.7 gm, Carbohydrate 6.4 gm, Dietary Fiber 0.1 gm, Fat 5.4 gm, Saturated Fat 1.3 gm, Sodium 479 mg
Meal Planning: 3 Lean Meat/Protein

Seafood Fettucine Alfredo

A long-time hit that's made it onto many "favorite recipe" lists.

1 tablespoon olive oil tub margarine
2 cloves crushed garlic
1 medium onion, chopped
1/4 cup dry white wine, optional
1/2 pound cooked crab meat (imitation, lump or canned)
1/2 teaspoon old bay seasoning
1 tablespoon dried parsley [or 2 tablespoons fresh chopped]
1/2 teaspoon salt
1/4 teaspoon fresh ground black pepper
1 can (12-ounce) evaporated skimmed milk [or fat-free half and half]
1 cup 1% milk
1/2 teaspoon butter-flavored sprinkles
2 tablespoons cornstarch *mixed in* 2 tablespoons water
1/4 cup freshly grated Parmesan cheese
4 cups cooked whole wheat spinach fettuccini

Melt margarine in a large skillet coated with nonstick cooking spray. Add garlic and onion; sauté over medium heat until golden brown; add wine. Cook until onions are opaque.

Add crab to onion mixture, flaking well. Season with old bay, parsley, salt and pepper. Mix well.

Add both milks and butter-flavored sprinkles. Stir continually to heat through. Do not allow to boil. Combine cornstarch and water to make a thick paste. Stir gradually into crab mixture; continue cooking until thickened. Remove from heat and stir in Parmesan cheese. Serve over whole wheat fettuccine. For a balanced meal, serve with a lowfat Caesar salad and fresh fruit salad. Makes 4 servings.

Nutrition Facts: Calories 421, Protein 26.1 gm, Carbohydrate 61.4 gm, Dietary Fiber 3.7 gm, Fat 7.8 gm, Saturated Fat 1.8 gm, Sodium 836 mg
Meal Planning: 3 Lean Meat/Protein, 4 Carbohydrate

Creamed Seafood Over Pasta

Lowfat canned soups are convenient and can produce a healthy recipe.

2 teaspoons extra virgin olive oil
3 cloves crushed garlic
1/2 package (16-ounce) Bird's Eye® Pepper Stir Fry
1/2 pound bay scallops
1/2 pound medium shrimp, peeled, deveined and tails removed
1 can Campbell's® Condensed Cream of Shrimp Soup
3/4 cup 1% milk
1 tablespoon dried parsley [or 2 tablespoons fresh chopped]
2 cups cooked whole wheat pasta

Place a large skillet coated with nonstick cooking spray over high heat. Add olive oil and heat. Add garlic and onion-pepper mixture; sauté for 1 minute; reduce heat to medium. Add scallops and shrimp; sauté for 1 minute. Cover with lid slightly ajar and continue cooking for 3 to 5 minutes or until shrimp and scallops are pearly opaque.

In a small bowl, combine soup and milk. Whisk to combine. Pour over seafood mixture and stir to combine. Cook over medium heat until bubbly. Add parsley and serve over pasta. For a balanced meal, serve with steamed broccoli with cauliflower and fresh fruit. Makes 4 servings.

Nutrition Facts: Calories 342, Protein 28.6 gm, Carbohydrate 35.2 gm, Dietary Fiber 2.8 gm, Fat 9.9 gm, Saturated Fat 3.2 gm, Sodium 1069 mg
Meal Planning: 3 Lean Meat/Protein, 2 Carbohydrate, 1 Vegetable

Recipe Tip: *Save time by using individually quick frozen shrimp or scallops— no peeling or deveining required.*

Swiss Crab Quiche

Use 1% milk in quiche recipes for a creamier texture.

1 (9-inch) unbaked lower fat pastry shell (*See Recipe on Page 82*)
1/2 pound cooked crab meat (imitation, lump or canned)
3/4 cup shredded lowfat Swiss cheese
3 green onions, chopped
1 jar (2-ounce) diced pimiento, drained and rinsed
1 eggs plus 4 egg whites [or 3/4 cup egg substitute]
1 cup 1% milk
1/4 teaspoon salt
1/4 teaspoon ground nutmeg
1/4 teaspoon ground white pepper

Bake pastry shell at 450 degrees F for 7 to 10 minutes or until crust is lightly brown. Remove from oven and reduce oven temperature to 350 degrees F.

Layer crab, cheese, onion and pimiento in baked pastry shell.

In a bowl, lightly beat eggs; stir in milk and seasonings. Gently pour over crab mixture. Bake at 350 degrees F for 45 minutes or until a knife inserted into center comes out clean. Let stand for 10 minutes before cutting. For a balanced meal, serve with fresh fruit and whole grain muffins. Makes 6 servings.

Nutrition Facts: Calories 304, Protein 21.2 gm, Carbohydrate 31.5 gm, Dietary Fiber 3.7 gm, Fat 9.1 gm, Saturated Fat 2.4 gm, Sodium 561 mg
Meal Planning: 3 Lean Meat/Protein, 2 Carbohydrate

Dijon Tilapia en Papillote

Tilapia is a mild-flavored fish– good in almost any fish recipe.

1 cup matchstick carrots
4 tilapia fillets (1/2 pound)
2 pieces (15 x 12-inch) parchment paper
2 teaspoons Dijon mustard
1/4 teaspoon dried basil
1 small zucchini, unpeeled and cut into 1/4-inch slices
1 teaspoon extra virgin olive oil
1/4 teaspoon garlic powder
1/4 teaspoon salt
1/4 teaspoon fresh ground black pepper
2 tablespoons fresh snipped chives [or 1 tablespoon dried]

In a covered saucepan or in microwave, cook carrots in a small amount of boiling water for about 3 minutes or until nearly tender; drain.

To assemble fish bundles, cut heart shapes from parchment paper then open. For each bundle, stack 2 tilapia fillets on right half of each heart, tucking under any thin edges. Spread mustard over fish. Sprinkle with basil. Top with carrot and zucchini. Drizzle with olive oil. Sprinkle with garlic powder, salt, pepper and chives.

Fold left half of each heart over fish. Starting at the top of the heart, seal each bundle by folding edges up together. Twist tip of heart to hold bundle closed. (A mixture of water and cornstarch brushed between the folded edges will assist in keeping the edges sealed.)

Place bundles on a baking sheet. Bake at 450 degrees F for 12 to 15 minutes or until paper puffs up and fish is done. To serve, cut bundles open by slashing a large X in the top then pull back paper. Transfer bundles to dinner plates. For a balanced meal, serve with brown rice pilaf and mixed greens tossed salad. Makes 2 servings.

Nutrition Facts: Calories 153, Protein 21.5 gm, Carbohydrate 7 gm, Dietary Fiber 2.3 gm, Fat 5.1 gm, Saturated Fat 1.4 gm, Sodium 423 mg
Meal Planning: 3 Lean Meat/Protein, 1 Vegetable

Don't be too sweet lest you be eaten up.
Don't be too bitter lest you be spewed out.
Yiddish Proverb

When the fruit is scarcest its taste is sweetest.
Irish Proverb

You never know what is enough
until you know what is more than enough.
William Blake

Many take by the bushel and give by the spoon.
German Proverb

Though honey is sweet, do not lick it off a briar.

Irish Proverb

Healthy people choose and cook with fewer processed sugars and limit ingredients high in refined sugars.

- Reduce sugar ingredients (granulated, brown or confectioners' sugar, honey, molasses, syrup, etc.) by 1/3 in most recipes.
- Realize that small amounts of sugar and related ingredients are often a necessary and acceptable addition to great tasting healthy food.
- Don't make dessert a regular part of every meal. Realize a meal is complete without dessert.
- Consider portion sizes. "Less fat, less sugar and fewer calories" does not imply "double the portion."
- Take advantage of the natural sweetness of fruit in recipes or for dessert.
- Substitute strong-flavored sweeteners such as dark brown sugar, pure maple syrup, dark molasses and honey.
- Do not eliminate sugar completely. Adding small amounts of sugar to healthy foods, such as oatmeal, tomato sauce and winter squash, may make them more flavorful and appealing.
- Substitute apple or white grape juice for water in recipes.
- Limit high sugar foods, beverages and other products with added or hidden sugars such desserts, candies, ice cream, sweet snacks, soft drinks, fruit drinks, sweetened teas, fat-free desserts and other related foods.
- Select unsweetened beverages and drink at least 6 cups of water daily. Cut back on sugar or honey in coffee and tea.
- Use a sugar substitute to reduce carbohydrate and/or calorie intake for certain health goals such as diabetes or weight control. *Cooking for the Health of It* recipes primarily use Splenda® sugar substitute.
- Look for sugarfree versions of favorite foods or ingredients to substitute in recipes.

Rosa Marina Salad

An updated old recipe my Aunt Margaret used to make.

8 ounces rosa marina (orzo) pasta
2 cans (20-ounce each) crushed pineapple, packed in juice
2 cans (8-ounce each) mandarin oranges, packed in juice or light syrup
3 tablespoons brown sugar
2 tablespoons all-purpose flour
Pinch salt
1/4 cup Splenda® sugar substitute
1 egg, lightly beaten
1 teaspoon pure vanilla extract
1 cup lite frozen whipped topping, thawed

In a large saucepan, cook rosa marina in a large amount of boiling water according to package directions. *Do not add salt or oil.* Stir occasionally while boiling. Drain and set aside to cool.

Drain pineapple, reserving juice. Drain mandarin oranges, discarding syrup. Combine drained pineapple and mandarin oranges and set aside.

Combine reserved juice, brown sugar, flour, salt, Splenda, egg and vanilla in a small saucepan. Cook over medium heat, stirring constantly with a wire whisk until thick. Remove from heat and set aside to cool.

In a large bowl, combine cooled rosa marina and cooled thickened juice mixture. Cover tightly and refrigerate overnight. Before serving, stir in reserved fruit and whipped topping. Makes 16 servings (approximately 3/4 cup per serving).

Nutrition Facts: Calories 122, Protein 2.6 gm, Carbohydrate 26.3 gm, Dietary Fiber 1.1 gm, Fat 0.6 gm, Saturated Fat 0.1 gm, Sodium 19 mg
Meal Planning: 1½ Carbohydrate

Almost Tollhouse® Cookies

This recipe illustrates reducing fat & sugar– adding good fats & fiber.

1/3 cup Promise® stick margarine
1/3 cup fat-free cream cheese, chilled
1/3 cup nonfat ricotta cheese
1/3 cup granulated sugar
1/3 cup brown sugar
1/3 cup Splenda® sugar substitute
2 eggs [or 1/2 cup egg substitute]
1 teaspoon pure vanilla extract
1½ cups all-purpose flour
1 cup whole wheat pastry flour
1/3 cup ground flax seed
1 teaspoon baking soda
Dash salt
1 cup miniature semi-sweet chocolate chips
1/3 cup finely chopped walnuts

In a large bowl, cream margarine, cream cheese, ricotta cheese, sugars, Splenda, eggs and vanilla with an electric mixer just until well combined.

In a medium bowl, combine flours, flax, baking soda, salt, chocolate chips and nuts. Add to creamed mixture, mixing just until combined. Do not overmix.

Using a cookie scoop, drop onto a baking sheet coated with nonstick cooking spray. Flatten slightly with the back of a nonstick spatula. Bake at 375 degrees F for 7 to 8 minutes or until lightly browned on the bottom of cookies. Cool slightly; remove to wire racks to cool. Makes about 3 dozen cookies (1 cookie per serving).

Nutrition Facts: Calories 95, Protein 2 gm, Carbohydrate 13 gm, Dietary Fiber 0.9 gm, Fat 3.9 gm, Saturated Fat 1.2 gm, Sodium 83 mg
Meal Planning: 1 Carbohydrate

Almost Brownie Cookies

Sure to satisfy any chocolate craving– do not overbake.

1/4 cup Promise® stick margarine
1/4 cup fat-free cream cheese, chilled
1/3 cup nonfat ricotta cheese
1 teaspoon pure vanilla extract
1 cup dark brown sugar
2 eggs [or 1/2 cup egg substitute]
3/4 cup all-purpose flour
3/4 cup whole wheat pastry flour
1/3 cup unsweetened cocoa powder
1/4 teaspoon baking soda
Dash salt
1/2 cup miniature semi-sweet chocolate chips

In a large bowl, combine margarine, ricotta cheese, cream cheese, vanilla and brown sugar. Beat at low speed with an electric mixer until well combined. Beat in eggs.

In a medium bowl, combine remaining flours, cocoa, baking soda, salt and chocolate chips. Stir into batter, mixing just until combined. Do not overmix.

Using a cookie scoop, drop onto a baking sheet coated with nonstick cooking spray. Flatten slightly with back of nonstick spatula.

Bake at 375 degrees for 9 to 11 minutes or until set. Cookies will appear wet. Let cool for 2 minutes then remove to wire racks to cool completely. Makes about 2 dozen cookies (1 cookie per serving).

Nutrition Facts: Calories 99, Protein 2.6 gm, Carbohydrate 14.8 gm, Dietary Fiber 1.2 gm, Fat 3.7 gm, Saturated Fat 1.2 gm, Sodium 67 mg
Meal Planning: 1 Carbohydrate

Nut & Orange Biscotti

Biscotti is a wonderful cookie without all the fat.

3/4 cup whole almonds
2 teaspoons extra virgin olive oil
3 eggs [or 3/4 cup egg substitute]
3/4 cup granulated sugar
2 tablespoons almond-flavored liqueur
1 tablespoon pure vanilla extract
1 tablespoon grated orange peel
1 teaspoon almond extract
1-1/3 cups all-purpose flour
1 cup whole wheat pastry flour
2 teaspoons baking powder
1/3 cup chopped dried cranberries

Toast nuts on a baking sheet at 325 degrees F until golden, about 15 minutes. Place oil and 1/4 cup hot nuts in a blender or food processor. Process to a buttery paste. Chop remaining nuts.

In a large bowl, combine eggs, almond paste and sugar. Beat with an electric mixer until blended. Add liqueur, vanilla, orange peel and almond extract.

Combine flours and baking powder. Gradually stir into egg mixture until well blended. Stir in chopped almonds and dried cranberries. Spoon batter onto a baking sheet coated with nonstick cooking spray. With floured hands, pat into a flat log about 3/4-inch thick and 3-inches wide. Bake at 325 degrees F for about 25 minutes or until golden.

Remove from oven and let cool for 5 minutes. Reduce oven heat to 225 degrees F. Cut log crosswise into 1/2-inch slices. Lay slices flat on baking sheet and return to oven. Continue baking until golden all over, about 45 to 55 minutes. Cool completely on wire racks. Makes 30 biscotti (1 biscotti per serving).

Nutrition Facts: Calories 99, Protein 2.9 gm, Carbohydrate 17.1 gm, Dietary Fiber 1 gm, Fat 3.3 gm, Saturated Fat 0.4 gm, Sodium 42 mg
Meal Planning: 1 Carbohydrate, 1/2 Fat

Cocoa Almond Biscotti

A mild cocoa cookie sure to please any sweet tooth.

2 cups all-purpose flour
1/2 cup unsweetened cocoa powder
2 teaspoons baking powder
1/3 cup sliced almonds
3/4 cup granulated sugar
1/2 cup Splenda® sugar substitute
3 eggs [or 3/4 cup egg substitute]
1/4 cup Promise® stick margarine, melted
1/2 teaspoon almond extract
Powdered sugar

In a small bowl, mix flour, cocoa and baking powder; stir in almonds. Set aside.

In a large bowl, beat sugar, Splenda, eggs, margarine and almond extract with an electric mixer at medium speed for 2 minutes. Stir in flour mixture and mix until well combined.

Divide dough in half. With floured hands, shape each half into a 14 x 2-inch log. Place on a baking sheet coated with nonstick cooking spray. Bake at 350 degrees F for 25 minutes.

Remove from oven and cut on the diagonal into 16 (1-inch) slices. Place biscotti, cut-side up, back onto baking sheet. Return to oven and bake for an additional 8 to 10 minutes on **each** side or until lightly toasted. Cool completely on wire racks. Dust biscotti tops with powdered sugar if desired. Makes 32 biscotti (1 biscotti per serving).

Meal Planning: Calories 81, Protein 2 gm, Carbohydrate 12 gm,
Dietary Fiber 0.6 gm, Fat 3.2 gm, Saturated Fat 0.6 gm, Sodium 52 mg
Meal Planning: 1 Carbohydrate, 1/2 Fat

Chocolate Chip Snack Squares

A unique blend of chocolate and orange– great with a glass of milk.

1/3 cup Promise® stick margarine, softened
2 tablespoons honey
1/3 cup fat-free or 1% milk
1 egg
1/3 cup unsweetened calcium-fortified 100% orange juice concentrate
1 teaspoon pure vanilla extract
3/4 cup all-purpose flour
3/4 cup whole wheat pastry flour
1 teaspoon baking soda
1/4 teaspoon salt
1/4 cup semi-sweet chocolate chips, chopped

In medium bowl, combine margarine, honey, milk, egg, orange juice concentrate and vanilla. Beat with an electric mixer until well combined.

In a medium bowl, combine flours, baking soda, salt and chocolate chips. Stir into liquid ingredients, mixing well.

Spread mixture into an 8-inch square baking dish coated with nonstick cooking spray. Bake at 350 degrees F for 20 to 25 minutes. Makes 16 squares.

Nutrition Facts: Calories 110, Protein 2 gm, Carbohydrate 14.7 gm,
Dietary Fiber 1 gm, Fat 5.2 gm, Saturated Fat 1.3 gm, Sodium 163 mg
Meal Planning: 1 Carbohydrate, 1 Fat

Mom's Carrot Raisin Bread

One of my favorite treats growing up– almost no added sugar.

2 cups 100% apple juice
3 tablespoons brown sugar
1¼ cups dark raisins
1 tablespoon margarine
3 large carrots, grated
1¾ cups all-purpose flour
1 cup whole wheat pastry flour
1/2 teaspoon salt
2 teaspoons baking powder
1 teaspoon baking soda
1 teaspoon ground cinnamon
1 teaspoon ground nutmeg

In a large saucepan, combine apple juice, brown sugar, raisins, margarine and carrots. Bring to a boil over high heat. Remove from heat and let stand 12 hours or until completely cool.

In a large mixing bowl, combine flour, salt, baking powder, baking soda, cinnamon and nutmeg. Make a well in center and add cooled carrot-raisin mixture. Mix lightly just until combined.

Divide batter evenly between 4 small (3 x 5-inch) foil loaf pans coated with nonstick cooking spray. Bake at 350 degrees F for 40 to 45 minutes or until toothpick inserted in center comes out clean. Makes 4 loaves (8 slices per loaf).

Nutrition Facts: Calories 71, Protein 1.5 gm, Carbohydrate 15.8 gm, Dietary Fiber 1 gm, Fat 0.6 gm, Saturated Fat 0.1 gm, Sodium 104 mg
Meal Planning: 1 Carbohydrate

Applesauce Gingerbread

Molasses, applesauce and spices blend together for a delicious dessert.

1 cup all-purpose flour
1 cup whole wheat pastry flour
1½ teaspoons baking soda
1½ teaspoons ground ginger
1/2 teaspoon ground cinnamon
1/4 teaspoon ground allspice
1/4 teaspoon ground cloves
1/4 teaspoon salt
1/4 cup canola oil
1/4 cup unsweetened applesauce
1/4 cup brown sugar
1/2 cup Splenda® sugar substitute
1 egg
2 tablespoons molasses
3/4 cup lowfat buttermilk

In a medium bowl, combine flours, baking soda, ginger, cinnamon, allspice, cloves and salt. Set aside.

In a large bowl, cream oil, applesauce, brown sugar and Splenda with an electric mixer. Beat in egg then beat in molasses and buttermilk. Continue beating until well blended. Gradually stir in dry ingredients just until blended.

Spoon batter into a 10-inch springform pan coated with nonstick cooking spray. Bake at 350 degrees F for 35 to 40 minutes or until a wooden pick inserted in center comes out clean. Cool on a wire rack for 10 minutes. Remove springform. Makes 12 servings.

Nutrition Facts: Calories 146, Protein 3.4 gm, Carbohydrate 21.8 gm, Dietary Fiber 1.3 gm, Fat 5.3 gm, Saturated Fat 0.6 gm, Sodium 226 mg
Meal Planning: 1½ Carbohydrate, 1 Fat

Cherry Streusel Coffee Cake

A lovely addition to any breakfast or brunch— fussy looking but easy.

1/4 cup Promise® stick margarine
1/4 cup nonfat ricotta cheese
1/2 cup granulated sugar
1 egg, lightly beaten
1 cup fat-free or lite sour cream
1 teaspoon pure vanilla extract
1/2 teaspoon almond extract
1/2 cup fat-free or 1% milk
1 cup all-purpose flour
1 cup whole wheat pastry flour
2 teaspoons baking powder
1/4 teaspoon baking soda
1/4 teaspoon salt
1 can (20-ounce) lite cherry pie filling

In a large bowl, beat margarine, ricotta cheese and sugar with an electric mixer until fluffy. Beat in egg, sour cream and extracts until well combined. Beat in milk.

In a medium bowl, combine flours, baking powder, baking soda and salt. Beat into creamed mixture, mixing just until combined. Spread 2/3 of the batter evenly into a 10-inch bundt pan coated with nonstick cooking spray. Spread pie filling on top of batter. Drop remaining batter by tablespoonfuls on top of filling.

To make **streusel**, combine *1/4 cup all-purpose flour, 1/4 cup old fashioned rolled oats, 3 tablespoons Splenda® sugar substitute [or granulated sugar] and 2 tablespoons Promise® stick margarine* in a medium bowl. Cut in margarine using a pastry blender until mixture resembles a coarse meal. Stir in *1/4 cup sliced almonds.* Sprinkle streusel over top of batter. Bake at 350 degrees F for 1 hour or until a toothpick inserted comes out clean. Cool for 10 minutes; invert and carefully remove from pan. Make 12 servings.

Nutrition Facts: Calories 236, Protein 5.5 gm, Carbohydrate 38 gm, Dietary Fiber 1.7 gm, Fat 6.9 gm , Saturated Fat 1.3 gm, Sodium 252 mg
Meal Planning: 2½ Carbohydrate, 1 Fat

Apple Pie Bars

Another family favorite– to keep it tender don't overwork the dough.

1½ cups all-purpose flour
1½ cups whole wheat pastry flour
1/4 teaspoon salt
1/2 cup Promise® stick margarine
1/2 cup fat-free cream cheese, chilled
1 egg yolk, beaten
Fat-free or 1% milk
6 to 8 large assorted variety apples (Golden, Gala, Mutsu, Fuji, etc.)
1/3 cup granulated sugar
1/2 cup Splenda® sugar substitute
1 teaspoon ground cinnamon

In a medium bowl, combine flours and salt. Cut in margarine and cream cheese with a pastry blender until crumbly.

Add enough milk to egg yolk to make 1/2 cup. Add to flour mixture; mix with a fork until moistened. Do not overmix. Gently press dough out onto a jellyroll pan coated with nonstick cooking spray.

Core and slice apples. Spread apples over prepared dough.

In a small bowl, combine sugar, Splenda and cinnamon. Sprinkle over apples. Bake at 375 degrees F for 45 minutes or until golden. Cut into 16 bars. Makes 16 servings.

Nutrition Facts: Calories 197, Protein 4.5 gm, Carbohydrate 30.6 gm, Dietary Fiber 2.9 gm, Fat 6.8 gm, Saturated Fat 1.2 gm, Sodium 119 mg
Meal Planning: 2 Carbohydrate, 1 Fat

Peach Custard Pie

Phyllo dough makes a nice flaky crust with less fat and calories.

6 sheets fresh or frozen (thawed) phyllo dough
Nonstick cooking spray
5 cups sliced fresh peaches, unpeeled
1/2 teaspoon ground cinnamon
1/2 teaspoon ground nutmeg
1/4 cup granulated sugar
1/4 cup Splenda® sugar substitute
2 tablespoons all-purpose flour
1/2 cup egg substitute [or 2 eggs]

Coat a 9-inch pie pan with nonstick cooking spray. Place 1 phyllo sheet in pie pan, pressing it lightly into bottom and sides (edges will over-hang). Spray entire sheet liberally with cooking spray. Repeat to make 5 more layers, crisscrossing each layer so edges are distributed around pie plate. (Do not allow phyllo dough to dry out; keep dough moist by covering sheets with a damp cloth while preparing the crust.) Twist the overhanging edges under to form a rim.

Place sliced peaches in prepared crust. Sprinkle with cinnamon and nutmeg.

In a blender or food processor, combine sugar, Splenda, flour and egg substitute. Process until combined. Pour over peaches. Bake at 400 degrees F for 30 for 35 minutes. If not set, reduce heat and bake 10 to 15 additional minutes. Makes 8 servings.

Nutrition Facts: Calories 144, Protein 3.6 gm, Carbohydrate 27.5 gm, Dietary Fiber 2.1 gm, Fat 2.6 gm, Saturated Fat 0.4 gm, Sodium 99 mg
Meal Planning: 2 Carbohydrate, 1/2 Fat

Pear Cranberry Crisp

Serve hot over lowfat ice cream for a spectacular dessert.

4 Barlett pears, unpeeled, cored and thinly sliced
1/2 cup dried cranberries
1/4 cup Splenda® sugar substitute [or granulated sugar]
1/4 teaspoon ground cinnamon
1 teaspoon ground nutmeg
1/3 cup old-fashioned rolled oats
2 tablespoons brown sugar
2 tablespoons Promise® stick margarine, melted
Nonstick cooking spray

Arrange pear slices in an 8 x 8-inch baking dish coated with nonstick cooking spray. Sprinkle with cranberries, Splenda, cinnamon and nutmeg.

In a small bowl, combine oats and brown sugar. Add margarine to oat mixture, mixing with a fork until well combined. Sprinkle crumb mixture over pears. Bake at 375 degrees F for 30 minutes or until pears are tender. Spray crumb top with nonstick cooking spray after 15 minutes of baking time. Makes 8 servings. For variety, substitute any fresh fruit– try mangos, papaya or nectarines for a delicious dessert.

Nutrition Facts: Calories 100, Protein 1 gm, Carbohydrate 17.8 gm, Dietary Fiber 2 gm, Fat 3.3 gm, Saturated Fat 0.6 gm, Sodium 36 mg
Meal Planning: 1 Carbohydrate, 1/2 Fat

Peachy Keen Crepes

Crepes are fun and easy to make– less fussy than they look.

3 large fresh peaches, unpeeled
3 fresh Bartlett pears, unpeeled
1 tablespoon water
2 tablespoons olive oil tub margarine
2 tablespoons brown sugar
1 teaspoon lemon juice
1/2 teaspoon pure vanilla extract
1/2 cup 100% white grape juice
2 teaspoons cornstarch
8 crepes - *See recipe below*
Lite whipped cream, optional

Core peaches and pears. Slice into very thin slices. Place peaches, pears and water in a microwave-safe bowl. Cover with wax paper and microwave on HIGH for 2 minutes to blanch fruit.

Coat a medium skillet with nonstick cooking spray. Add margarine to skillet and melt over medium heat. Add brown sugar and cook until caramel-like. Add peach and pear slices, lemon juice and vanilla. Stir to combine. Combine juice and cornstarch together and stir into fruit. Continue cooking until thickened and hot.

To assemble crepes, spoon 1/4 cup peach-pear mixture on each crepe. Fold left and right edges to center; then roll up jellyroll-style. Top with lowfat whipped cream if desired. Makes 8 servings.

Crepes: In a food processor or blender, combine *1 cup all-purpose flour, 1 cup fat-free or 1% milk and 1 egg.* Process on low speed until combined. Coat a 10-inch skillet with nonstick cooking spray; place over medium heat. Remove hot skillet from heat and spoon in a scant 1/4 cup of batter. Lift and tilt skillet to quickly and evenly spread batter. Return to heat; brown crepe on 1 side only. Invert skillet over paper towels; remove crepe. Repeat to make 8 crepes coating with cooking spray each time. Cover crepes and chill until needed.

Nutrition Facts: Calories 146, Protein 3.6 gm, Carbohydrate 25.1 gm,
Dietary Fiber 1.3 gm, Fat 3.8 gm, Saturated Fat 0.7 gm, Sodium 62 mg
Meal Planning: 1½ Carbohydrate, 1/2 Fat

Chocolate Fluff Dessert

Top with gummy worms and serve in a bucket to make "Dirt."

2 small packages sugarfree instant chocolate fudge pudding mix
4½ cups cold 1% milk, divided
1 envelope whipped topping mix
1 teaspoon pure vanilla extract
3 cups chocolate graham snacks, finely crushed

In a large bowl, prepare pudding according to directions, using 4 cups milk. Set aside.

Prepare whipped topping mix according to directions, using 1/2 cup milk and vanilla extract. Fold into prepared pudding.

In a large glass bowl, layer 1/3 pudding mixture and 1/3 crushed graham snacks. Repeat layers. Finish layers with crushed graham snacks. Makes 12 servings.

Nutrition Facts: Calories 126, Protein 5 gm, Carbohydrate 21.4 gm, Dietary Fiber 1.1 gm, Fat 2.2 gm, Saturated Fat 1.2 gm, Sodium 213 mg
Meal Planning: 1½ Carbohydrate, 1/2 Fat

Banana Cream Crisp

A lower calorie alternative to banana cream pie.

1 small package sugarfree instant vanilla pudding mix
1 small package sugarfree instant banana pudding mix
4 cups 1% milk
1 envelope whipped topping mix
1 teaspoon pure vanilla extract
1 cup crushed honey graham cracker snacks
4 ripe bananas, peeled and sliced
Lite whipped cream, optional

In a large bowl, prepare pudding according to package directions using only 3½ cups milk. Set aside.

Prepare whipped topping, according to directions, using 1/2 cup milk and vanilla extract. Fold into reserved pudding.

In individual parfait glasses or cups, layer bananas, pudding mixture and crushed grahams. Repeat layering twice. Top with crushed grahams. Garnish with 1 banana slice and a dollop of lite whipped cream if desired. Makes 8 servings (approximately 1 cup or one 8-ounce parfait glass per serving).

Nutrition Facts: Calories 170, Protein 6.6 gm, Carbohydrate 31.3 gm,
Dietary Fiber 2.2 gm, Fat 2.7 gm, Saturated Fat 1.5 gm, Sodium 244 mg
Meal Planning: 2 Carbohydrate

Thousands in the mouth, peanuts in the pocket.

Krio Proverb

Healthy people use moderate amounts
of monounsaturated, nut and plant oils
in place of saturated and trans fats.

- Use moderate amounts of olive, canola, peanut or other nut oils in cooking.
- Snack on moderate amount of nuts. Toast nuts to enhance the flavor.
- Select trans fat free olive or canola oil tub margarines.
- Select salad dressings made with canola or olive oil. Read ingredients list on food labels.
- Blend together melted butter and pure olive oil for a delicious alternative to butter or margarine.
- Top mixed greens tossed salads with a variety of olives.
- Use a brand name peanut butter or natural peanut butter that contains 0 grams trans fat per serving.
- Add chopped nuts to rice or pasta dishes.
- Use moderate amounts of nuts or sliced avocado to top salads and other dishes. Add sliced avocado to sandwiches.
- Top cold or hot cereals with a handful of chopped nuts.
- Combine olive oil with fresh or dried herbs, crushed garlic, whole peppercorns and honey for a delicious homemade dressing.
- Place peanuts and other nuts in candy dishes rather than candy.
- Select unsalted nuts when available.
- Recognize the satiety value of fats. Small amounts of fat at meals can provide tremendous "staying power" and help control appetite.
- Understand that "good" fats are part of a healthy diet.

Fruity Chex® Party Mix

The more cinnamon, the better– a great healthy snack.

1 tablespoon canola oil
6 cups Multi-Bran Chex® cereal
3 cups Honey-Nut Chex® cereal
1 cup walnuts or pecans, broken
1 cup dry roasted soynuts
1 cup whole flax seed
1 cup chopped dates, dusted with flour
1 cup golden raisins
1 cup dark raisins
Nonstick cooking spray
4+ tablespoons ground cinnamon, divided

Preheat oven to 325 degrees F. Brush a large, deep baking pan with oil. Combine cereals, walnuts, soynuts and flax seed in the pan. Coat heavily with nonstick cooking spray. Sprinkle liberally with cinnamon and toss to coat. Bake for 15 minutes.

Remove from oven and spray top heavily with nonstick cooking spray. Sprinkle liberally again with cinnamon, tossing to coat. Return to oven and bake another 15 minutes. Remove from oven and repeat cooking spray and cinnamon process again.

Stir in dates. Return to oven and bake for a final 15 minutes. Remove from oven and add raisins, tossing to combine; do not bake raisins. Cool on paper towels and store in an airtight container. Total baking time is 45 minutes. Makes 50 (1/2 cup) servings.

Nutrition Facts: Calories 88, Protein 2.5 gm, Carbohydrate 16.3 gm,
Dietary Fiber 2.8 gm, Fat 2.3 gm, Saturated Fat 0.2 gm,
Monounsaturated Fat 0.8 gm, Sodium 71 mg
Meal Planning: 1 Carbohydrate, 1/2 Fat

Peanut Butter Muffins

A hearty great tasting muffin— a great way to begin any day.

2 cups whole wheat pastry flour
1/2 cup soy flour
1/2 cup all-purpose flour
1/3 cup dark brown sugar
1/4 cup Splenda® sugar substitute
1 tablespoon baking powder
Pinch salt
1/2 cup unsalted chopped peanuts
1/2 cup chunky peanut butter
2 eggs, lightly beaten [or 1/2 cup egg substitute]
1/4 cup nonfat ricotta cheese
1 tablespoon canola oil
1¼ cups fat-free or 1% milk

In a large bowl, combine flours, brown sugar, Splenda, baking powder, salt and peanuts. Set aside.

In a blender or food processor, combine peanut butter, eggs, ricotta cheese, oil and milk. Process until smooth. Add mixture to dry ingredients, stirring with a flat wooden spoon just until combined. Do not overmix.

Spoon or scoop batter into muffin cup pans coated with nonstick cooking spray. *Do not use paper liners.* Bake at 400 degrees F for 20 to 25 minutes or until done. Makes 15 muffins.

To make **Peanut Butter and Jelly Muffins**, after scooping batter into muffin pans, drop 1 teaspoon 100% pure fruit spread on the center tops of each muffin. To make **Chocolate Chunk Peanut Butter Muffins**, stir 1/3 cup chopped semi-sweet chocolate chips into dry ingredients.

Nutrition Facts: Calories 199, Protein 8.9 gm, Carbohydrate 23.1 gm, Dietary Fiber 3.2 gm, Fat 9.1 gm, Saturated Fat 1.6 gm, Monounsaturated Fat 4.2 gm, Sodium 152 mg
Meal Planning: 1 Lean Meat, 1 Carbohydrate, 1 Fat

Oriental Salad

This salad is so delicious— everyone will ask for the recipe.

2 packages *lower fat Oriental-style Ramen noodles
1 pound broccoli coleslaw
1 cup matchstick carrots
1 cup toasted sunflower seeds
1/2 cup sliced almonds, toasted
1/4 cup canola oil
1/4 cup apple cider vinegar
1/2 cup water
1/4 cup granulated sugar
1/4 cup Splenda® sugar substitute

Break up uncooked Ramen noodles while still in package. Pour into a large bowl, reserving 1 seasoning packet. Add broccoli coleslaw, sunflower seeds and almonds.

In a small bowl, combine remaining ingredients and add reserved Ramen seasoning packet. Toss to combine. Refrigerate for at least 1 hour before serving for flavors to blend and noodles to soften. Makes 20 servings (approximately 1/2 cup per serving.)

Lowfat ramen-style noodles are available at health food and specialty stores. Nissin® and Maruchan® brands Ramen noodles are available at most grocery stores and contain 7 to 8 grams total fat per serving– less than half of most brands.

Nutrition Facts: Calories 142, Protein 3.2 gm, Carbohydrate 11.7 gm, Dietary Fiber 1.7 gm, Fat 9.9 gm, Saturated Fat 1.5 gm, Monounsaturated Fat 4.6 gm, Sodium 187 mg
Meal Planning: 2 Vegetable, 2 Fat

Original Oriental Salad recipe from my sister-in-law Sandra Livingston from Jamestown, Pennsylvania.

Fabulous Falafel

Baking rather than deep-frying makes this falafel healthy and tasty.

1 can (15-ounce) garbanzo beans, drained and rinsed
3 green onions, sliced
1 tablespoon sesame oil
1 egg white
2 tablespoons fresh chopped parsley
2 teaspoons lemon juice
1 teaspoon ground cumin
2 cloves crushed garlic
1/4 teaspoon crushed red pepper
1/3 cup toasted wheat germ
1/4 cup dry whole wheat bread crumbs
1 cup nonfat sour cream
1 tablespoon dried chives [or 2 tablespoons fresh chopped]
1/8 teaspoon fresh ground black pepper
5 whole wheat pita halves
Tomato slices
Alfalfa sprouts

In a food processor or blender, combine garbanzo beans, onions, oil, egg white, parsley, lemon juice, cumin, garlic and red pepper. Process until nearly smooth. Transfer to a medium bowl and stir in wheat germ and bread crumbs. Shape mixture into five patties.

Coat a shallow baking pan with nonstick cooking spray. Place patties in pan and bake at 350 degrees F for 15 minutes or until heated through.

In a small bowl, combine sour cream, chives and black pepper. Whip with a wire whisk until smooth. Serve falafel in whole wheat pita bread with tomato slices, alfalfa sprouts and sour cream-chive mixture. For a balanced meal, serve with a fresh fruit salad and lowfat yogurt. Makes 5 servings.

Nutrition Facts: Calories 339, Protein 14.2 gm, Carbohydrate 59 gm, Dietary Fiber 10 gm, Fat 5.9 gm, Saturated Fat 0.9 gm, Monounsaturated Fat 3.8 gm, Sodium 456 mg
Meal Planning: 2 Lean Meat/Protein, 3 Carbohydrate, 1 Vegetable

Monterey Lentil Burgers

Another great alternative to burgers.

1/3 cup dried lentils
1/4 cup bulgur
1¾ cups water
 1 egg white, lightly beaten
1/3 cup dry whole wheat bread crumbs
1/4 cup shredded lowfat Monterey Jack cheese
1/4 cup shredded carrot
2 tablespoons fresh chopped parsley [or 1 tablespoon dried]
1/2 teaspoon dried basil
1/4 teaspoon ground cumin
1 clove crushed garlic
1/8 teaspoon salt
1/8 teaspoon fresh ground black pepper
2 tablespoons sesame or extra virgin olive oil

Rinse, sort and drain lentils. In a small saucepan, combine lentils, bulgur and water. Bring to a boil; reduce heat. Cover and simmer for 30 to 40 minutes or until tender. Drain off any liquid.

In a medium bowl, mash lentil mixture slightly. Add egg white, bread crumbs, cheese, carrots, parsley, basil, cumin, garlic, salt and pepper. Mix well with a fork. Shape into four patties.

Spray a large skillet with nonstick cooking spray. Heat skillet over medium heat. Add olive oil and heat. Place prepared patties in hot oil and cook for 6 minutes or until golden, turning once. Recoat skillet with nonstick cooking spray before turning to cook second side. For a balanced meal, serve with whole grain rolls, lettuce and tomato slices, homemade lowfat potato chips and sliced nectarine. Makes 4 servings.

Nutrition Facts: Calories 205, Protein 9.9 gm, Carbohydrate 22.9 gm, Dietary Fiber 7.6 gm, Fat 8.9 gm, Saturated Fat 1.8 gm, Monounsaturated Fat 5.5 mg, Sodium 199 mg
Meal Planning: 1 Lean Meat/Protein, 1 Carbohydrate, 1 Vegetable, 1 Fat

Olive-Caper Sauce

For the olive lover.

1/3 cup coarsely chopped walnuts
1 tablespoon extra virgin olive oil
1 small red onion, chopped
20 small Calamata olives, pitted and chopped
10 sun-dried tomato halves, rehydrated and chopped
1/4 cup fresh coarsely chopped basil
1 tablespoon dried marjoram
1/8 teaspoon fresh ground black pepper
1/2 cup low sodium vegetable broth
2 tablespoons dry white wine, optional
2 tablespoons capers, well drained and rinsed
1/4 cup freshly grated Romano cheese

Coat a large skillet with nonstick cooking spray. Heat skillet over medium-high heat. Add walnuts and toast, stirring constantly, about 1 minute. Remove walnuts from skillet and set aside.

Add oil to skillet and heat. Add onion, olives, tomatoes, basil, marjoram and pepper. Sauté for 1 minute. Reduce heat to medium and continue cooking, stirring frequently, until onion is tender. Stir in broth, wine and capers. Reduce heat to low and simmer for 10 to 12 minutes, until liquid reduces slightly.

Serve over whole wheat pasta, couscous or brown rice. Sprinkle with Romano cheese. For a balanced meal, serve with Romaine lettuce salad and lowfat cottage cheese topped with fresh fruit. Makes 4 servings.

Nutrition Facts: Calories 129, Protein 4.5 gm, Carbohydrate 7.6 gm,
Dietary Fiber 1.4 gm, Fat 9.3 gm, Saturated Fat 2.1 gm,
Monounsaturated Fat 5.1 gm, Sodium 614 mg
Meal Planning: 1/2 Lean Meat/Protein, 1 Vegetable, 1½ Fat

Ziti Medley

A fantastic combination of flavors, aromas and textures.

6 ounces whole wheat penne pasta
2 teaspoons extra virgin olive oil
1 large red bell pepper, seeded and cut into thin slices
1 large green bell pepper, seeded and cut into thin slices
1 pound fresh asparagus, cut into 1½-inch pieces
2 cloves crushed garlic
1 tablespoon lemon juice
3/4 cup nonfat ricotta cheese
3/4 cup nonfat sour cream
1/4 cup freshly grated Parmesan cheese
1/4 cup almond slivers, toasted

In a large stockpot, cook pasta in a large amount of boiling water according to package directions. *Do add salt and oil.* Stir occasionally while boiling. Drain and set aside.

Meanwhile, coat a large skillet with nonstick cooking spray. Place skillet over medium heat and add oil. Add peppers, asparagus and garlic. Sauté for 3 minutes or until tender-crisp. Stir in lemon juice. Remove from heat; set aside.

Combine ricotta cheese and sour cream in a food processor or blender. Cover and process until smooth. Add ricotta mixture to reserved pepper mixture; toss well to mix thoroughly.

Combine cooked pasta and pepper-cheese mixture in a large bowl. Toss well and sprinkle with Parmesan cheese and almonds. For a balanced meal, serve with mixed baby greens and arugula salad with fresh raspberries and lowfat vinaigrette dressing. Makes 6 servings (approximately 1 to 1¼ cups per serving).

Nutrition Facts: Calories 240, Protein 14.2 gm, Carbohydrate 28.7 gm, Dietary Fiber 4.8 gm, Fat 7.4 gm, Saturated Fat 1.8 gm, Monounsaturated Fat 4.2 gm, Sodium 169 mg, Calcium 242 mg
Meal Planning: 2 Lean Meat/Protein, 1 Carbohydrate, 2 Vegetable

Roma & Pine Pasta Salad

A great pasta salad sure to ward off any vampires— lots of garlic!

8 ounces angel hair pasta
8 ounces whole wheat angel hair pasta
3/4 cup red wine vinegar
1/2 cup extra virgin olive oil
1/4 cup water
6 cloves crushed garlic
1/2 teaspoon salt
1/2 teaspoon fresh ground black pepper
4 teaspoons granulated sugar
8 to 10 large Roma tomatoes, chopped
1/4 cup fresh chopped basil
1/2 cup toasted pine (pignolia) nuts
1/3 cup freshly shaved Parmesan cheese

In a large stockpot, cook pasta in a large amount of boiling water according to package directions. *Do add salt and oil.* Stir occasionally while boiling. Drain and place in a large pasta bowl. Set aside.

In a small bowl, combine vinegar, oil, water, garlic, salt, pepper and sugar. Whip with a wire whisk to blend and pour over reserved pasta. Toss to combine.

Stir in chopped tomatoes, basil, nuts and cheese. Toss to combine. For a balanced meal, serve with grilled chicken breasts, lowfat Caesar salad and fresh fruit slices. Makes 10 servings (approximately 1 cup per serving).

Nutrition Facts: Calories 327, Protein 10 gm, Carbohydrate 38.4 gm, Dietary Fiber 4.2 gm, Fat 15.8 gm, Saturated Fat 2.9 gm, Monounsaturated Fat 9.5 gm, Sodium 170 mg
Meal Planning: 1 Lean Meat/Protein, 2 Carbohydrate, 1 Vegetable, 2 Fat

Original Roma & Pine Pasta Salad recipe from my sister-in-law Joy Livingston from Mission Viejo, California.

Chesapeake-Style Soy Cakes

Using canned soybeans saves so much time– these cakes are great.

1 can (15-ounce) soybeans, drained and rinsed
2 tablespoons fresh chopped parsley [or 1 tablespoon dried]
1 cup fresh whole wheat bread crumbs
1/2 teaspoon crushed thyme
1/2 teaspoon salt
1/2 cup finely chopped onion
1/4 teaspoon fresh ground black pepper
2 cloves crushed garlic
1 egg, lightly beaten [or 1/4 cup soy yogurt or silken tofu]
1/4 cup shredded carrots
1/4 cup texturized soy protein [or 1/4 cup whole wheat bread crumbs]
1 fresh lemon
1 to 2 tablespoons extra virgin olive oil

Place soybeans in a large bowl. Coarsely mash soybeans. Add remaining ingredients, except lemon and oil.

Cut lemon in half and squeeze juice from one-half into soy mixture. Reserve other half for another use. Mix with a fork until soy mixture is well combined. Form into 8 patties.

Coat a large skillet with nonstick cooking spray. Heat over medium heat. Add oil and heat. Place patties into hot skillet and flatten with a nonstick spatula. Cook for 2 minutes or until bottom is golden. Turn and cook second side until golden and heated through. Recoat pan with nonstick cooking spray before turning to cook second side. Makes 4 servings (2 patties per serving).

Nutrition Facts: Calories 313, Protein 18.1 gm, Carbohydrate 31.4 gm,
Dietary Fiber 9.2 gm, Fat 14.7 gm, Saturated Fat 2.5 gm,
Monounsaturated Fat 7.8 gm, Sodium 529 mg
Meal Planning: 2 Lean Meat/Protein, 1 Carbohydrate, 1 Vegetable

Chocolate Walnut Brownies

Use cocoa powder in baking to avoid the saturated fat in cocoa butter.

1/3 cup canola or extra virgin olive oil
1/2 cup granulated sugar
1/4 cup Splenda® sugar substitute
1 teaspoon pure vanilla extract
1/2 cup egg substitute
1/2 cup all-purpose flour
1/3 cup chopped walnuts
1/3 cup unsweetened cocoa powder
1/4 teaspoon baking powder
Pinch salt

Line a 9-inch square baking pan with foil, leaving edges of foil hanging out over the edges of the pan. Coat with nonstick cooking spray and set aside.

In a large bowl, combine oil, sugar, Splenda, vanilla and eggs. Whip with a wire whisk or electric mixer.

In a small bowl, combine flour, walnuts, cocoa, baking powder and salt. Stir into oil mixture just until moistened.

Spread batter into prepared baking pan. Bake at 350 degrees F for 20 to 25 minutes. Brownies should be set but shiny on top. Remove from pan by lifting edges of foil and placing on a flat surface to completely cool before cutting. Makes 12 brownies.

Nutrition Facts: Calories 131, Protein 2.3 gm, Carbohydrate 14 gm,
Dietary Fiber 1 gm, Fat 8.0 gm, Saturated Fat 1.2 gm,
Monounsaturated Fat 4.9 gm, Cholesterol 0 mg, Sodium 39 mg
Meal Planning: 1 Carbohydrate, 1½ Fat

Peanut Butter Brownies

Be sure not to overbake these yummy brownies.

2 eggs [or 1/2 cup egg substitute]
1/4 cup pure maple syrup or honey
1/3 cup Splenda® sugar substitute
1/4 cup dark brown sugar
1/4 cup chunky peanut butter
1 tablespoon canola oil
3 tablespoons evaporated skimmed milk
2 teaspoons pure vanilla extract
1 cup whole wheat pastry flour
1/3 cup all-purpose flour
1 tablespoon baking powder
Pinch salt
1/4 cup unsalted chopped peanuts, optional

Line a 9-inch square baking pan with foil, leaving edges of foil hanging out over the edges of the pan. Coat with nonstick cooking spray and set aside.

In a large bowl, combine eggs, syrup, Splenda, sugar, peanut butter, oil, milk and vanilla. Beat with an electric mixer at medium speed until thoroughly blended.

In a medium bowl, combine flours, baking powder and salt. Add to peanut butter mixture and beat at low speed until mixture is smooth.

Spread batter in prepared baking pan. Sprinkle with chopped peanuts if desired. Bake at 350 degrees F for 30 minutes or until lightly golden. Brownies should be set but shiny on top. Remove from pan by lifting edges of foil and placing on a flat surface; cut into 12 squares while warm. Makes 12 brownies.

Nutrition Facts: Calories 142, Protein 4.6 gm, Carbohydrate 19.3 gm,
Dietary Fiber 2 gm, Fat 5.9 gm, Saturated Fat 1.0 gm,
Monounsaturated Fat 2.8 gm, Sodium 141 mg
Meal Planning: 1 Carbohydrate, 1 Fat

Sticks and stones
may break my bones.
African Proverb

Healthy people ensure an adequate daily calcium intake to build adequate bone mass and prevent osteoporosis.

- Choose 2 to 3 servings of lowfat (1%) or fat-free milk and dairy products everyday. The lower in fat the higher in calcium— 1% lowfat milk provides 300 milligrams (mg) calcium and fat-free milk provides 302 mg.
- Got milk? Take advantage of the lactose in milk, which helps our bodies better absorb calcium. Plus the vitamin D in milk helps deposit calcium in our bones.
- Drink a full 8 ounces of lowfat or fat-free milk at breakfast rather than just a splash on your cereal. Or try a fruited yogurt or yogurt smoothie for a quick breakfast.
- Drink a refreshing, satiating glass of lowfat milk for coffee breaks, lunch and dinner rather than bone depleting soft drinks, coffee, alcohol or other caffeinated beverages.
- Select calcium-rich snacks such as fruited yogurt, lowfat cheesesticks or sugarfree pudding.
- Other foods that contain calcium include tofu, soybeans, canned fish with bones and dark-green leafy vegetables.
- Choose 2 to 3 daily servings of calcium-fortified soy milk products, orange juice and cereals if lactose or milk intolerant.
- Substitute pureed cottage or ricotta cheese for cream in cream sauce or soup recipes. Or use fat-free half and half in place of whole or 2% milk in cream soup recipes.
- Limit caffeine, soda pop and coffee intake, which can inhibit calcium absorption.
- Take 1,000 to 1,200 milligrams calcium daily, if necessary, to ensure adequate daily calcium intake. For optimal absorption, take calcium supplements with food and do not take them with soft drinks, coffee or iron supplements.

Hot Pepper Cheese Dip

This has been a staple appetizer in our family for many years.

1 cup nonfat sour cream
8 ounces (2 cups) shredded lowfat hot pepper cheese
4 ounces (1 cup) shredded lowfat extra sharp Cheddar cheese
1 cup chopped fresh mushrooms
1 cup diced fresh tomatoes
3 green onions, finely chopped
1 large green bell pepper, seeded and finely chopped
10 black olives, chopped
Lowfat or baked tortilla chips

Spread sour cream on a large round platter. Sprinkle cheeses evenly over sour cream. Top with mushrooms, tomatoes, onions, pepper and olives. Cover and refrigerate until ready to serve.

Serve with lowfat or baked tortilla chips. Makes approximately 12 appetizer servings (1/4 cup per serving).

Nutrition Facts: Calories 113, Protein 9.1 gm, Carbohydrate 5.4 gm, Dietary Fiber 0.5 gm, Fat 5.5 gm, Saturated Fat 3.1 gm, Sodium 222 mg, Calcium 197 mg
Meal Planning: 1 Lean Meat/Protein, 1 Vegetable

Original Hot Pepper Cheese Dip recipe from my sister Jill Livingston from Hartstown, Pennsylvania

Radish Dip

This cruciferous dip has a nice zip to it.

1/2 cup plain nonfat yogurt
1/2 cup lite sour cream
1 cup radishes, cut in half
1/4 cup lite mayonnaise
1/4 teaspoon hot sauce
1/4 teaspoon salt
1/8 teaspoon fresh ground black pepper

Drain yogurt using a cheese cloth. Place in a medium bowl and stir in sour cream. Set aside.

In a food processor or blender, coarsely chop radishes, pulsing several times.

Add mayonnaise, hot sauce, salt and pepper. Pulse several times or until well combined. Add to yogurt mixture; stir well. Cover and chill to blend flavors. Garnish with sliced radish, if desired.

Serve with assorted cruciferous vegetables such as broccoli, cauliflower, broccoflower and kohlrabi. Makes 1½ cups dip (1/4 cup per serving).

Nutrition Facts: Calories 30, Protein 1.8 gm, Carbohydrate 3.6 gm, Dietary Fiber 0.3 gm, Fat 1 gm, Saturated Fat 0.3 gm, Sodium 163 mg, Calcium 49 mg
Meal Planning: 1 Vegetable

Walnut Cheese Ball

A cheese ball that rivals all others but without all the fat.

8 ounces fat-free cream cheese
8 ounces reduced fat cream cheese
8 ounces (2 cups) shredded lowfat extra sharp Cheddar cheese
1/4 cup lite mayonnaise
1/4 cup finely chopped green bell pepper
1 small onion, finely chopped
1/3 cup finely chopped walnuts
Lowfat crackers or whole grain melba toast

In a medium bowl, soften cream cheeses with a wooden spoon.

Add cheddar cheese, mayonnaise, green pepper and onion. Mix with a wooden spoon until well combined. Refrigerate for 1 hour to firm.

With hands, roll into a ball or log. Refrigerate for at least 1 hour.

Roll in chopped nuts when firm enough to handle. Serve with lowfat crackers or melba toast. Makes 1 large cheese ball (approximately 2 tablespoons per appetizer serving).

Nutrition Facts: Calories 98, Protein 7.8 gm, Carbohydrate 2.1 gm,
Dietary Fiber 0.1 gm, Fat 6.4 gm, Saturated 3.7 gm,
Sodium 233 mg, Calcium 137 mg
Meal Planning: 1 Lean Meat/Protein, 1/2 Fat

*Original Cheese Ball recipe from my friend and fellow dietitian
Brenda Warren, RD from Conneaut, Ohio*

Stuffed Mushrooms

A quick and easy appetizer to serve before any meal.

12 extra large fresh mushrooms
4 teaspoons low sodium soy sauce
1/2 cup shredded lowfat Jarlsberg cheese
2 cloves crushed garlic
1/4 teaspoon fresh ground black pepper

Wash and scrub mushrooms. Carefully twist and remove stems. Set mushroom caps aside. Finely chop mushroom stems.

In a small bowl, combine chopped stems with soy sauce, cheese, garlic and pepper. Stuff into reserved mushroom caps.

Place caps in a 9 x 13-inch baking pan coated with nonstick cooking spray. Broil several inches from heat source until cheese melts, using caution not to burn.

Remove from baking dish with a slotted spatula and transfer to a serving platter. Makes 6 appetizer servings (2 mushrooms per serving). May also be prepared in the microwave.

Nutrition Facts: Calories 40, Protein 3.6 gm, Carbohydrate 2.5 gm,
Dietary Fiber 0.6 gm, Fat 1.8 gm, Saturated Fat 1.0 gm,
Sodium 162 gm, Calcium 57 mg
Meal Planning: 1 Vegetable, 1/2 Fat

Clam Pie Appetizer

Vary the garlic in this appetizer for a great spread– pass out the mints!

2 cans (8-ounce each) minced clams, undrained
1 cup dry whole wheat bread crumbs
2 tablespoons extra virgin olive oil
4 tablespoons olive oil tub margarine, melted
2 to 3 cloves crushed garlic
1 tablespoon dried oregano
2 tablespoons dried parsley
1/4 teaspoon fresh ground black pepper
1/4 teaspoon ground white pepper
1 cup shredded part-skim mozzarella cheese
1/2 cup shredded nonfat mozzarella cheese
1/4 cup freshly grated Parmesan cheese

In a medium bowl, combine clams in juice, bread crumbs, oil, melted margarine, garlic, oregano, parsley and pepper. Spread mixture evenly in a deep 9-inch pie pan coated with nonstick cooking spray.

Combine cheeses and sprinkle evenly over clam mixture.

Bake at 350 degrees F for 30 minutes or until cheese melts and starts to brown. Serve hot with lowfat crackers or whole grain melba toast.

Clam Pie may be assembled in advance and frozen prior to baking. Thaw in the refrigerator before baking. Makes 24 appetizer servings (approximately 2 tablespoons per serving).

Whole Wheat Bread Crumbs: *To make soft whole wheat bread crumbs, crumble 2 to 3 day old whole wheat bread into small bits using your hands or shred between 2 forks. For dry bread crumbs, spread on a baking sheet and bake at 350 degrees F for 10 to 12 minutes or until toasted. Let cool.*

Nutrition Facts: Calories 44, Protein 2.6 gm, Carbohydrate 1.2 gm, Dietary Fiber 0.1 gm, Fat 3.2 gm, Saturated Fat 1 gm, Sodium 132 mg, Calcium 84 mg
Meal Planning: 1/2 Lean Meat

Original Clam Pie recipe from my friend and fellow dietitian Eileen Scutella, RD from Erie, Pennsylvania

Artichoke-Parmesan Spread

Everyone digs into this spread– artichokes are surprisingly popular.

1 cup 1% lowfat cottage cheese
1/2 cup freshly grated Parmesan cheese
2 tablespoons nonfat mayonnaise
2 tablespoons nonfat sour cream
1 tablespoon extra virgin olive oil
2 cloves crushed garlic
1 can (14-ounce) marinated artichoke hearts, packed in olive oil

In a food processor or blender, combine cottage cheese, Parmesan cheese, mayonnaise, sour cream and garlic. Process until mixture is smooth, scraping sides of processor bowl as needed.

Add artichokes and 2 tablespoons of the olive oil marinade. Pulse several times to chop artichokes.

Spoon artichoke mixture into a 1-quart baking dish coated with nonstick cooking spray. Bake at 350 degrees F for 20 minutes or until thoroughly heated.

Serve Artichoke-Parmesan Spread with whole grain melba toast or lowfat crackers. Makes 16 appetizer servings.

Nutrition Facts: Calories 50, Protein 3.6 gm, Carbohydrate 3.5 gm,
Dietary Fiber 1.1 gm, Fat 2.6 gm, Saturated Fat 0.8 gm,
Sodium 150 mg, Calcium 55 mg
Meal Planning: 1/2 Lean Meat/Protein/ 1 Vegetable

Pistachio Salad

Adding dry milk powder is an easy (and sneaky) way to boost calcium.

1 can (20-ounce) crushed pineapple, packed in juice
1 can (8-ounce) mandarin oranges, packed in juice, well drained
1 small package sugarfree instant pistachio pudding
1¼ cups plain nonfat yogurt
1/2 cup nonfat dry milk powder
1/3 cup chopped pistachios

Drain crushed pineapple, reserving juice. Set aside. Drain mandarin oranges and discard juice.

In a deep bowl, add reserved pineapple juice, pudding mix, yogurt and dry milk. Whip with a wire whisk for 1 to 2 minutes or until well blended.

Stir in crushed pineapple and mandarin oranges. Pour at once into 8 serving dishes. Pistachio Salad is best if refrigerated before serving. Makes 8 servings (approximately 1/2 cup per serving).

Nutrition Facts: Calories 129, Protein 6.2 gm, Carbohydrate 24 gm,
Dietary Fiber 1.8 gm, Fat 1.5 gm, Saturated Fat 0.3 gm,
Sodium 123 mg, Calcium 181 mg
Meal Planning: 1 Lean Meat/Protein, 1 Carbohydrate

Cottage Cheese Pancakes

Using a few yolks maintains the flavor— the whites provide the fluff.

6 eggs, separated
1/8 teaspoon cream of tartar
2¼ cups 1% lowfat cottage cheese
2/3 cup whole wheat pastry flour
3 tablespoons nonfat dry milk powder
2 tablespoons granulated sugar
1/8 teaspoon salt
Dash of ground cinnamon

Separate eggs. Reserve all 6 whites. Reserve 2 yolks and discard the remaining yolks. Set aside.

In a deep bowl, beat the egg whites with cream of tartar until stiff but not dry. Set aside.

In a large bowl, beat the 2 egg yolks, cottage cheese, flour, dry milk, sugar, salt and cinnamon with an electric mixer. Gently fold stiff egg whites into cottage cheese mixture.

Coat a griddle or skillet generously with nonstick cooking spray. Heat for a few minutes over medium heat. (Griddle is ready when a drop of water skids across the griddle.) Drop batter by large spoonfuls onto the heated griddle or skillet. Grill the pancakes over medium heat until puffy and golden brown. Turn to brown second side. Serve at once with pure fruit spread, pumpkin butter, apple butter, fresh grated nutmeg or a small amount of Pennsylvania pure maple syrup. For a balanced meal, serve with fresh fruit salad. Makes 6 servings (approximately 4 to 5 pancakes per serving).

Nutrition Facts: Calories 167, Protein 17.5 gm, Carbohydrate 17.7 gm, Dietary Fiber 1.6 gm, Fat 2.9 gm, Saturated Fat 1.1 gm, Sodium 458 mg, Calcium 100 mg
Meal Planning: 2 Lean Meat/Protein, 1 Carbohydrate

Winter Vegetable Soup

One of the best soups you'll ever taste– surprisely sweet.

2 tablespoons olive oil tub margarine
1 medium onion, sliced
2 cups diced carrots (fresh or frozen)
1½ cups rutabaga, peeled and diced
1 medium potato, unpeeled and diced
2 large parsnips, peeled and diced
2 cups low sodium vegetable broth
1 bay leaf
1 tablespoon cornstarch
1½ cups 1% milk
1/2 cup evaporated skimmed milk
1/2 teaspoon salt
1/4 teaspoon fresh ground black pepper
1/4 teaspoon ground white pepper
1 cup frozen petite green peas, thawed

Coat a large saucepot with nonstick cooking spray. Add margarine and melt over medium heat. Add onion, carrots, rutabagas, potato and parsnips. Reduce heat, cover and cook over low heat for 10 minutes. Add broth and bay leaf and simmer for 30 minutes.

In a small bowl, blend cornstarch with a small amount of 1% milk, then add to soup. Pour remaining 1% milk and evaporated milk into soup and heat, stirring until soup thickens. Do not boil. Remove bay leaf and season with salt and pepper.

Stir in green peas and simmer over low heat to heat peas. Adjust seasonings. For a balanced meal, serve with mixed greens tossed salad and lowfat yogurt topped with fresh fruit and lowfat granola. Makes 4 servings (approximately 2 cups per serving).

Nutrition Facts: Calories 244, Protein 10.7 gm, Carbohydrate 38.5 gm,
Dietary Fiber 8 gm, Fat 5.6 gm, Saturated Fat 1.2 gm,
Sodium 651 mg, Calcium 305 mg
Meal Planning: 1 Lean Meat/Protein, 2 Carbohydrate, 1 Vegetable

Golden Vegetable Soup

Rutabaga is not the prettiest vegetable but it has a great sweet flavor.

4 cups diced carrots (fresh or frozen)
1½ cups rutabaga, peeled and chopped
2 small leeks, chopped
1 large Yukan gold potato, unpeeled and diced
4 cups low sodium vegetable broth
3/4 cup 1% milk
1/2 cup fat-free half and half
1/2 teaspoon salt
1/4 teaspoon fresh ground black pepper
1/4 teaspoon ground white pepper

In a large saucepot, combine all vegetables and broth. Bring to boil over medium-high heat. Reduce heat, cover and simmer for 30 minutes.

In a food processor or blender, process cooked vegetable mixture to a puree.

Return puree to saucepot. Gradually stir in milk and half and half. Season with salt and peppers.

Reheat over low heat. Do not boil. Adjust seasonings. Makes 4 servings (approximately 2 cups per serving).

Nutrition Facts: Calories 159, Protein 8.3 gm, Carbohydrate 30.9 gm,
Dietary Fiber 5.3 gm, Fat 1 gm, Saturated Fat 0.4 gm,
Sodium 677 mg, Calcium 266 mg
Meal Planning: 1 Lean Meat/Protein, 1 Carbohydrate, 2 Vegetable

Florentine Asparagus Soup

Spinach and asparagus combine for a delicious cream soup.

1½ pounds fresh spinach
1/2 pound fresh asparagus
2 tablespoons olive oil tub margarine
1 medium vidalia onion, chopped
1/4 cup all-purpose flour, divided
2½ cups low sodium vegetable or chicken broth
1/2 teaspoon salt
1/4 teaspoon fresh ground black pepper
1/4 teaspoon ground white pepper
1/4 teaspoon freshly grated nutmeg [or 1/4 teaspoon ground]
2 cups 1% milk
3/4 cup fat-free half and half

Wash spinach thoroughly and discard stalks. Wash and trim hard stalks from asparagus. Cook spinach and asparagus in a large saucepot over medium heat until tender. Set aside.

Coat a large saucepot with nonstick cooking spray. Add margarine and melt over medium heat. Add onion and cook until soft. Blend in 2 tablespoons flour and cook for 1 minute. Add cooked vegetables and broth. Simmer for 15 minutes. Season with salt and peppers. Add nutmeg.

In a food processor or blender, process soup mixture to a puree. Return to saucepot.

In a small bowl, combine remaining 2 tablespoons flour with a small amount of 1% milk. Gradually add flour mixture and remaining milks to soup. Reheat gently until thickened. Do not boil. Adjust seasonings. Makes 4 servings (approximately 1½ to 2 cups per serving).

Nutrition Facts: Calories 206, Protein 13.9 gm, Carbohydrate 25.5 gm,
Dietary Fiber 4.3 gm, Fat 6 gm, Saturated Fat 1.5 gm,
Sodium 729 mg, Calcium 452 mg
Meal Planning: 2 Lean Meat/Protein, 1 Carbohydrate, 1 Vegetable

Mushroom Crusted Quiche

The mushroom crust is so unique you'll use it again and again.

2 tablespoons extra virgin olive oil
1/2 pound mushrooms, coarsely chopped
1/2 cup finely crushed saltine or lowfat butter-flavored crackers
3/4 cup chopped green onion
3/4 cup shredded lowfat Jarlsberg cheese
1 cup 1% lowfat cottage cheese
3 eggs [or 3/4 cup egg substitute]
1/4 teaspoon ground cayenne pepper
1/4 teaspoon fresh ground black pepper
1/4 teaspoon ground paprika

Coat a large skillet with nonstick cooking spray. Heat skillet. Add oil and heat over medium heat. Add mushrooms and cook until limp. Stir in crushed crackers, then turn mixture into a deep 9-inch pie pan coated with nonstick cooking spray. Press mixture evenly over pan bottom and up the sides.

Coat skillet again with nonstick cooking spray. Add onion and cook until limp. Spread onions over mushroom crust. Sprinkle Jarlsberg cheese evenly over onions.

In a food processor or blender, process cottage cheese, eggs, cayenne and black pepper until smooth. Pour into crust and sprinkle with paprika. Bake at 350 degrees F for 20 to 25 minutes or until a knife inserted just off center comes out clean. Let stand for 10 to 15 minutes before cutting. For a balanced meal, serve with lowfat muffins and fresh melon slices. Makes 6 servings.

Nutrition Facts: Calories 301, Protein 13.8 gm, Carbohydrate 32.2 gm, Dietary Fiber 1.8 gm, Fat 12.9 gm, Saturated Fat 3.0 gm, Monounsaturated Fat 7 gm, Sodium 732 mg, Calcium 127 mg
Meal Planning: 2 Lean Meat/Protein, 2 Carbohydrate, 1 Fat

Cheese Vegetable Fajitas

Take advantage of seasonal vegetables to add variety to this recipe.

1 tablespoon sesame oil
3 cloves crushed garlic
1 large vidalia onion, sliced
1 large red bell pepper, seeded and sliced
1 large green bell pepper, seeded and sliced
1 large yellow bell pepper, seeded and sliced
1/2 teaspoon ground cumin
1/4 teaspoon fresh ground black pepper
1/2 cup green enchilada sauce
4 tablespoons fat-free cream cheese
1 cup part-skim mozzarella cheese
1 cup nonfat mozzarella cheese
1/2 avocado, cut into thin slices
4 fajita-style whole wheat or spinach tortillas

Coat a large skillet with nonstick cooking spray. Heat over medium-high heat; add oil and heat. Add garlic and sauté for 30 seconds until golden. Add sliced onions and peppers and sauté for 1 to 2 minutes to begin to carmelize vegetables. Season with cumin and black pepper. Add enchilada sauce and stir to thoroughly coat.

To serve, spread fat-free cream cheese over each tortilla. Evenly distribute cheeses, sautéed vegetables and avocado slices between tortillas. Top with coarsely chopped lettuce and chopped tomatoes if desired. Fold up bottom of tortilla; fold in both sides and roll up. For a balanced meal, serve with refried black beans and sliced papaya. Makes 4 servings.

Nutrition Facts: Calories 278, Protein 15.1 gm, Carbohydrate 27.9 gm, Dietary Fiber 5.7 gm, Fat 12.2 gm, Saturated Fat 3.8 gm, Monounsaturated Fat 4.2 gm, Sodium 640 mg, Calcium 388 mg
Meal Planning: 2 Lean Meat/Protein, 1 Carbohydrate, 2 Vegetable, 1 Fat

Cheese Enchiladas

A super quick meal to throw together after a long day.

1/2 cup shredded lowfat Monterey Jack cheese
1/2 cup shredded lowfat extra sharp Cheddar cheese
1/2 cup shredded nonfat mozzarella cheese
3 green onions, minced
1 tablespoon fresh chopped cilantro [or 1 teaspoon dried]
6 (6-inch) white or yellow corn tortillas
1 can (15-ounce) green enchilada sauce
1/2 cup nonfat sour cream

In a medium bowl, combine Monterey Jack cheese, 1/4 cup Cheddar cheese, mozzarella cheese, green onions and cilantro.

Spread about 1/4 cup cheese filling down the center of each tortilla. Roll up and place in a 9-inch microwave-safe dish. Repeat with remaining tortillas.

Pour enchilada sauce over prepared enchiladas. Sprinkle with remaining Cheddar cheese.

Cover loosely with wax paper and microwave on HIGH for 3 to 4 minutes or until steaming.

To serve, spoon sour cream down the center of enchiladas. For a balanced meal, serve with coarsely chopped Romaine lettuce, chopped tomatoes, refried beans and sliced mangos and bananas. Makes 6 enchiladas.

Nutrition Facts: Calories 188, Protein 11.4 gm, Carbohydrate 20.2 gm, Dietary Fiber 2.1 gm, Fat 6.7 gm, Saturated Fat 3.7 gm, Sodium 337 mg, Calcium 336 mg
Meal Planning: 1½ Lean Meat/Protein, 1 Carbohydrate, 1 Vegetable

Quick Macaroni & Cheese

Quick doesn't always mean it has to come from a blue box.

4 ounces farfalle (bow-tie) pasta
4 ounces whole wheat farfalle pasta
1 cup 1% milk
2 tablespoons all-purpose flour
2 ounces (1/2 cup) diced lowfat American cheese
2 ounces (1/2 cup) shredded lowfat extra sharp Cheddar cheese
3 tablespoons freshly grated Parmesan cheese
1 teaspoon extra virgin olive oil
1/2 teaspoon salt
1/2 teaspoon butter-flavored sprinkles
1/4 teaspoon ground white pepper
1/4 teaspoon fresh ground black pepper

In a large stockpot, cook pasta in a large amount of boiling water according to package directions. *Do not add salt or oil.* Stir occasionally while boiling. Drain well.

Meanwhile, combine remaining ingredients in a large saucepan. Cook over medium heat until thickened and cheese melts, stirring constantly with a wire whisk.

Pour cheese sauce over cooked pasta and stir to combine and coat pasta. For a balanced meal, serve with steamed baby carrots and broccoli, mixed greens tossed salad and fresh melon slices. Makes 4 servings (approximately 1 cup per serving).

Nutrition Facts: Calories 349, Protein 20.1 gm, Carbohydrate 44.2 gm, Dietary Fiber 3.7 gm, Fat 8.9 gm, Saturated Fat 4.8 gm, Monounsaturated Fat 2.4 gm, Sodium 555 mg, Calcium 293 mg
Meal Planning: 3 Lean Meat/Protein, 3 Carbohydrate

Fettucine Spinach Toss

Nonfat ricotta cheese makes a rich fat-free cream sauce.

4 ounces whole wheat fettucine
Olive oil nonstick cooking spray
1 tablespoon extra virgin olive oil
1 clove crushed garlic
1 teaspoon dried basil leaves
1/8 teaspoon salt
1/8 teaspoon ground white pepper
2 tablespoons all-purpose flour
1 cup 1% milk
1 package (10-ounce) frozen chopped spinach, thawed
1/3 cup freshly grated Parmesan cheese
2 cups nonfat ricotta cheese

In a large stockpot, cook pasta in a large amount of boiling water according to package directions. *Do not add salt or oil.* Stir occasionally while boiling. Drain and set aside.

Coat a large skillet with nonstick cooking spray; add oil and heat over medium heat. Add garlic, salt, basil, pepper and flour. Remove from heat and coat flour mixture with cooking spray. Return to heat and stir until smooth and golden. Add milk. Cook over medium heat, stirring constantly with a whisk until mixture thickens. Do not boil.

Puree ricotta cheese in a food processor or blender until smooth. Add spinach, Parmesan cheese and pureed ricotta cheese to milk mixture. Stir until cheese melts and heats through. Do not boil.

Add cooked noodles to spinach mixture and stir to thoroughly combine. For a balanced meal, serve with steamed baby carrots and mixed grape salad. Makes 4 servings (approximately 1½ cups per serving).

Nutrition Facts: Calories 316, Protein 28.5 gm, Carbohydrate 36.2 gm,
Dietary Fiber 3.5 gm, Fat 8.1 gm, Saturated Fat 2.2 gm,
Monounsaturated Fat 3.3 gm, Sodium 585 mg, Calcium 744 mg
Meal Planning: 3 Lean Meat/Protein, 2 Carbohydrate

BrocCauli Alfredo

Save time by using frozen broccoli and cauliflower for this rich sauce.

4 ounces whole wheat linguine
4 ounces linguine
1 medium head cauliflower, cut into florets
1 large bunch broccoli, cut into florets
2 tablespoons olive oil tub margarine
2 tablespoons all-purpose flour
1/4 teaspoon salt
1/2 teaspoon fresh ground black pepper
1/2 teaspoon ground white pepper
1/2 teaspoon garlic powder
1½ cups 1% milk
1 cup evaporated skimmed milk
1/2 cup freshly grated Parmesan cheese

In a large stockpot, cook pasta in a large amount of boiling water until al dente, about 7 minutes. *Do not add salt or oil.* Stir occasionally while boiling. Drain. Return to stockpot and keep warm.

Meanwhile, in a covered microwave-safe bowl, microwave cauliflower and broccoli in 1/2 inch water until crisp-tender, about 5 minutes. Stir after 3 minutes. Drain and keep warm.

While vegetables are cooking, coat a large skillet with nonstick cooking spray. Add margarine and melt over medium heat. Add flour, salt, peppers and garlic powder. Cook, stirring constantly, for 1 minute or until flour begins to brown. Gradually stir in milks. Cook, stirring constantly, until mixture begins to thicken. Remove from heat and stir in Parmesan cheese.

In a large pasta bowl, combine linguine, vegetables and cheese sauce until well mixed. For a balanced meal, serve with baby mixed greens salad and fresh fruit. Makes 4 servings (approximately 2 cups per serving).

Nutrition Facts: Calories 408, Protein 22.6 gm, Carbohydrate 57 gm,
Dietary Fiber 8.1 gm, Fat 9.3 gm, Saturated Fat 3.7 gm,
Monounsaturated Fat 3.5 gm, Sodium 523 mg, Calcium 480 mg
Meal Planning: 3 Lean Meat/Protein, 2 Carbohydrate, 3 Vegetable

Never eat more than you can lift.

Miss Piggy

Healthy people balance their calorie intake to achieve or maintain a healthy weight throughout their lifetime.

- Focus on proper weight early in life and maintain weight as a lifelong strategy.
- Eat 3 meals daily and do not skip meals.
- Pay attention to hunger signals. If you eat in response to hunger, your body will signal when you've had enough to eat.
- Fill up and stay full on high fiber foods. Select foods with 3 or more grams of dietary fiber per serving. Strive for 25 to 40 grams daily or about 10 grams per meal.
- Reduce portion sizes and choose "human-sized" portions. Read food labels for serving sizes.
- Provide an abundant supply of fruits and vegetables. Save calories by filling half your plate with vegetables.
- Choose lowfat foods with 0 to 3 grams of fat per serving. Cut back on high fat foods such as fried foods and snack chips.
- Include protein at each meal for satiety. Select from fish, soy, poultry, lean meats, lowfat or fat-free milk products, dried beans and peas and other vegetarian alternatives.
- Monitor your weight on a regular basis and nip weight gain in the bud. Set weight loss goals in 10 pound increments.
- Limit the purchase and availability of empty calorie (high calorie, low nutritional value) foods and beverages.
- Practice positive self-talk. Focus on enjoying healthful foods.
- Celebrate the wide diversity of healthy foods to ensure variety of foods and freedom from boredom.
- Drink at least 6 cups of water daily.
- Use **Hand Planning**, the *Cooking for the Health of It* **Pyramid Planning** or *Eating for the Health of It* **Plate Planning** as guides for planning, balancing and portioning meals.

Hand Planning
for Portion Control

Plan a balanced meal using your hand as a guide for portion control. Your hands are appropriate in size to your body and may be used to approximate portion sizes to meet your nutritional needs for optimal health and wellness.

Your Fist
Portion of Whole Grain
Portion of Fresh Fruit

Your Open Hand
Portion of Vegetables

Your Palm
Portion of Meat/Protein

Tip of Your Thumb
Portion of Added Fat

242

Cooking for the Health of It
Pyramid Planning

Lowfat Milk Products
Choose 2 to 3 servings daily.

High Fiber Foods
Look for 3 or more grams of dietary fiber per serving.

Fats and Oils
Olive, Canola, Peanut & Nuts

Fish, Poultry, Lean Meat, Eggs, Soy and Alternatives

Fat-Free or Lowfat Milk & Milk Products

Whole Grain Breads & Cereals, Brown Rice, Pasta, Legumes, Potatoes and Other Minimally Processed Starches
Choose 1 to 2 servings per meal.

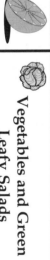

Fresh Fruit and Fruit Salads
Choose 3 to 4 servings daily.

Vegetables and Green Leafy Salads
Choose 3 to 5 servings daily.

Added Fats
Choose 1 to 2 servings per meal.

Fish, Poultry, Fish, Lean Meat, Eggs, Soy and Protein Alternatives
Choose 2 to 3 daily servings.

Low Fat Foods
Look for 3 or less grams of total fat per serving.

243

Plate Planning
Eating for the Health of It

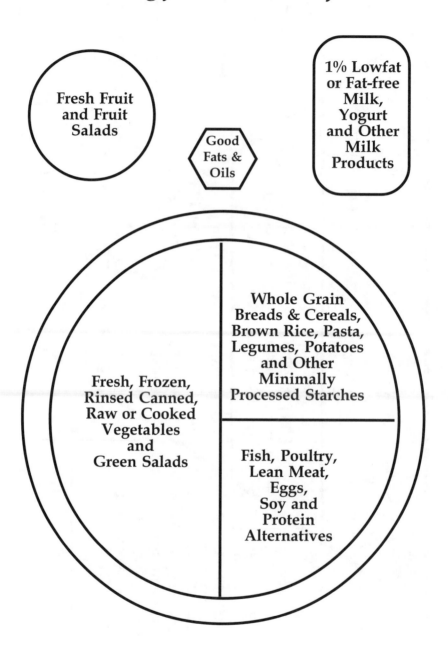

Fresh Fruit and Fruit Salads

1% Lowfat or Fat-free Milk, Yogurt and Other Milk Products

Good Fats & Oils

Fresh, Frozen, Rinsed Canned, Raw or Cooked Vegetables and Green Salads

Whole Grain Breads & Cereals, Brown Rice, Pasta, Legumes, Potatoes and Other Minimally Processed Starches

Fish, Poultry, Lean Meat, Eggs, Soy and Protein Alternatives

Give neither counsel nor salt till you are asked for it.

Italian Proverb

Healthy people enjoy the natural flavor of foods without excessive use of salt, sodium and salted foods.

- Limit daily sodium intake to less than 2,400 to 3,000 milligrams daily unless directed otherwise by your healthcare provider.
- Balance sodium intake throughout the day— consider 800 to 1,000 milligrams of sodium per meal.
- Choose more foods averaging less than 140 to 200 milligrams of sodium per serving.
- Select fewer processed and convenience foods. Be aware of very high sodium foods.
- Balance high sodium foods with low sodium foods.
- Most fresh, dried and canned fruit and fruit juices have little or no sodium content.
- Season with more dried or fresh herbs and spices.
- Use fresh lemon or lime juice to enhance the flavor of foods without salt.
- Be aware of salt (i.e. sodium chloride) in seasoning mixes, seasoning salts and herb and spice combination seasonings.
- For optimal flavor cook with fresh chopped onions, celery, peppers, chilies, parsley, chives and other fresh vegetables and herbs rather than ground, dried or powder seasonings.
- Select more highly flavored foods, such as reduced-fat extra sharp and aged cheeses, rather than mildly flavored foods, which often require more salt.
- For the best flavor cook with more garlic, using fresh garlic cloves or ready-to-use garlic rather than garlic powder or dried minced garlic.
- Take the salt shaker off the table.
- Recognize that a healthy diet does not mean sodium-free.

Cooking for the Health of It
Reduced-Sodium Seasoning

For recipes that serve 4 to 6 portions, use a combination of 1/2 teaspoon salt, 1/4 teaspoon fresh ground black pepper and 1/4 teaspoon ground white pepper. To save time, combine two parts salt, one part fresh ground black pepper and one part ground white pepper in a spice jar and use in *Cooking for the Health of It* recipes. This reduced-sodium seasoning will provide:

Number of Servings	Sodium Per Serving
4 Servings	266 milligrams
6 Servings	178 milligrams

A Well-Stocked Kitchen
Herbs & Seasonings

Fresh Lemons	Lemon Juice
Fresh Limes	Lime Juice
Garlic Cloves	Ready-to-Use Chopped Garlic
Onions — Vidalia, Sweet & Red	Frozen Chopped Onions
Celery and Celery Leaves	Frozen Chopped Peppers
Canned Diced Green Chilies	Fresh and Dried Parsley
Fresh and Dried Chives	Fresh and Dried Cilantro
Whole and Ground Cinnamon	Whole and Ground Nutmeg

Assorted Bell Peppers — Red, Green, Yellow & Orange

- Fresh grind whole spices for the best flavor and aroma using a mortar and pestle or coffee mill.
- Purchase high quality herbs and spices– do not be tempted by dollar store bargains.
- Use dried herbs within six months and ground spices within one year for optimal flavor.
- Plant an indoor or outdoor herb garden for the best herb flavor. Quick dry herbs in the microwave. Or puree in a blender or food processor and freeze in ice cube trays for use in soups, sauces and other recipes.

About Nutrition Facts

Nutrition Facts are provided for all recipes. Nutrition Facts were calculated using **MasterCook Deluxe**, Version 3.03, 1995 (Sierra® On-Line, Incorporated). All recipes provide nutrition analysis for:

Calories Per Serving
Protein [grams]
Carbohydrate [grams]
Dietary Fiber [grams]
Total Fat [grams]
Saturated Fat [grams]
Sodium [milligrams]

Selected recipes contain nutrition analysis for:
Monounsaturated Fat [grams]
Calcium [milligrams]

About Meal Planning

Meal Planning guidelines or servings are provided for all recipes. These meal planning guidelines are similar to diabetes and other diet exchanges:

1 Meat/Protein Serving = 35 to 55 Calories/1 to 3 grams Fat
1 Carbohydrate* = 70 to 80 Calories/15 grams Carbohydrate
1 Vegetable = 25 Calories
1 Fat = 45 Calories

*Dietary Fiber is subtracted from carbohydrate calculations when fiber exceeds 5 grams per serving.

Many recipes provide menu suggestions for balanced meal planning using the *3 Food Rule*. A balanced meal should consist of at least 3 foods:

1 Serving of Meat/Protein-Rich Food
1 Serving of Whole Grain or Minimally-Processed Starch
1 Serving of Fruit and/or Vegetable

References

1. National Health and Nutrition Examination Survey III, 1988-94, CDC/NCHS and the American Heart Association.

2. U.S. Decennial Life Tables for 1989-91, Vol. 1, No. 4, Sept 1999.

3. AHA *2002 Heart and Stroke Statistical Update*. AHA 2001.

4. Krauss RM, et al. AHA Dietary Guidelines: Revision 2000. *Circulation* 2000; 102:2284-99.

5. U.S. Department of Health and Human Services (HHS). HHS, ADA Warn Americans of "Pre-Diabetes." HHS News. March 27, 2002.

6. U.S. Department of HHS. The Surgeon General's call to action to prevent and decrease overweight and obesity. U.S. Department of HHS, Public Health Service, Office of the Surgeon General 2001.

7. Allison DB, et al. Annual deaths attributable to obesity in the United States. *JAMA* 1999; Oct 27;282(16):1530-8.

8. Flegal K, et al. Prevalence and Trends in Obesity Among U.S. Adults, 1999-2000. *JAMA* 2002; 288:1723-1727.

9. The Food Guide Pyramid. Adapted from U.S. Department of Agriculture (USDA), Center for Nutrition Policy and Promotion. Home and Garden Bulletin No. 252, 1996.

10. Dietary Guidelines. USDA and U.S. Department of HHS. Fifth Edition. Home and Garden Bulletin No. 232, 2000.

11. "America's Bone Health: The State of Osteoporosis and Low Bone Mass In Our Nation." National Osteoporosis Foundation 2002.

Health & Nutrition Resources

1. **American Diabetes Association** [www.diabetes.org]
   1701 North Beauregard Street, Alexandria VA 22311

2. **American Dietetic Association** [www.eatright.org]
   216 West Jackson Boulevard, Chicago IL 60606

3. **American Heart Association** [www.americanheart.org]
   7272 Greenville Avenue, Dallas TX 75231

4. **American Institute for Cancer Research** [www.aicr.org]
   1759 R Street NW, Washington DC 20009

5. **Centers for Disease Control & Prevention** [www.cdc.gov]
   1600 Clifton Road, Atlanta GA 30333

6. **National Cancer Institute** [cis.nci.nih.gov]
   Building 31, Room 10A16, 9000 Rockville Pike, Bethesda MD 20892

7. **National Heart, Lung & Blood Institute** [www.nhlbi.nih.gov]
   National Cholesterol Education Program
   [www.nhlbi.nih.gov/about/ncep]
   PO Box 30105, Bethesda MD 20824

8. **National Health Information Center** [www.healthfinder.gov]
   healthfinder® — Gateway to Reliable Consumer Health Information
   PO Box 1133, Washington DC 20013

9. **National Osteoporosis Foundation** [www.nof.org]
   1232 22nd Street NW, Washington DC 20037

10. **Office of Disease Prevention & Health Promotion**
    Office of Public Health & Science [www.odphp.osophs.dhhs.gov]
    200 Independence Avenue SW, Room 738G, Washington DC 20201

11. **Shape Up America!** [www.shapeup.org]
    4500 Connecticut Avenue NW, Suite 414, Washington DC 20008

12. **National Institute of Diabetes & Digestive & Kidney Diseases**
    [www.niddk.nih.gov]
    Building 31, Rm 9A04 Center Drive, MSC 2560, Bethesda MD 20892

13. **Mind-Body Wellness Center** [www.mind-body.org]
    18201 Conneaut Lake Road, Meadville PA 16335

Index of "Good-for-You" Recipes

Dessert Recipes

Fish and Seafood Recipes

Fruit, Vegetable and Salad Recipes

Potato, Pasta, Rice and Other Starch Recipes

Sauce Recipes

Soup and Stew Recipes

Tofu, Soy and Other Meatless or Vegetarian Recipes

About the Author

Jane M. Livingston, RD, CDE is a registered dietitian and certified diabetes educator from Erie, Pennsylvania. She is Director of Nutrition and Diabetes Education Programs and nutrition therapist at the Mind-Body Wellness Center in Meadville, Pennsylvania where she coordinates the diabetes education, weight management, cardiac risk reduction and other nutrition and wellness programs at the Center. She is also a faculty member of ECaP (Exceptional Cancer Patients) Professional Training. Jane received a Bachelor of Science Degree in General Dietetics from Villa Maria College in Erie. Over the past 16 years Jane has held various clinical and management positions at Hamot Medical Center in Erie and the Department of Veterans Affairs where she facilitated regional and national health promotion and Healthy Veterans 2010 initiatives. As a counselor and educator Jane has developed many health education programs and travels throughout the tri-state region promoting her no-nonsense message of eating right, cooking light and living well. Contact Jane Livingston, RD, CDE at:

Mind-Body Wellness Center
18201 Conneaut Lake Road • Meadville PA 16335
Phone (814) 333-5060 • Fax (814) 333-5067
www.mind-body.org • jlivingston@mmchs.org

Dear friend, I pray that you may enjoy good health
and that all may go well with you,
even as your soul is getting along well.
3 John 1:2